Ceasefire City

M

Ceasefire City

Militarism, Capitalism, and Urbanism in Dimapur

Dolly Kikon
Duncan McDuie-Ra

OXFORD
UNIVERSITY PRESS

OXFORD
UNIVERSITY PRESS

Oxford University Press is a department of the University of Oxford.
It furthers the University's objective of excellence in research, scholarship,
and education by publishing worldwide. Oxford is a registered trademark of
Oxford University Press in the UK and in certain other countries.

Published in India by
Oxford University Press
22 Workspace, 2nd Floor, 1/22 Asaf Ali Road, New Delhi 110 002, India

First Edition published in 2021

ISBN-13 (print edition): 978-0-19-012973-6
ISBN-10 (print edition): 0-19-012973-5

ISBN-13 (eBook): 978-0-19-099267-5
ISBN-10 (eBook): 0-19-099267-0

Typeset in ScalaPro 10/13
by The Graphics Solution, New Delhi 110 092
Printed in India by Rakmo Press, New Delhi 110 020

Contents

Images

Acknowledgements

Dimapur is no longer an obscure place. It is my good fortune that I witnessed a town turn into a city, but it is even more exciting that I wrote a book about this exceptional city. I want to thank my co-author Duncan McDuie-Ra for taking this adventurous journey with me to explore and wander through Dimapur. Thank you for your courage to dream with me and write this book together. Your friendship, commitment, and wisdom to collaborate and write about a city where desires, dreams, death, and danger surround its residents have profoundly shaped my understanding about frontier urbanism. I am deeply indebted to your intellectual generosity and fellowship.

I was born in Dimapur and grew up absorbing the magic of this place. This book was made possible because of the love and faith of the city's extraordinary residents. Their lives, despite the everyday hardship, inspired me to complete this project. As an anthropologist, I traced the accounts of ordinary citizens who navigate a ceasefire city like Dimapur. I am grateful to Anungla Zoe Longkumer, Tali Angh, Alobo Naga, and Kevi Kiso for helping me connect with the social life of music in the city. I also owe my gratitude to Senti Toy who fostered my intellectual curiosity about the transformation of music in Naga society. Her music, writings, and friendship made me reflect upon the concepts of audibility and musical sensibilities. A community of elders and hunters from Dimapur shared their wisdom and accounts of hunting, and opened up my world to an enchanting yet complex world of urban hunting. The wit, terror, and violence involved in hunting, I hope, will initiate conversations about animals and humans who cohabit in frontier urban spaces like Dimapur. I would also like to thank Abraham Lotha for his generosity and friendship over the last decade during which we shared notes about Naga nationalism and anthropology. His role in documenting the life of our Naga leader Late Khodao Yanthan helped me gain an important insight about the politics of belonging and homeland. I am extremely grateful to the team at Home Trust Shop, a coffin store. They are responsible for showing me the everyday experience of living and dying in a ceasefire city.

I also want to thank Nchumbeni Merry for her generosity and time during my fieldwork in Dimapur. She fed me and made sure I had a home to rest. Mhademo Kikon helped me with the logistics of fieldwork; Azung and James offered their hospitality, food, and wonderful friendship; and Susan Lotha took me for a lovely walk around the ADC Court colony and shared her experiences of the city. Akum Longchari and the *Morung Express* team have always inspired me to embrace Dimapur and engage with the city and its residents. I deeply treasure their friendship and affection. I am grateful to the tribal associations in Dimapur who allowed me to attend their community meetings, picnics, and cultural events.

Finally, I would like to thank my family for being my greatest supporters. The affection of my sisters Julie and Rosemary goes beyond any academic writing project. My mother Mhalo Kikon raised me as a single mother in Dimapur. This book is for your irresistible tribal spirit of survival and living life with courage. My father-in-law Bijoy Barbora and my sister-in-law Moushumi are my biggest cheerleaders, and it is impossible for me to put it in words how dearly I hold them in my heart. Mhademo, Longshibeni, Kimiro, Samantha, Ishaanee, Chichano, and Tuki: all of you allow me to dream about a meaningful future. And my gratitude to Sanjay (Xonzoi) Barbora, my beloved partner who has supported me throughout the course of this project. Thank you, as always, for your patience and wisdom. To the readers ready to flip through the pages of this book, thank you because you will never ever ask me again, 'So, where is Dimapur?'

—Dolly Kikon

I would like to thank my co-author and dear friend Dolly Kikon, my friends and family, and the multitude of people in Dimapur who helped with this research.

—Duncan McDuie-Ra

Introduction

In academic research, the challenge for researchers is to convince their peers and audience that the research is significant, that it is worthwhile. During our research in Dimapur, a far greater challenge was convincing the city's residents, the people who know the city—or at least patches of it—intimately, that the city itself is even worth talking about. This project began as an exploration of tribal masculinity in 2015. In the course of that research, it became clear that Dimapur was becoming the arena where masculinity plays out, where it is challenged, re-asserted, and fragmented. It is where anxieties over migration, poverty, wealth, corruption, and gender have produced urban crises. These crises happened during the life of this project, and this is the point from where the city took over as our focus. Soon it was clear that Dimapur is not simply an arena or stage for the performance of gender and identity politics or for experiments in different forms of governance; rather, the city is both an arena and a performer. Amin and Thrift (2017: 3) task us with thinking about the 'overlapping socio-technical systems' that undergird cities. Socio-technical systems are not just the material backdrop to a city, the infrastructure upon which life is performed, but also attain relevance in the way in which they 'insatiate and sustain life' by 'allocating resource and reward, enabling collective action, shaping social dispositions and affects, marking time, space and map, maintaining order and discipline, sustaining transactions, moulding the environmental footprint' (Amin and Thrift 2017: 3). This is an invitation to think of the urban landscape not just as an arena or stage but as a machine. If Dimapur is a machine then the metaphor can be reworked in many ways: a broken machine, certainly, but also a machine that hums away, with half of its parts missing or dangling off the sides. The machine keeps going, more parts get added, it sucks in more energy. People fight over it; they are repulsed by it. It breaks down often, and people want to fix it. Yet, those charged with fixing it disagree on what is to be done and even on the nature of the breakdown itself. Some even struggle to see the machine they are to fix.

We encountered this all the time. Once we started to put the city at the centre of the project, the relationship between the city and its residents began to emerge, and it usually emerged when we first broached the topic. Whenever we told respondents, friends, and acquaintances that we were writing a book about Dimapur, their usual response was confusion: Were we really writing a book about the city? *This* city? Such a response was not a surprise, as we will discuss later in the book, Dimapur remains 'off the map' for most people, even its residents. This response would be unlikely if we were writing about Mumbai or Chennai or even a medium-sized city like Amritsar. These are cities with glorious pasts, alternative lives and circulations in literature and film, and arenas where events of consequence to mainstream India have taken place. They are on the map. Dimapur is not. Despite this, we must point out here that Dimapur has been embroiled in the everyday militarization and violence of Asia's longest-running separatist conflict—the Indo-Naga armed conflict. Along with numerous security camps of the Indian Armed Forces, two designated ceasefire camps of the Naga insurgents—the National Socialist Council of Nagaland Isak-Muivah (NSCN-IM) and the National Socialist Council of Nagaland-Unification (NSCN-U)—in the peri-urban areas make Dimapur an exceptional city.

Upon clarifying to our respondents that we were indeed writing about the city, our conversations would go either of the two ways: One, the person in question would try to redirect us to more legible and legitimate themes of social and political significance. They might suggest customary law, corruption, in-migration, state neglect, and erosion of Naga culture as things that deserve scholarly attention. We would try to explain to them that all of this can be witnessed in Dimapur. Sometimes this worked, but even when it did, the person in question would try to convince us to focus on another place, a 'better' place, such as Kohima, the state capital, or one of the district headquarters that are 'more Naga'. It was as if even though the respondents could accept that we were studying things that mattered, we were trying to study them in a place that did not really matter. Two, the person in question would remain doubtful that such an endeavour is even possible and, more commonly, worthwhile. Dimapur is difficult to grasp spatially and socially, and even more so politically and economically. This is not only true for researchers and new arrivals but for residents as well. Even if we were able to pin down aspects of the city's spatial politics and the ways in which residents and transients experience the city, what would it prove? Who really cares about Dimapur? We begin our book with this question firmly in mind.

Who Cares about Dimapur?

The rapid urbanization of India's Northeast frontier is one of the most crucial transformations the region has witnessed, yet it remains *relatively* understudied. In the Northeast states, the land being classified as 'urban' is expanding, creating new opportunities for developers and capitalists from within the region and beyond, and existing urban areas are becoming denser, more diverse, and more 'developed' (McDuie-Ra and Lai 2019). Development in urban areas is material, driven by state and private finance, and ideational in the continued imagining and re-imagining of urban modernity among planners, consultants, and citizens. This is significant anywhere, but in a region where vast tracts of territory and entire communities have been categorized as 'backward' for well over a century—a status now coveted and defended by those subject to it—imaginations of urban life and an urban future are in constant circulation.

For us, Dimapur is a fascinating manifestation of urbanization in the Northeast, and, we argue, epitomizes the social, political, and economic changes taking place in the region (and to the region) and the continuities from a past of violence, brutality, exploitation, and resistance to these incursions. Dimapur is a window into contemporary tribal life. It is a place of dreams and nightmares, pride and shame, refuge and insecurity, soldiers and insurgents, priests and politicians, emigration and return, potholes and flyovers, and ruin and rejuvenation. These are not contradictory dynamics; they are routine to the rhythm of the city and to the everyday lives of its inhabitants. Dimapur is, like other militarized landscapes, a landscape 'of contact, tension and negotiation between civilians and the military, soldiers and the environment, and between humans and non-humans' (Pearson 2012: 126). These encounters are not simply between inhabitants of diverse ethnic and racial backgrounds, but between people from all sides and factions in a long-running armed conflict followed by a period of peace and reconciliation. These are not just encounters between people but among different technologies, infrastructures, and socio-legal regimes. Analysing contemporary Dimapur is a window into how a society heals, or tries to, after a long conflict, where those affected are in close proximity to one another, to those who inflicted wounds directly and indirectly. Though not all wounds were inflicted in Dimapur itself, it is a place where many of the wounded and their descendants end up. Furthermore, Dimapur gives insights into governance in a post-conflict setting, a setting located in an economically dependent frontier state with specific constitutional provisions for tribal communities. Although Kohima is the state capital and administrative centre, Dimapur is where the spoils of political life are transformed into mansions, buildings, and businesses. Indeed, Dimapur was the epicentre of an unprecedented political crisis in 2017, a crisis that laid bare the contentious politics between customary and municipal orders, politics that is unlikely to wither in Dimapur or in other tribal cities in the frontier.

There are many cities and sites in South Asia, and even in the Northeast, where the cliché of 'needing no introduction' is true. Dimapur is the inverse of such places. It *needs* an introduction, a sense of the fabric of urban space. And there are precious few existing accounts that we can defer to and build upon. Even residents joke about not knowing the city: partly owing to the migrant flows from the hills and plains to settle in for short and long periods; partly to the village nature of urban space—few spend a lot of time outside their localities except to go to the commercial heart or to their workplaces; and partly as a legacy of decades of violence and insecurity that prevented residents from roaming and wandering around the city

Dimapur is a spectator to the contemporary knowledge of Nagaland. It rarely features in travel writings on Nagaland, despite the lavish attention given to the state by domestic and global travel writers, filmmakers, and guidebook series. If knowing Nagaland means knowing its festivals and exotica, Dimapur is excluded from knowledge production and circulation about Nagaland and its peoples. Furthermore, it has rarely featured in literature—though this is changing—or films, aside from a few local features, and barely has an online presence. Given this deficit, one of the primary aims of this book is to produce and analyse knowledge of the city, and in turn, the elements of the present conjuncture interwoven into the material and social fabric of Dimapur (Image I.1).

Dimapur is the largest city in Nagaland by population and the third-largest city in the region after Guwahati (Assam) and Agartala (Tripura). It has a population of somewhere between 378,811 (Census of India 2011) and 450,000. The fluctuations really depend upon whether one considers the entire 'urban agglomeration', the district, or just adds tens of thousands of people onto official figures to account for the rapid growth since the last Census and the challenges of capturing the city's floating population. The city is the largest among the hill states of the region that hug the border between India and Myanmar to the east, Bangladesh to the southwest, and China to the

Image I.1 Big-city capitalism following the ceasefire: A Toyota showroom near North Angami Colony

Source: Duncan McDuie-Ra

north. Dimapur is not situated in the hills and, thus, has had more room for growth, though sharing a border with Assam has halted this in parts of the city. It is the largest city in a tribal state, though the city itself is not located in the tribal heartland.

Dimapur presents an urban form that is particular, shaped by decades of conflict followed by 20 years of (partial) peace on the one hand, and instructive of urban dynamics in other parts of Northeast India, on the other. Yet exploring Dimapur is more than a story about growth. It is a story of *militarism, capitalism, and urbanism*, the three themes that we unravel throughout this book and the themes we believe are integral to understanding contemporary Northeast India, frontier urbanization elsewhere in Asia, and the feasibility of India's urban fixation in its border areas.

Frontier Urbanism

In this book, we focus on frontier urbanism to tell a story of the present. The social and political changes in the last two decades, starting with the Indo-Naga ceasefire agreement in 1997, led to the rise of numerous peace processes, development programmes, and economic programmes oriented towards propagating 'progress and development' across Northeast India. Yet, the last two decades have also recorded increasing unemployment, land alienation, and out-migration from Nagaland and its neighbouring states. At the same time, business deals and contracts primarily centred on mega construction projects, such as new malls, housing projects, and highways, have proliferated. Images of shopping malls and concrete structures are signs of progress and a return to normalcy from decades of armed conflict. We explore the lives and experiences of people within tropes of infrastructure and development discourse, a more conventional approach, and we also present frontier urbanism as a relationship that people create with their surroundings through sound (music), movement (hunting), and loss (dying).

We move away from describing the ongoing developments in the region such as the construction boom, militarization, and the experiences of unemployment as contradictory or distinct historical moments. Rather, we assert that these processes constitute the logic of frontier urbanism. To consider the urban sensibilities and activities in cities like Dimapur as solely founded on the figure of the Naga insurgent or the Indian security forces is to reject new political and social engagements. In addition, frontier urbanism also helps us to move beyond the dominant framework of studying tribal societies in India. For instance, dominant literature on Naga society is focused on the past or on traditions on the verge of disappearing. While we acknowledge the importance of these conversations, in this book, we focus on the experiences of people who live in the present and deal with the complexities of changes and transformation as urban dwellers. We trace how residents in Dimapur mobilize and ascribe values, and find new ways of defining the meaning of community, identity, and aspirations.

Our aim is to focus on the processes of urbanization and open up new ways of thinking about the city and the complexity of urban life (Brash 2006). By presenting an ethnography of Dimapur, we adopt an analytical lens that interrogates the boundaries that construct Northeast India as an underdeveloped and backward region. In this book, we explore how a distinctive form of urban process comes alive through social relations, networks, and mobility. We refer to this as frontier urbanism. This allows us to examine contemporary lives and how people's mobility and aspirations shape new relations (musicians as new communities), political imaginations (urban hunting and the dog meat debate), and public spaces (the overflowing graves of Dimapur and anxieties of being buried in a foreign land).

We are firm in our view that urbanization in the Northeast is an essential and under-studied phenomenon that needs to be explored in order to better understand the frontier, its past, and visions for its future. Cities in the hill states of the Northeast do not have a celebrated or even noted urban history, unlike many settlements in the valley areas complete with attention from state archaeologists and archivists. Cities in the hill areas can be considered emerging urban forms that dissolve the urban–rural distinction, particularly when analysed alongside changes in rural areas. This is particularly true of Dimapur where many of the localities outside the commercial centre are still governed as villages and maintain strong connections to 'home villages' in the various districts of Nagaland. If we can accept that urban areas in the Northeast are important sites for research into the frontier, change, and continuity, then what makes Dimapur itself worthy of this level of attention? Why Dimapur? We argue that there are six reasons for focusing on Dimapur, and these also undergird our arguments in the book. We will expand on these in depth here and return to them at various points throughout the book and in the epilogue that concludes the book.

First, as mentioned earlier, Dimapur is the largest city in a tribal-majority state. It is a rapidly urbanizing space in a rapidly urbanizing region. The Census notes a 22 per cent growth rate in Dimapur's population between 2001 and 2011, a figure for the entire district. The district is divided into eight circles, only three of which are considered urban (and not in their entirety): Dimapur Sadar, Chumukedima, and Medziphema. The population growth rate in these circles over the same period was 72.66 per cent. The population in rural circles declined in the same period (–6.3 per cent), with dramatic declines in Niuland (–62.27 per cent) and Nihokhu (–36.84 per cent). These figures have several issues. The degree of land reclassification and misclassification (as either urban or rural) is difficult to determine in this data, though it has some interesting effects on the ground in the city where several areas outside the municipal boundaries are urban in form. Furthermore, and most significantly, there has been controversy over the 1991 and 2001 censuses in Nagaland. The censuses were marred by suggestions that the population figures were inflated to boost numbers of certain communities, a suspicion highlighted following an overall population decrease in the 2011 Census (see Agrawal and Kumar 2012; Jeermison 2011). Indeed, Chief Minister Neiphiu Rio publicly refuted the data from the 2001 Census in 2011 (*Nagaland Post* 2011). If inflated, the 2001 figures would mask the pace of urban growth even further, assuming 2011 is more rigorous. Going back further, the first Census record of Dimapur's population was 5,753 in the 1961 Census, before Nagaland had been officially created; 12,426 in 1971; and 32,315 in 1981, though these predate the formation of the Dimapur District in 1997 (Census of India 2011). Perhaps the most useful figure to draw out from all this is that between 1981 and 2011 the population increased by a factor of ten. Despite limitations, it is possible to conclude at the very least that urban Dimapur is growing rapidly and the rural areas on the fringes are shrinking. And if the 2011 figure is to be trusted, it is the third biggest city in the Northeast and *the biggest in a tribal majority state.*

This brings us to our second point. Dimapur is the epitome of an emerging urban form and thus gives us the opportunity to frame, albeit tentatively, frontier urbanism as a research agenda in India. The transformations taking place in the frontier are largely urban, with consequences for rural areas to be sure, yet the relationship between the two is constitutive. As Verstappen and Rutten (2015: 232) demonstrate in their study of Anand in Gujarat, towns and small cities function as 'node(s) of interconnection between rural urban and local global mobility'. Dimapur functions in a similar way, yet it also draws migrants from other parts of India and across international borders; migrants instrumental in shaping the city through its infancy. In McDuie-Ra's (2016) book on Imphal, a centuries-old city and the capital of neighbouring Manipur, the city is analysed as the site of several projects aimed at recalibrating the city through exogenous and endogenous imaginations of connectivity. Imphal's location close to the border with Myanmar and to infrastructure connecting it with other parts of India (via Dimapur) is instrumental in reimagining the city as a gateway, a corridor of dual connectivity linking India to Southeast Asia, and in the process, linking the frontier to India. At the same time, the city is the site of intensive and often violent politics of belonging and exclusion between Manipur's ethnic communities and 'outsiders', culminating in vociferous demands to implement the restrictive Inner Line Permit system. Thus, the city is simultaneously viewed as a transnational hub and an exclusive domain. Dimapur, by contrast, is a kind of blueprint to be emulated.

Dimapur is located in a tribal majority state protected by various constitutional provisions, yet it is a migrant city, attracting people from across the Northeast, from other parts of India, and from across international borders, drawn to its opportunities and peculiar cosmopolitanism. We believe that Dimapur is indicative of the kinds of urban futures that will shape the region in the coming decades. Baruah (2015: 1) alludes to this when discussing the anxiety over migration in Dimapur and suggests that

> What worries so many Naga activists and politicians about Dimapur are exactly the things that serious thinkers about northeast India's economic future find promising. The region's future prosperity, they believe, lies in the ability to create more Dimapur-like open economic spaces in the hill states of the region.

Whether one agrees that this will be beneficial or not, as successive Indian governments look for ways to integrate the frontier into the nation beyond (but not instead of) military occupation, market expansion is crucial and the development of urban areas is a vital mechanism to accumulate capital and assuage the highly protective land regimes in tribal areas. Dimapur is perhaps the ideal urban environment: it is situated in a tribal state but somehow separate, a zone of ethnic, legal, and political pluralism. However, as two urban crises demonstrate, the first in 2015 following a public lynching (discussed in Chapter 1) and the second in 2017 over proposed changes to municipal governance (discussed in Chapter 2), there is delicacy here too.

This brings us to our third point: Dimapur is more than just a city. As a zone between the hills and plains, between tribal and non-tribal space, between shifting cultivation and settled agriculture, between civilization and savagery, Dimapur is a spatial experiment. Kar (2009: 60) proposes that the British Inner Line Permit System, which separated hills and plains into different administrative regimes and has persisted into postcolonial India, is 'a line in time'. He adds that the 'advance of the Line on map was read as the progress from pre-capital to capital, from the time of "no law" to the time of "law"' (Kar 2009: 60). If we keep the metaphor of the line in mind, then Dimapur is a squiggle in that line: a dip, a loop, or perhaps an inkblot. It is situated in the foothills that are subject to territorial claims by the Indian state, the federal state governments of Assam and Nagaland, and various non-state actors (see Kikon 2019), yet in Dimapur, these claims are tempered. This does not mean such claims are absent, and, as we will discuss in later chapters, the borders and edges of the city are in a constant flux through expansion, contraction, and transgression. Furthermore, the city can be cut off from other parts of the frontier by blockades, protests, and *bandhs* emanating from these claims.

Our point here is that Dimapur is an experimental territorial form. It is an in-between zone, an enclave carved out of Assam to connect the newly formed state of Nagaland to India in the process of an ongoing armed conflict. It is a swathe of terrain straddling Nagaland and Assam, hills and plains, tribal land and non-tribal land, simultaneously remote and connected, parochial and cosmopolitan, and for our purposes, knowing Dimapur grounds the politics and past of the frontier in lived urban space. We regard the city itself as a frontier of sorts, echoing what Eilenberg (2014) refers to as a 'frontier constellation'. In discussing agrarian expansion in the Indonesia–Malaysian borderlands, Eilenberg uses 'frontier constellation' to analyse 'the multiple meanings and notions associated with regions where resource frontiers and national borders interlock' (Eilenberg 2014: 159). By exploring militarism, capitalism, and urbanism in Dimapur, we analyse the meanings produced and affixed to this in-between space, the territorial units it rubs up against, and the flows that pass through it. In doing so, we argue that Dimapur reveals what Rasmussen and Lund (2018: 389) call 'the vernacular political forms that constitute emergent institutions and struggles over legitimate rule'. We are interested in attempts by a raft of state, non-state, and state-like actors to exert spatial control in Dimapur, the places where it succeeds, breaks down, is resisted and contested, and where no one seems to bother. These attempts, we argue, reveal dynamics of territory, rule, and rupture that are commonly abstracted in studies of the region, taken at face value from the claims of key actors, or unravelled through discussions of identity politics and ethno-nationalist movements. We explore them on the ground in a city, an enclave, where they converge.

Fourth, despite the booming commercial veneer and the ceasefire agreement between the NSCN-IM and the Indian government in 1997, Dimapur is a city governed under extraordinary laws with a substantial military presence. As noted earlier, Dimapur not only hosts the Indian military and paramilitary, but it is also home to the ceasefire camps for the NSCN-IM and the NSCN-U—a veritable city within the city—known as Camp Hebron and Camp Vihokhu. Both 'sides' in the decades-long conflict now cohabit the city in their various fortifications with the civilian population strewn in between. The city is simultaneously a post-conflict city and an occupied city, suggesting the limits, and perhaps the nature, of demilitarization in the Northeast and its coexistence with market expansion (Image I.2).

Fifth, Dimapur has been a city of conflict but also a city of refuge for people escaping the direct impact of conflict in Nagaland, in neighbouring polities, and the ecological and economic ruin of militarization. It is, as Debbarma (2017) points out in the case of

Image I.2 A post-conflict city and an occupied city: Indian Reserve Battalion cadre patrolling the Super Market

Source: Duncan McDuie-Ra

Agartala in nearby Tripura, a kind of 'colonial settler town', yet the colonizers in Dimapur, as in Agartala, are not always obvious. At the same time, this conflict brought migrants to the city from other directions seeking opportunities that had accelerated after the ceasefire. It is a city of migrants, of settlement and resettlement, owing to its geography, topography, and its place—or non-place—in the political and cultural imagination of communities of the frontier. Despite its size and commercial significance, Dimapur is 'off the map'. The map here refers to the political and cultural map of Nagaland, furthering the notion of an enclave, a zone, a constellation of undeclared exception from the authorities that govern the territories surrounding it; except, of course, the laws protecting the armed forces. Given this diversity and this history, Dimapur is a city where the 'recovery of the everyday', the coming to terms with 'the fragility of the normal' (Mehta and Chatterji 2001: 202), is being 'refashioned' after decades of extreme violence and brutality. Much of the population is in a perpetual attempt to recover the everyday; an everyday that is itself unstable in urban space lived among barracks and under extraordinary laws (Image I.3).

Finally, Dimapur allows the opportunity to begin an account of the Northeast, and Nagaland in particular, from a position of modernity. Wouters and Heneise (2017: 8) posit that the richness of ethnographic writing on Nagaland in the colonial period is not matched by the post-colonial, creating 'a decades-wide ethnographic void'. Indeed, studies of tribal communities in the Northeast rarely begin with modern subjectivities, instead locating modern subjectivities (if at all)

Image I.3   Peace monument at the Police Colony

Source: Duncan McDuie-Ra

as antagonisms for traditional practices and worldviews, temptations responsible for inter-generational schisms, or the teleology of social change. Taking tribal communities seriously as active (rather than passive) modern subjects continues the work that we have started elsewhere, exploring migration, work, and race (Kikon and Karlsson 2019; McDuie-Ra 2012a, 2015a). It also builds upon the work of scholars exploring the formation of class in the Northeast and Nagaland in particular (Küchle 2019); sacral worlds, their politics, and their global connections (Joshi 2007; Mepfhü-o 2016; Pongen 2016; Thomas 2015); religious revivals (Longkumer 2016); engagement with Indian politics and consumer cultures (Longkumer 2019; Wouters

2015); and emerging film, photography, art, literature, and material cultures (Baishya 2018; Kaisii 2017; Kuotsu 2013; Pachuau and van Schendel 2015; Toy 2010; von Stockhausen 2014).

As Mbembé and Nuttall (2004: 352) have argued in their work on African cities, attention to urban spaces serves 'to identify sites within the continent, entry and exit points not usually dwelt upon in research and public discourse, that defamiliarize common-sense readings of Africa'. They add, 'such sites would throw people off their routine readings and deciphering of African spaces. Identifying such sites entails working with new archives—or even with old archives in new ways. One such archive, as we explore in detail in this issue as a whole, is the metropolis itself' (Mbembé and Nuttall 2004: 352). This mirrors our intention to approach contemporary tribal worlds, and those who dwell in them, through a study of the largest city in a tribal state.

Starting with Dimapur enables us to begin the process of 'defamiliarization' in a multi-ethnic, mostly non-agrarian, consumer-driven, densely populated space, where the daily tactics, aspirations, and activities of urban dwellers narrate a very different Northeast, a very different Nagaland, and a very different tribal society than depicted in studies that have dominated the field in the past. We hope this will also destabilize 'routine readings' of Nagaland and Northeast India more broadly.

Militarism, Capitalism, and Urbanism

Dimapur's present conjuncture is poised between order and crisis. It is a pivotal moment, and one that is instructive for other parts of the frontier. We characterize Dimapur's conjuncture through three themes: militarism, capitalism, and urbanism; themes that we analyse through a set of linked concepts discussed here. 'Conjuncture' is a concept with a long history in Gramscian thought and varies in different disciplinary traditions (see Hall 1986; Jessop 2005; Kipfer and Hart 2012). It disappears and reappears, and these trajectories are complex and beyond the scope of what we are trying to achieve in this work. For our purposes, we take a fairly loose definition of conjuncture as a 'complex formation of an historical moment' (Koivisto and Lahtinen 2012: 276). It is not the 'conceptual dictator' but an analytical tool to identify the 'many determinants of concrete reality, and thus open up new possibilities for political interventions' (Koivisto and Lahtinen 2012: 276). Crucial for us is Hall's well-known imploration to see things 'not as you'd like them to be, not as you think they were ten years ago, not as they're written about in sacred texts, but as they really are: the contradictory, stony ground of present conjuncture' (Hall 1989: 151). This is essential both for our research on Dimapur and for research on the Northeast in general, which *can* be characterized by dated assumptions and predetermined arguments rather than attention to circumstances. Focusing on conjuncture asks us to analyse continuity and change, the material and social, as constitutive of the present, the stony ground.

In short, we are interested in the forces that have shaped contemporary Dimapur (even if we cannot fully explain them), the ways they manifest in the city, and the ways people navigate these in their everyday lives. We have grouped them into three loose themes: militarism, capitalism, and urbanism. Capitalism captures the history of Dimapur as a supply outpost, a frontier between hills and plains bound up in resource extraction, infrastructure expansion, and the expansion of the conflict economy. Following the ceasefire in 1997, capital has expanded rapidly and has transformed urban space: former insurgents have turned to business; migrants send remittances back to families in Dimapur to start ventures; money from resource extraction on tribal lands is ploughed into property and business ventures; the 'easy money' culture buoyed by transfers from the Indian government takes material form in similar ways; and Dimapur is an integral node in the recalibration of the Northeast from a frontier to a market for everything from consumer goods to personal finance.

Militarism traces the centrality of the Indian Armed Forces in the development of the city materially and the lived experience of the city socially. The military is not just a presence, it is an active agent in shaping the city and the lives of those who live in it and move through it. Military infrastructure ('developed', technologically advanced, and gated) is juxtaposed with civilian infrastructure (broken, uneven, and impractical) and community infrastructure (improvised, pragmatic, and exclusive). The size and scale of military infrastructure in Dimapur is astounding and has extended the city in various directions as the land in between military barracks and housing is gradually filled with new settlements. These 'encampments', to use Pieris's phrase in reference to military barracks in Colombo and Jaffna, serve to normalize military presence as part of the fabric of the city and also serve as a 'concealer' of violence (Pieris 2014: 395).

Dimapur is militarized outside the barracks too. Any space is open to the armed forces. They are mobile throughout the city and, under the extraordinary provisions of the Armed Forces Special Powers Act 1958 (AFSPA), can go wherever they please: public and private, street and house, and market and pathway. The AFSPA gives legal protection to the Indian military and paramilitary for any acts committed against the civilian population in 'disturbed' areas (see Mathur 2012). It also grants the armed forces the right to enter any premises, arrest and detain civilians suspected of committing or of being 'about to commit' any 'cognizable' offence indefinitely, and prevents the gathering of more than five people. The presence of other armed forces under local command adds another layer of militarism, one with a local face and local ties. These overlapping authorities have given rise to a 'culture of impunity', a term Kikon uses to describe the rise in domestic and sexual violence in Naga society during the time of the ceasefire (Kikon 2016). Outside Dimapur, soldiers of the NSCN-IM are housed in Camp Hebron and the NSCN-U cadres live in Camp Vihokhu, sites that function as both settlements and offices of these parallel governments. Hebron and Vihokhu loom over the city; taxation and other payments made by city businesses to the insurgent organizations are processed in these camps, but these sites are more than that. Based on how the ceasefire talks have progressed in the 2010s, decisions made in the ceasefire camps around Dimapur (and beyond) could have a major impact on the city depending on the nature of sovereignty agreed upon and the reactions of excluded NSCN factions and neighbouring states, especially Manipur (see Chasie and Hazarika 2009; Kolås 2011; Misra 2003; Shimray 2004). As with the armed forces, former insurgents and their kin groups including clan members and families exist throughout the city and shape the urban environment as members of communities, activists, politicians, and capitalists. Some thrive, some struggle. The point here is that all 'sides' in a long-running conflict live in the city, making claims and counterclaims on urban space, on symbols of sovereignty, and on who does what, when, where, and at what cost.

We use 'urbanism' as an umbrella term for the near and far processes of making Dimapur look and function 'like a city'. An urban focus at the national level has redirected development towards urban development through various schemes and institutional restructuring, discussed in Chapter 2. At the same time, the dismantling of the Planning Commission in 2015, which was replaced with National Institution for Transforming India (NITI) Aayog (see Patnaik 2016), has major implications for the Northeast as it was the main source of annual budget for a Special Category 1 state like Nagaland. This has given new impetus to states to gain funds for urban development by making urban areas in the frontier more 'city-like'. Obviously, this has major consequences for a city the size and importance of Dimapur. There are also local drivers of urbanism, including the revised Nagaland Municipal Act 2001, reviving a formerly weak form of governance in India (Denis et al. 2012), one that created incentives for classifying areas as rural rather than urban in the past. This is shifting. However, the revised Nagaland Municipal Act 2001 has been a source of tension in Nagaland.

Most areas of the city that lie away from the commercial centre operate as villages despite being urban in form, and are governed by village authorities under customary law. Governing neighbourhoods as villages in the city can be highly effective in some areas and ineffective in others. The locality *goanbura* or the 'headman' is the go-to person for all kinds of works, ranging from attesting documents and getting proof of residence to resolving disputes between neighbours. However, sanitation work, such as garbage collection or maintaining sewage, falls outside the control of a customary authority like the headman. The municipal authority takes up these matters, yet fails to connect localities and the infrastructure needed to extend and maintain pipes, roads, wires, and so on across the city. Irrespective of these complex and overlapping authorities, attempts to change the existing structure are emotive as some groups see them as a threat to customary law, as shown in the political crisis of 2017, a theme we discuss later in the book. Urbanism is not solely about governance: it is about making order by policing space; marking boundaries within the city and on its edges; creating showpiece developments, such as the Eiffel-esque City Tower and the neo-traditional market space known as Urban Haat; and it is about the ways in which Dimapur's residents respond, resist, and make place and mark it 'from below'.

The task we undertake in this book is to explore the present conjuncture in Dimapur. Militarism, capitalism, and urbanism have shaped the present order, and have the city poised between becoming a model for urban development in the region and descending into crisis. Picking apart these elements through reading the material and social worlds of the city is the main task of Part I of this book. We then focus on narratives of people, places, and objects that reveal the ways people (and some animals) navigate the city, its order, and its conjuncture and disjuncture. As Li (2014) demonstrates in her recent work on capitalist relations in upland Sulawesi, ethnographic approaches animate conjunctures by unravelling the ways in which people experience a particular conjuncture and the ways it shapes their subjectivities and their agency. Indeed, in Dimapur, the conjuncture is not simply the result of things being done *to* the frontier (by India, and before that, by the British), but things that happen *in* the frontier caused by an array of subjects with varied forms of agency.

Approaching Dimapur

This book is a collaboration between two scholars whose primary research field is Northeast India and primary method is ethnographic. We have worked together previously, and this book developed out of conversations during our regular trips to the Northeast with friends and peers. From 2015 to 2019, we worked closely to portray the images of everyday lives in Dimapur, a city we started visiting together. Without making a spectacle of the militarized lives and the distressing stories about loss, migration, poverty, and corruption that we heard during our visits, we began to reflect on the ways of surviving and living in this city. These stories were connected to people across the city who became our friends and interlocutors, granting us access to their dreams and aspirations of making it in Dimapur. Collaborative ethnography holds many possibilities for capturing and harnessing the craziness of Dimapur. Collaborative ethnographies can offer us improvised 'ethnographic technique and analysis' (Bourgois and

Schonberg 2009: 11). We undertook some parts of the fieldwork in Dimapur together and some parts individually. We shared our field notes, images, transcriptions of interviews, and updated each other about our fieldtrips. We feel that this approach has produced coherent material for the arguments we are making and thus will not detail the individual tasks *ad nauseam*, however, in discussing our approach there are a few important points to note.

As an urban sociologist, Duncan McDuie-Ra focused on the spatial dimensions of Dimapur, while Kikon focused her anthropological lens on understanding the lived experiences of the city. Interdisciplinary collaborative research can be challenging. On occasions, we had to move into our respective disciplinary fields to develop the analytical framework of our study. At other times, we made it a point to improvise our approaches to study and understand the social world of Dimapur. Rather than focusing on the divisions and the distinct analytical approaches, we were able to create trust and generosity to draw out the best from our respective trainings and disciplines. Curiosity and our drive to produce a work that brought out the intensity and spirit of Dimapur without compromising on the quality of this collaboration was key.

As an outsider, McDuie-Ra (2016) utilized techniques used in other cities in the Northeast and among Northeast migrants in Delhi (McDuie-Ra 2012b, 2013) to explore space and place-making. McDuie-Ra undertook the walking ethnography of urban space (discussed later) alone, with Kikon, and with other friends and contacts in Dimapur. He took thousands of photographs of surfaces, objects, texts, wastelands, and buildings, and discussed these images with residents and Kikon to gain a sense of the urban fabric, the changes taking place, and how residents, visitors, and sojourners contend with these through their engagements with space.

By contrast, Kikon grew up in Dimapur and has experienced the city through conflict and ceasefire. She has returned to the city time and again for personal and professional reasons, including for extensive research on the foothills of Assam and Nagaland, and as an advocate and activist. In recent years, she has written about people's experiences of living in this city. From militarization and sexual violence (Kikon 2016) to everyday violence and conflict economy (Kikon 2015a) and matters of governance and prohibitions (Kikon

2017a), she has drawn on her anthropological training to make militarized cities like Dimapur visible in the public imagination. With intimate knowledge of the city, Kikon focused on bringing the stories of the city to the forefront of this project. For Kikon, this project is also a personal narrative, and her personal reflections, friendships, and ties to the city shaped the research we both undertook, giving depth and clarity to many of the seemingly unexplainable and incredible sites, events, and personalities.

Mapping the elements of the present conjuncture and narrating the stories of people, places, and objects that navigate through it give the opportunity for a multifaceted and, in part, experimental approach. This is not a classical methodology section per se and, given the way in which we undertook the research, it is difficult to sequence our approach into distinct phases with a linear order. With this in mind, we will discuss the components of our research approach.

Learning to Love Dimapur

Our approach to Dimapur seeks to first establish a sense of the city and then tell stories of those experiencing it. Besides interviews, conversations, and cultural and social events that are evident in the chapters of this book, we were keen to learn about life on the streets, the new construction boom, roadside bazaars, and residential areas. In order to immerse ourselves in every level of Dimapur's urban life, we realized that it was important to get a sense of this frontier city by walking through it. This was not easy. Walking might appear as a way of meandering aimlessly or as an easy method to pick only selective parts (read safe and gentrified sections) of the city. We adopted walking in addition to the interviews and conversations as part of our ethnographic method to establish a self-reflective approach in the field and also to highlight the importance of embracing the city as a whole. This meant we walked to the rough neighbourhoods and spent time in the eating joints and shops. We entered the wealthy gated localities around the city as well. We feared for our safety at times because our mere presence in certain spaces attracted the attention of law enforcement agencies.

For instance, during a walking tour of a wealthy suburb in the city in December 2016, we stopped by the roadside to see a crowd of Nagaland Armed Police (NAP) personnel, all bare-chested and sweating, digging a pond. We sat beside a mound of mud and watched the action in front of us. Suddenly, two armed policemen walked towards us and started interrogating us. Later, we realized that the fear and anxiety of our mere presence by the roadside stemmed from something deeper. The NAP personnel were digging the pond for a Naga politician (a minister). This activity was 'outside' the ambit of what constituted as work for the NAP. Initially we were fearful, but as we stood conversing with the armed policemen about our research, this moment led to a series of events such as having access to the minister's house and witnessing the lives of the wealthy tribal elites, fieldwork experiences that would have otherwise never taken place. For us, walking during fieldwork was not an insular activity to shut off one's surroundings or to justify one's awkwardness to connect with people around us. On the contrary, it is because we adopted walking as an ethnographic method that we engaged in deep conversations with each other as co-authors and also with people we met in parks and on the street. We also took field notes, stood and read road signs at leisure, and absorbed the signboards and posters on the streets.

Therefore, our immediate sense of Dimapur came from what we saw and felt as we entered the exceptional surroundings of the city. Images, signs, conversations, and moods we gauged from our fieldwork and developed into themes for this book emerged from closely putting together the visuals (posters and signboards) and engagements (first-person meetings with informants). In addition, McDuie-Ra's photographs illustrated the characters of the city we wanted to highlight in the book and helped us to frame the theoretical themes across our chapters.

Purposeful mobility from designated points—government office to NGO rally (often in a vehicle)—are common routes, yet emerging urban areas can best be captured on foot, and in many instances by accident, as we noted earlier. As Edensor (2010: 69) argues, walking reveals rhythms that intersect, 'adding to the complex polyrhythmy of place'. A mobile sense of place/s can be produced (and identified) 'through longer immersion by the walking body across a more extended space' (Edensor 2010: 70). In their introduction to a collection on walking ethnography, Ingold and Vergunst (2008: 3) argue, 'It is along the ground, and not in some ethereal realm of discursively constructed significance, over and above the material world, that lives are paced out in their mutual relations'. Cheng (2014: 213) also argues, '[w]alking not only guides us through encounters with other human beings, but also embeds us in a dense network of materials, ranging from skyscraping buildings to the most mundane of everyday objects such as lampposts or sidewalks'. He stresses the importance of objects encountered and discovered during walking and their power to 'disrupt the rhythm of walking, their power to affect our spatial orientations, as well as capture our attentiveness to their weighty existence' (Cheng 2014: 214). And in a region where research can often take a predictable trajectory, any opportunity to encounter something new, unexpected, and (hopefully) significant was welcomed.

We walked together, individually, in winter, in summer, in dust, and in rain. We walked between appointments, and eventually, instead of appointments. We discovered places, people, objects, and events accidentally and incidentally. We were able to revisit places and routes on foot that Kikon had walked through while growing up in Dimapur. The transformation of urban sites like Friends Line and Eros Line—famous cinema halls where thriving localities had come up decades earlier—allowed us to reflect about the distinct experiences of militarized urbanism in frontier regions like Northeast India. Our conversations during these walks, often accompanied by other friends and residents, helped to narrate change in a particular area, to a particular building, to note what had disappeared and what had emerged.

In a city with no official public transport, walking also helps us to embody some of the burdens that residents, especially the poor, bear in their everyday lives. Dimapur is a difficult city to walk; few pathways, wide-open drains, potholes, dust, and mud, as well as heavy traffic can make parts of the city very challenging to traverse on foot. Away from main roads, though, the narrow thoroughfares and shortcuts through localities, fields, and wastelands are easier to move through, and bring more unexpected sites for research. Walking also gives an embodied sense of the stark spatial shifts. In the course of an hour, one can pass through a commercial space full of people from all over the city and frontier and goods from all over the world teeming onto the pavement, through a timber yard where shirtless men pile logs under the hot sun, into a densely built locality of multi-floor rental properties, past an extravagant church with elegantly dressed parishioners stepping carefully over open drains, along the concrete outer wall of a military barracks under careful (or perhaps cursory) surveillance, and through an ornate gate into a tribal locality where houses are ordered into neat lots with gardens, animals, and hybrid concrete and bamboo architecture. Through this same journey the posters, graffiti, memorials, debris, sounds, and smells begin to change, along with the people visible in public, suggesting zones—edges within the city—that denote different places of belonging and exclusion.

One of the hazards of seeking to establish a sense of the city, and indeed of walking it, is that *everything* appears relevant: every corner, every street, every shop, every park, every state development project, every memorial, and every building. Everything tells you *something* about the city, but not everything can be seen, felt, understood, or explained. We focused on three parts of the urban landscape that we feel exemplify the militarism, capitalism, and urbanism thematic triumvirate: (*i*) visual culture, (*ii*) infrastructure and the built environment, and (*iii*) consumer spaces. We consider these to be a starting point rather than a definitive model for reading urban Dimapur.

Visual Culture

Visual culture in the urban Northeast is astounding and Dimapur is perhaps the richest repository. Freitag encourages the use of visual resources for understanding public culture in urban South Asia. She posits that in such rapidly changing sites, paintings, photographs, posters, maps, and three-dimensional objects are 'witnesses to the changing "communication context" predicated on visual literacy that transcended multiple languages and scripts' and depend 'on new dissemination networks, repletion ... and thickly-entwined inter-ocular references' (Freitag 2014: 401). Dimapur is covered in images and text that reflect a lived cosmopolitanism—and its limits—that both accompanies and challenges dominant ways of understanding the city, its component parts, and its particular 'frontier constellation'. Consider advertisements (government and private) on billboards, painted directly on walls, shutters, or handed out on flyers. Some advertisements are vandalized, some are defaced, some are pasted over with political posters that turn conventional advertisements for, say, telecommunications companies into statements about place and territory. Billboards for education fairs, training colleges, apartment complexes (often in other cities), cars, or global restaurant chains reveal changing perceptions of the frontier as a consumer market producing and reflecting the aspirations and desires of the residents, visitors, and interlopers.

They also provide fascinating insights into the global, national, and regional circuits and flows that pass through the city. At some point, someone, somewhere thought that extending a retail chain, opening a franchise, including the city in a concert tour or a healing ministry, or exporting to or importing from Dimapur was a good idea. Evidence of these circuits challenge ideas of remoteness, the fall-back descriptor of the frontier vis-à-vis the rest of India, recalling Shneiderman's idea of 'relational remoteness' she develops in the Nepal context in the collaborative article led by Erik Harms (see Harms et al. 2014: 373–4), something we will discuss further in Chapter 1. Remoteness has been challenged by a number of recent studies of the contemporary Northeast and the past. Kikon's work on resource extraction and militarization challenges categories applied to the region. She asserts how the politics of resource extraction in the region helps us understand 'new forms of heterogeneity, citizenship, indigeneity, legitimacy, and gender relations in contemporary India' (Kikon 2019: 10). She asserts how the politics of resource extraction situates the region as an 'important location' to understand 'new forms of heterogeneity, citizenship, indigeneity, legitimacy, and gender relations in contemporary India' (Kikon 2019: 10). Pachuau and van Schendel's (2015: 4) work on Mizo modernity through private photography through the twentieth century also explores 'multiple forms of modernity ... [and] how local people produced these, how they engaged with them and how they established and used links beyond their world and region' in what is typically described as a remote and far-flung frontier.

For us, the visual culture of Dimapur offers similar possibilities. Recognized global circuits are an obvious draw, but most fascinating to us in understanding the fabric of the city are the 'low-end' circuits, akin to Mathews's description of 'low-end globalization' as 'the transnational flow of people and goods involving relatively small amount of capital and informal, sometimes semi-legal or illegal, transactions' (Mathews 2011:

20). Indeed, while Dimapur features Toyota showrooms, a Pizza Hut, and retailers selling the latest Samsung mobile phones, it is also part of other circuits: circuits that reach a far greater mass of the population (Image I.1). Through his ethnography of Chungking Mansions in Hong Kong, Mathews (2011: 20) adds that large multinational corporations 'have only a limited impact on the consciousness of much of the world's population. Globalization for these people consists, in large part, of the goods, ideas, and media brought in by small traders and illegal workers'. We would add several other carriers of globalization to this list in considering Dimapur, and also note the national and regional origins of the goods, ideas, and media too, and a great place to find evidence of these flows is in the visual culture of the city, which we will turn to throughout the book.

Take for example, the posters pasted onto the walls around Dimapur train station announcing the visits of Dr Sheikh (Image I.4) in mid-2017. Dr Sheikh is promoted as a 'famous sexologist physician for male[s] and female[s]' with a registration in Patna, Bihar. In Hindi and English, his poster lists ailments that he can cure, his fees, and— judging by the additional fees—his prized 'Japani Body Analyser Scanner Machine', suggesting that he is versed in both Ayurvedic and high-tech medicine. He claims to be able to cure a range of ailments without operation, while also offering penis enlargement and 'Freedom From Alchole [sic] (100 per cent cure Treatment)': a bold promise to make in this part of the frontier! The poster announces that he consults from hotels in three locations across the border with Assam: Diphu, Lumding, and Haflong. Dr Sheikh spends three weeks of the month circulating through towns in the border region and is trying to either encourage patients from Dimapur to visit him in these towns or to begin operating out of the city. Registered in Bihar and advertising in English and Hindi (not in any Naga languages), Dr Sheikh has found his way to the frontier to try to make a living with his 'Japani' scanner. Being this far from Bihar means few people will be able to check if he is a 'famous sexologist' or scrutinize the credentials of the mysterious 'MIMS' to which he claims past affiliation. At the same time, Dr Sheikh's presence suggests the frontier is not remote either; it is integrated into his own low-end circuit of travelling treatment.

Other posters locate Dimapur in global circuits of faith. For instance, a poster mounted on wooden frames and affixed throughout

Image I.4   Dr Sheikh: Kiosk wall in front of Hotel Acacia

Source: Duncan McDuie-Ra

the residential areas of Dimapur and along the main highways spotted throughout the winter of 2016–17 announced a Christmas Gospel Revival and Healing Festival to be held at the local sports ground in Chumukedima, the circle on the eastern edge of the city, in the urban fringe of Dimapur. The main attraction is 'Messenger of God: Rev. Dr. Len Lindstrom' from 'Canada North America'. Lindstrom is photographed in a suit, the Bible in hand, smiling with a brilliantly coiffured blond bouffant, superimposed on a background of worshippers who appear to be at an outdoor field. Inserted into the poster in a circular frame is a headshot of Dr Alem Meren, a Naga described as a 'Global Missionary at Large', and in the bottom corner is Rev. Dillip Singh, photographed from the knees up playing a lute and wearing a shirt and tie, billed as the 'First Nagamese Gospel Composer and Singer'. The Christmas Gospel Revival and Healing Festival poster not only locates Dimapur on a global circuit toured by a Canadian missionary, but a Naga, Dr Meren, is also part of that circuit as a globally mobile missionary and Singh, a non-Naga, is a composer in the Nagamese creole language. Scores of similar posters can be found throughout the city at any given time advertising healing missions from Korea, from Bodoland in Assam, and from various districts in Nagaland.

Common, too, are billboards publicizing the armed forces and paramilitary, marking sites of control and littering the landscape with propaganda such as 'Friends of the Hill People' and publicity for community initiatives. Civilian governments, both local and national, and customary authorities mark space with their presence on foundation stones, inauguration plaques, and details of funding schemes utilized to build a bridge, seal a road, or upgrade a bus station. Sovereign claims are matched by sovereign counterclaims: for instance, following the death of Isak Chishi Swu, the chairman of the NSCN-IM, images of him transposed on the flag of an independent Nagalim could be found throughout the city, pasted onto walls, billboards, and even on the City Tower (Image I.5).

Image I.5   Isak Swu's birth anniversary celebration at Camp Hebron (ceasefire camp)

Source: Duncan McDuie-Ra

Alternative scripts appear as graffiti made with etchings, spray paint, stencils, and even printouts from a computer on white A4 paper announcing support for a particular underground group or declarations of undying love in multiple languages. Handwritten signs direct people to funerals, weddings, and prayer meetings, often wedged onto an existing signboard or affixed to a bamboo stake. Red stains from betel nut and white clumps of lime paste mark the built environment with the presence of passers-by, often haphazardly, but occasionally with purpose targeting the face of a politician or a particular storefront. Less obvious yet also instructive are the names on businesses and publicly displayed licences revealing the commercial power of particular ethnic communities, and these change as one moves through different localities. Hand-painted locality maps, snippets of religious texts, and civic and moral instructions add further layers of text and image.

Dimapur is such a fascinating repository for visual culture because seemingly nothing is removed from walls, poles, and shutters. The result is an astounding visual archive of commercial, political, and social initiatives in Dimapur and the territories it rubs up against, the flows that pass through it, the imaginaries lodged in its urban space. All of these reveal elements of the present conjuncture; the stony ground of the present moment.

Infrastructure and the Built Environment

Dimapur's infrastructure, its lack, and the politics around who should provide it and what this entails for governance, rule, and territorial control are perhaps the most contentious of all urban issues in the city. In his review of ethnographic approaches to infrastructure, Larkin (2013: 329) urges us to consider infrastructures as 'matter that enable the movement of other matter. Their peculiar ontology lies in the facts that they are things and also the relation between things'. Infrastructures go beyond their immediate functionality and, as Larkin (2013: 329) argues, 'need to be analysed as concrete semiotic and aesthetic vehicles oriented to addressees'. There is a rich literature that shows how studies on infrastructure offer an important theoretical lens to understand hopes, anxieties, disrepair, citizenship, and governance (Anand 2016; Chu 2014; Harvey and

Knox 2015; Schwenkel 2013). As the largest city in the hill states, Dimapur is a magnet for infrastructure schemes and scheming: a site to search out subcontracts (and sub-sub-subcontracts) through tribal and kin networks, connections to politicians, and commercial ties to the suppliers of materials and cheap labour—often non-tribal capitalists and their own cheap labour force. Dimapur exemplifies Amin's explorations of the co-production of infrastructure in Brazil. He writes: '[T]his is the ground of making life livable, the city a plural ontology, and power more decentered, with much of this given collective orientation through joint effort in securing everyday infrastructure' (Amin 2014: 157). The city features many projects of dubious needs and suspect quality, along with seemingly genuine attempts to make urban life better. Some of these projects inspire pride, hope, embarrassment, or disgust, while others are repurposed for entirely different uses as they age, become dilapidated, and go to ruin. The search for exceptional spaces—spectacular and/or useless infrastructure—also needs to account for normalcy, and indeed the unstable ground upon which 'normal' and 'exceptional' can be understood in Dimapur.

Infrastructure draws our attention to the providers and intended beneficiaries, the public or *publics*, or the addressees, to recall Larkin. As Collier et al. (2016) argue, 'it is not only the things extracted, transformed, and circulated through infrastructures that are today being reshaped, but the public—or publics—of infrastructure'. Being 'developed' and gaining distance from 'backward' pasts is crucial for many people in Dimapur, it is part of what draws them to the city, and this feeling is shaped through the material presence of infrastructure. And yet the condition of the infrastructure, the unevenness, the dilapidation, the corruption—proven and rumoured—turns people off the city, especially young people, many of whom leave to pursue their dreams elsewhere. As Collier et al. (2016) add, '[i]f at one time the public was imagined as a homogenous and passive subject of need, today multiple publics are involved in contesting and making (differential) claims on the state'. This is challenging in Dimapur where the state itself is fragmented: it is a multi-ethnic city in a tribal state ruled by a constellation of state and non-state actors operating at different scales serving different publics. An outcome of this is the coexistence of adjacent publics in the same city.

A common preoccupation in public life is lamenting a lack of development, usually imagined as infrastructure. This fractured modernity of Dimapur also generates citizen campaigns for better roads and more participatory planning. Yet military infrastructure, housing, technology, surveillance, and weaponry provide a hyper-modern contrast. Bases and barracks are integral to this contrast along with advanced technologies like weaponry (on display in the patrolling vehicles and bodies of armed forces personnel), telecommunications and information technology (especially on demography, topography, geology, and geography—most of which is unavailable to the public), and properties featuring swimming pools, clubs, schools, cafés, movie theatres, and medical facilities inside garrisons and military housing. Yet military modernity is excluded from accounts of development in Dimapur and the frontier generally, a testament to the separation between military and civilian space.

Although these spaces overlap, the overlap is uneven—military personnel often enter civilian space, yet the reverse is far less common. However, in pockets of Nagaland (even in cities like Dimapur), daily tasks like visiting an ATM, walking between work and home, or crossing district boundaries necessitates crossing the lines between 'developed' military space and 'undeveloped' civilian space. It is among the civilian government that the desire for infrastructure, and eventually extraction, is so pronounced.

In neighbourhoods, even deep in the centre of the city, customary authority in tribal councils provides community infrastructure and exercises a degree of spatial control. In some localities with more than one dominant tribal community, there are parallel figures of authority managing the same territory through different forums. Some of this infrastructure is provided through funds from the state, both local and national, while some is provided through contributions of residents, often for purposes of infrastructure development to offset state neglect—patching up holes in the cement pavement, organizing private waste collection, extending a neighbourhood road to new settlements, and so on.

We pay attention to infrastructure on its own but also as part of the built environment more generally. Herscher and Siddiqi ask us to consider the spatial histories of political violence, with their own sequences, continuities, and ruptures. Spatial violence calls for us to hone our understanding of the deeper and slower structural forms of violence that contour political historical categories such as 'development', 'reconstruction', 'modernity', 'peace', 'progress', and so on, which they argue is 'a constitutive dimension of architecture, urbanism, and their epistemologies' (Herscher and Siddiqi 2014: 270–1). In Dimapur, neighbourhoods, public buildings, commercial areas, houses, slums, parks, ceasefire camps, barracks, and memorials tell stories of past and present relationships of power and violence (Image I.6). Juxtapositions help to illustrate these relationships. King (2011: 12) describes juxtapositions as attention to the positioning 'of the dissimilar and even the incompatible', drawing attention to the ways in which space is appropriated, officially and unofficially, temporarily and more permanently, all of which drive change, reflecting past and present configurations of power and their accompanying imaginations.

It is not just fissures between the civilian and military space that are striking; multi-storeyed houses of the elite and well-connected (to both state and non-state power), with high fences and a fleet of cars parked on the lawn, rise adjacent to bamboo thatch and mud shacks. Even more common are reinforced concrete buildings with bamboo thatch extensions (see Image I.7), bringing the material of modernity and urbanity—concrete—in concert with the material of the village—bamboo—to create a vernacular architecture that suggests improvisation, mobility, and the ceaseless flow of kin and family in and out of residences in the city. If we agree with Forty (2012: 41) when he argues that 'seen from the developed world, part of what makes reinforced concrete disagreeable is precisely its poverty', then vernacular housing in Dimapur narrates poverty at the intersection of urban and village, planning and improvisation: tactics gleaned through decades of conflict and erratic settlement.

Mansions designed by architects sit behind high fences (Image I.8), while imitation architecture can be spotted on segments of houses—columns and balconies—along with do-it-yourself extensions; many Dimapur house owners, especially men, are in constant renovation mode as funds appear from remittances, contracts, pensions, or revenue from land sales outside the city. Settlements started by families seeking refuge from violence have grown into neighbourhoods and communities. Some become legible parts of the

Image I.6   Tribal capitalism at Shijo complex

Source: Duncan McDuie-Ra

Image I.7   Do-it-yourself extensions using cement and bamboo at Supply
Colony

Source: Duncan McDuie-Ra

Image I.8   Grand residence in Dimapur's 'Beverly Hills', Sovima

Source: Duncan McDuie-Ra

city, others remain distant from state authority, and yet others have residents who are struggling against threats of eviction.

Spaces of Consumption

Consumer spaces are the ideal sites to witness the encounters of the in-between zone that is Dimapur. During our fieldwork, we paid attention to where goods were being sold, what was being sold, who was selling them, in what type of building or market, the manner in which objects were sold (clandestine, open), and visual, aural, and olfactory accompaniments to these activities. As with the visual culture mentioned previously—and indeed much of the visual culture is tied to selling goods—we were drawn by the goods being sold and the circuits they reflected. We were also drawn to the customers and the interactions between them and sellers—interactions that frequently cross linguistic, ethnic, and tribal/non-tribal boundaries—and to the various authorities that collect fees and taxes from vendors, including uniformed tax collectors for the NSCN-IM.

Consumer spaces reveal other dynamics too. Meat is sold in the open in many parts of Dimapur just like many urban hubs across India: pork and beef are sold out of small butchers in neighbourhoods throughout the day; chicken is available strung up on bamboo racks on street corners; and dogs and other animals can be bought in local markets—though dogs are subject to anxiety by the authorities and some residents, as we will discuss later. There is much to be said about the politics of food in Dimapur, but the open sale of pork and beef, meats that are categorized as taboo for dominant religious groups like Hindus and Muslims, signifies that this is tribal space—at least in parts—and tribal eating habits will prevail over the food taboos of other communities.

Peddlers of various goods are mobile throughout the city, entering neighbourhoods, commercial areas, and setting up on pavements selling everything from second-hand clothes to silkworms (to eat). Mobile peddlers are also adept at repurposing infrastructure, ruins, and wastelands as sites to sell, keep stock, and rest. Indeed, consumer spaces have developed purposefully in zoned areas for non-tribal and later tribal capitalism—showrooms, shopping centres, and malls—but also organically underneath raised overpasses, on railway tracks, and out of residences.

Traders are drawn to the frontier, to the in-between zone between hills and plains, non-tribal space and tribal space, and the railway has long brought goods and traders to the city. And the city has developed around these sites. A reading of Dimapur's history is possible by mapping established spaces of consumption such as the Hong Kong market and Marwari Patti, as well as alternative areas for tribal traders such as the Super Market and temporary locations utilized by different communities.

We were able to grasp a sense of the way flows of movement through different parts of the city—flows continually in flux following the creation and destruction of new walkways (above and underground), transport routes and hubs, vehicle and pedestrian thoroughfares, competing sites and vendors, extortion attempts, pockets of gentrification and urban decline—shape and are shaped by the desire to buy and sell goods.

Stories

During this research, we heard stories from all kinds of people in all kinds of settings. But why did we turn to stories for direction to understand urban experiences in Dimapur? Stories offer us rich experiences about place-making and memories of places and social relations. In addition, storytelling involves an active process of speaking and communicating a plot that includes performances to represent and promote distinct meanings about encounters. Drawing from ethnographic methods about studying everyday lives in urban spaces (Biehl 2005; Bourgois and Schonberg 2009; O'Neill 2017), our approach was to present the urban scene we experienced during our fieldwork. Eating, talking, walking, and attending cultural events, we gained access to both spaces and stories. As will be evident from the ethnographic chapters in Part II of the book, we present stories as an integral part of the ethnographic method. As such, telling stories about Dimapur means writing ethnography with care and considering the voices of communities and life stories on the ground. We take ethnography as 'a site of expression for politics, economics, justice, and the ethical' (Pandian and McLean 2017: 22) and, hence, decided to carry out a collaborative form of ethnographic writing to tell stories of a frontier city. The experiences of co-authoring an ethnographic text where we present stories as an integral part of the book require trust and the scrutinizing of one's individual ability to collaborate and listen to insights from the collaborating researcher. Stories, for example, provoke emotions and enable us to record the lives of people who otherwise might be in positions of power as leaders, politicians, or tribal elders. We identified field notes, images, and interviews jointly to portray the lives and complexities of living in a militarized violent city. So, how did we start the process?

We began with friends, relatives, and past acquaintances. For some aspects of the fieldwork, we had a 'wish list' of respondents and had to utilize contacts to get in touch with them. We met some of our respondents while walking around, some while waiting for other appointments, and some found us! Others refused to meet us. We conducted interviews in music studios, offices, businesses, colleges, seminaries, workshops, guesthouses, households, in cars, and while walking around. We interviewed respondents over several hours in large groups—including a 20-strong group of urban hunters, in shifts—as with students at a theological college who came in batches determined by cohort, and one-on-one. Some interviews were long, some were short, and some were just conversations that happened by accident. During some interviews, both of us (Kikon and McDuie-Ra) were present; at others, there was only one of us, and this has been mentioned wherever we believe it matters for the content.

In seeking stories of Dimapur, the most common element was agency: stories of people making things happen in the city or failing to. The explanations people give for success or failure connect their lives to bigger things, to factors shaping their reality, even if articulating these factors with precision is difficult. Common to most accounts of agency, the possibilities for action and the limitations, is the reference to the multifarious and ambiguous networks of power that operate in the city and shape its material and social form. These networks are legacies of the conflict, the ceasefire, and the geopolitics of the frontier.

At their simplest, accounts of everyday politics in the Northeast envisage a powerful and brutal Indian state and military apparatus that alienates and suffocates the local population, conceptualized through Agamben's (1998, 2005) notion of 'bare life' under a 'state of exception' in recent times (Basavapatna 2012; Chakravarti 2010; Gaikwad 2009; Kshetrimayum 2009; McDuie-Ra 2009; Sundar 2011; Vajpeyi 2009). Others will situate local populations between the overbearing state and the coercive and extortive practices of insurgent groups and ethnonationalist organizations. Less common are analyses that break down the components of the state, particularly the vicissitudes in relations between Indian and federal state governments—Nagaland *and* Assam in the case of Dimapur—and local authorities: a complex assemblage of district, municipal, spiritual, and customary authorities and figures who move among and between them. The Indian state and military *are* brutal (and have been for a long time). The local population *does* line up behind racial categories; tribal and non-tribal from time to time, but also behind narrower groupings (tribe and clan) and groupings that do not fit identity narratives. Local authorities are beset by competition, contradiction, and corruption. Alliances are made among the powerful, and those who aspire to power, that cut across assumed tribal/non-tribal, secular/sacral, and pro/anti-India lines. All of these readings are necessary, and all of them emerged in our conversations, interviews, and shared adventures with residents of the city.

Focusing on the city, on the space where these converge, collapses multiple forms of authority and a diverse population with shifting affinities into a tight space (Bollens 2012), where kin, friends, enemies, lovers, strangers, 'big shots', and nobodies develop tactics and networks to get by, to make it, seek healing (corporeal and spiritual), and to disappear, drop out, or dissolve into the fabric of Dimapur. This resonates with Dunn and Cons's description of 'burdened agency', the agency of subjects 'who, in struggling to recreate normal lives on an uneven terrain shaped by competing projects of rule, must negotiate conflicting projects of sovereignty and necessarily transgress the visions and plans that undergird attempts to control them' (Dunn and Cons 2014: 93–4). Authority, violence, and coercion have vastly different origins in varied constellations and negotiating these in everyday life brings them into sharp relief, regardless of success or failure. And this, we argue, brings Dimapur to life and goes a long way in animating our arguments and bringing the city, the frontier, and the Northeast, generally, to life.

Structure of the Book

The book is organized in two parts: the first focuses on space and the second on stories. Along with this 'Introduction', Part I contains two chapters that explore militarism, capitalism, and urbanism through an analysis of spatial politics leading to two definitive crises in the city in recent years: the lynching of 2015 and the month-long *bandh* of 2017. Chapter 1 unravels the core tensions at the heart of Dimapur's urban politics: the growth of a migrant city in tribal territory. Beginning with the public lynching of rape accused Syed Farid Khan, whose dead body was strung on City Tower, a notable piece of 'modern' urban symbolism in a city with few others, we analyse the incident as an opening to the territorial politics at the heart of Dimapur's demographic anxieties. Unlike other cities and towns in tribal states in the Northeast, Dimapur is not a tribal settlement that has suddenly been invaded by migrants, who are aided in this by lax enforcement of protective laws, it is a space settled from multiple directions by different communities (tribal and non-tribal) that engage in a variety of tactics turning settlements into neighbourhoods. We focus on place-making in Dimapur to explore the ways in which different communities from within and outside Nagaland create a sense of belonging in patches of the city, arguing that the tensions between migrant city and tribal territory produce and reflect a spatial order particular to Dimapur. This order appears cosmopolitan, though as the lynching showed, it can also be extremely fragile.

Chapter 2 analyses the attempts by local and central governments to make Dimapur more city-like. Beginning with the crisis that erupted following attempts to hold municipal elections with reserved seats for women in 2017, we navigate the deeply contentious politics around the classification and re-classification of space in Dimapur. In particular, we focus on the threat—or imagined threat—to the power and legitimacy of tribal councils as urban space is produced out of Dimapur's patchwork. Producing a legible urban space from the collection of settlements, villages, barrack, commercial zones, ceasefire camps, encroached tracts, and wastelands under various socio-legal regimes is an immense challenge. There are several drivers of the production of urban space in the present era, most notably the urban turn in Delhi's development agenda, a turn felt heavily in the financially dependent Nagaland. As the largest city in a tribal state, Dimapur is also an experiment in the production of legible urban space in areas with customary law and constitutional protection. We argue that the city is a space to challenge and transgress customary law in ways unthinkable at the village level. However, transgression was a catalyst for crisis, a scenario likely to remain constant in urban politics for the conceivable future.

Part II departs in structure. The chapters are deeply ethnographic in nature and contain arguments and analysis that are drawn from our field interviews and field notes. Methodologically drawing from the conceptual themes discussed in Part I of the book, Part II focuses on the relationship between the lived experiences and the meanings that are forged in Dimapur. Putting the themes of militarism, urban space, and territoriality side by side (Part I) with the conversations and challenges of living in Dimapur (Part II), our understanding of the character of the city is founded on relationships and interactions that urban dwellers forge with the city. At times, these appear as dialogues, at other times as emotional reflections or outrageous satires about the harsh reality. Part II offers an ethnography of people, places, and objects. We have organized these accounts and experiences around the themes of the book: militarism, capitalism, and urbanism. Most notably, the ethnographic chapters are organized around gendered spaces and interpersonal relations that are captured in the backdrop of a social and political hierarchy (traditional authorities, state organs, and non-state actors). We pull these stories and spaces together in our conclusion.

Part II of the book focuses on the experiences of Dimapur and its spatial politics discussed in Part I through the lives of different communities, individuals, and through the witnessing of particular events. We have sought voices that are both central to how Dimapur is imagined among its residents—around music, hunting, and death—and are unconventional in the ways in which most cities are researched. We have not gravitated to the usual voices of authority or expertise on urban matters. This is in part a testament to Dimapur's experimental territorial form, as discussed in Chapter 1. Challenging these nodes of power, these elements in the machine of Dimapur, is to challenge gender relations as we will see in Chapter 2 and as will become clearer in the following chapters. The focus on stories in Part II is also a response to the call by Simone and Pieterse (2017) to rethink the ways in which we approach research on cities in the Global South, and to that we would add cities in the backroads, frontiers, and borderlands within the Global South. They advance a research agenda for urbanization in Asia and Africa that pays little heed to established approaches imported from the Global North. One of their key arguments is that urban knowledge and practice needs to be considered as 'a permanent site of experimentation' (Simone and Pieterse 2017: 154). They identify initiatives by artists, writers, and non-academics to capture urban worlds and urge scholars to 'remain committed to an epistemological adventurism that can take in numerous forms of representation, critique, proposition and, especially, provocation' (Simone and Pieterse 2017: 174). Part II of the book takes on the call for epistemological adventurism by focusing on the lives of music makers, animal hunters and protectors, and coffin makers, and the ways in which their lives are entangled with the city. In keeping with this spirit of adventurism, Chapters 3–5 of this book are drawn from encounters and conversations, images and events. We have included interviews, field notes, and documents that we collected during our fieldwork to compel the reader to engage and reflect on frontier militarized urbanisms. At the same time, we underline relationships and networks that flourish in Dimapur to highlight the significance of frontier urbanism. We will draw these stories together with the spaces discussed in Part I in the book's closing epilogue.

Chapter 3 follows the sounds of Dimapur through the lives of musicians and the nascent music industry. Dimapur has become a home for Naga musicians to establish music schools and recording studios and to hold events. Indeed, for a city with restrictions on mobility and a history of curfews, there are a surprising number of music performances across many genres throughout the year. Yet Dimapur is also the subject of the city's music. Musicians write and sing about the city, giving the urban landscape a presence in popular culture. The city also appears in music videos, circulated digitally through YouTube and other platforms, putting it 'on the map' for consumers of contemporary Naga music, whether in the frontier, in cities in other parts of India, or in diaspora. Through these networks, Dimapur is experienced as sound and image, some of which draw conspicuously on the past of militarism, though much eschews the past to project notions of a future, a capitalist future of wealth and conspicuous consumption played out in the urban landscape.

Chapter 4 explores the ways in which Naga hunting traditions are recast in the city. As discussed in the previous chapters, Dimapur is an enclave surrounded by Assam, and most of the remaining forest lies in Assam. Hunting expeditions bring hunters from the city into Assam's territory and into encounters with different security forces, other hunters, insurgents, and otherworldly spirits. And while intergenerational change and urbanization have reduced the desire to hunt, for many urban residents, hunting is a way to keep their connections to the village alive, blurring urban and rural boundaries. Yet even these illicit hunting grounds are disappearing with deforestation within and beyond tribal territory. Meanwhile in the city, the debate on selling dog meat has reconfigured human–animal relationships in a different way. Pressure to ban the sale of dog meat and make Dimapur more city-like has been met with opposition and approval from different urban residents. The dog-meat debate extends our point that the fringes (where hunters live) and the centre (of trade and market) are both founded on tribal authority and identity, with the urban landscape taking form around these.

Chapter 5 highlights the corporeal elements (dead bodies) and material artefacts (coffins) of death in Dimapur. We examine the processes of living and dying in Dimapur as a practice of place-making. The contestations and ambiguities of belonging emerge in death, as relatives want the bodies sent back to ancestral villages. Dimapur is not a final resting place, at least if it can be avoided. In this sense, Dimapur remains a migrant city where a sense of impermanence always dwells among the numerous tribal residents settled here. Increasing numbers of Nagas living in Dimapur are not associated with their ancestral villages in their everyday lives. They enjoy the benefits of modernization and consider their lives in Dimapur as an improved way of living given the easy accessibility of the market, communication, and mobile lives. Yet, conversation about dying in the city presents a compelling portrait of tribal alienation, exclusion, and disenchantments of modern living. This chapter asks: Where do these conversations take place? In what kinds of gatherings can we identify these emotions about living and dying in Dimapur? These questions led us to different locations and sites within the city, from a tribal women's association meeting, to reflections on an NSCN-IM leader's funeral, to the memorial schools and parks (dedicated to the deceased) that have been built across the city, to the philosophy and life-story of a coffin-maker.

The book closes with a short 'Epilogue'. It draws together the two parts of the book, the *meanings* granted and contested in particular spaces in the city and the embodied *experiences* of the city by its residents, to capture the dynamics of the ceasefire city—dynamics we describe as militarism, capitalism, and urbanism. We use a description of a single site visited by both authors together in early 2018 as the catalyst for drawing these parts together: the collapsed bridge over the Chathe River also known as the *Pagla Nodi* (Mad River) in Nagamese at Naga United Village, a large locality skirting the eastern edge of Dimapur along its border with Assam. During our visit in 2017, the bridge was being rebuilt with construction expected to be fully complete by late 2020. In 2019, residents living around the Naga United Village and beyond continued to cross over to Dimapur on a temporary bridge spanning the river further north—a crossing that caused traffic jams and was precarious during the monsoon season mid-year. It is also this temporary bridge that connects the city to one of the designated ceasefire camps, the Vihokhu Camp, where NSCN-U cadres are stationed. Perhaps most symbolic is the beautiful entry gate to Naga United Village, opened by the deputy transport commissioner of Nagaland in 2011. The gate no longer marks the connection between the village and the rest of the city, and immediately outside the gate is a steep drop into the riverbed. In 2017, the site of the collapsed bridge had become a magnet for protest signs bemoaning development failure and corruption, as well as attempts at DIY urban development by citizens trying to ensure that Naga United Village does not remain entirely cut off from the rest of the city. At the collapsed bridge, the visions of Dimapur as a cohesive urban space, as city-like, meet the reality of its patchwork of places demarcated and governed as almost distinct units. The common spaces in between fall into disrepair and become a locus for community frustrations; frustrations materialized in concrete slabs collapsed into the riverbed and an ornate village gate leading nowhere.

Finally, it is important to state clearly what this book is not about. First, many of the events of the last seven decades in what is presently Nagaland (and Assam and Manipur) appear from time to time in this book. They are integral in shaping urban space, fuelling migration, and producing the forms of capitalism that power Dimapur. They also come up in the stories of residents. However, this is a book about Dimapur as an enclave and in-between space, and not an account of Naga politics, history, or the struggle against the Indian state. We feel that the Naga struggle has been analysed with skill and diligence in a range of works and that we could not hope to improve upon these in any way (see, for example, Chasie and Hazarika 2009; Longkumer 2018b; Lotha 2016; Shimray 2005; Wouters 2018). Second, we do not detail the ceasefire process and the various territorial proposals offered or the process of reconciliation between different armed factions and Naga communities. The hard-working activists and community members involved in the processes and the journalists and scholars who witness it relate these events best. Third, we do not seek to resolve questions of customary law versus so-called 'modern' democratic reforms. Events in Dimapur have brought the question of customary law to the forefront of Naga politics once again and we are interested in the unfolding of these events and the ways in which urbanization is implicated in them. However, we do not provide a history of customary law or detail the intricacies of its variations between different tribal groups, nor do we opt for crowd-pleasing platitudes celebrating its longevity. Fourth, this is not a history of Dimapur 'since time immemorial'; it is an account of its recent past. It is not ahistorical, yet we do not go through the motions of Dimasa settlement, dispossession, colonial incursion, and the Second World War accounts. We are far more interested in history as evinced in the spaces of the city and the stories of its residents. Finally, this book is not another exploration of identity, the fallacies of categories like tribal or Naga, or the fragility of traditions. These issues continue to be studied at great length in and outside the region and if readers are interested, such works can be found without much difficulty.

Part I

Space

1

Migrant City, Tribal Territory

In March 2015, a group described in media outlets throughout the world as a 'mob' broke into the Dimapur Central Jail, dragged out rape accused Syed Farid Khan, beat him to death, and carried his body for over eight kilometres through the city to City Tower, a recognizable landmark. Here, Khan's corpse was strung up on the outer fence before a large crowd packed into the circular space surrounding the tower, blocking police and security access until they were eventually dispersed. The 'mob'—described variously as 'murderous', 'frenzied', and 'gruesome'—was alleged to be between 8,000 and 10,000 people. Forty-three were arrested, many of whom were college students. Footage of Khan's body being hauled through the crowd and hanging from the tower was circulated through social media and was quickly picked up by the press. The event triggered a week-long curfew under Section 144 of the Indian criminal code, counter-protests in Assam and elsewhere, blockades of roads to Dimapur from Assam, cutting off of the Internet, a probe by the Central Bureau of Investigation, a judicial probe (Agarwal Commission), police suspensions, and (though far less reported) plenty of soul-searching and condemnation among Dimapur's residents. The then-chief minister, T.R. Zeliang, posited that the incident was an attempt to create chaos and bring down the state government (Mitra 2015).

The horrific event became a staple of news coverage all over the world, and as Kikon noted in her essay on the lynching and its aftermath, it was the first time she could remember Dimapur ever receiving this much attention. She writes, '[w]hen I was growing up, I could never imagine that my hometown Dimapur would become a front-page or a national television "breaking news" material, or for that matter, that it would be associated with a lynching incident' (Kikon 2015a). The media focused on several aspects of the incident: the nature of the mob and the intolerance of migrants in Nagaland—an argument which extended to all of the Northeast; the build-up of anti-illegal migrant activity on the preceding day—including protests specifically mentioning Khan; his real name (Syed Farid Khan) and family background (including the fact that his family has military ties and he had a Naga wife); his citizenship (eventually verified by the chief minister of Assam); the sexual incident in question, particularly the charge of rape versus the claim of consent and alleged payment; essentialist commentary on Naga temperament and propensity for violence; tribal xenophobia; the complicity of the local media; government failure (both state and national); government collusion; claims that members of the NSCN-IM were also freed by the 'mob'; the economic motivations for the incident (Laskar 2015); and even the place of the incident in national memory (Kurian 2015).

There was far less consideration of Dimapur itself, of what the lynching said about the city: about who belongs and who does not, and how this is changing. Writing in the widely circulated *Economic and Political Weekly* in the aftermath of the lynching, Laskar, a former State Bank of India employee-turned-journalist posted in Dimapur for a period in the mid-1990s, seeks to explain the incident as an inevitable outcome of the city's demography. It is worth quoting at length as it crafts an image of uncivility and disorder that is (apparently) not found in the rest of the state. Laskar (2015) writes:

> Dimapur is not typical of the rest of Nagaland. Had something similar [to the lynching] taken place elsewhere in the state, the outcome would not have been as savage and uncivilised as what we saw in Dimapur.... While Indians living outside Nagaland need an Inner Line Permit (ILP) to enter the state, this does not apply to Dimapur town. As a result, you have people from all over India living in Dimapur, something you do not see in the rest of the state.... What makes things worse is that Dimapur is also a safe haven for criminals of all kinds.... The administration in Dimapur is spineless and the rule of law is as good as non-existent.

Perhaps his endorsement of the 'exclusive homelands' (Baruah 2003) discourse that has dominated the region is unintended, but the point made is a common one. Dimapur's diversity is the cause. It violates the territoriality inscribed in the Indian Constitution and its colonial genealogy: the line between tribal and non-tribal, savage and civilized, hills and plains. Such accounts are limited not only because of their assumptions about violence but because they identify migration as the movement of 'outsiders' from other parts of India (and possibly Bangladesh) to Dimapur and ignore migration from other parts of the hills, return migration from Nagas who have been living outside the state, and the state-driven migration and occupation of the city by the military. Dimapur is not a tribal settlement suddenly invaded by migrants aided by the lax enforcement of laws imposed stringently in other parts of the state. It is a space where people from different communities have settled in and engage in a variety of tactics in turning settlements into neighbourhoods.

Khan had lived in Dimapur for nearly two decades and was married to a local woman but was (apparently) singled out for violence because he was an illegal immigrant, a Bangladeshi, who had (allegedly) raped a tribal woman who filed a case with the police, leading to his arrest. Several writers have pointed out that Khan was an Indian citizen, a long-term resident of Dimapur, and thus undeserving of such treatment. Even the 'illegal Bangladeshi' narrative grafts a national anxiety onto a tribal territory, where citizenship is less important than status as a tribal or non-tribal. Dimapur is, after all, a tribal territory, though it is a migrant city. As Achumi (2019: 213) notes, in Dimapur, '[t]raders migrating to Nagaland mostly locate themselves in an [sic] unrecorded post-colonial relationships and encounters. The parochial politics between Hindus and Muslims present in other parts of India is absent in Nagaland because both Hindus and Muslims are outsiders for the Nagas'.

Kikon is one of the few commentators on the incident to situate Khan—a used-car dealer—in Dimapur's ethnic diversity. Kikon (2015a) writes:

> Like many traders in Dimapur, Farid Khan moved within the labyrinth and nurtured friendships and alliances to seek new contacts and connections. Some commentators who painted the life of Farid Khan solely as a family man, and a Muslim victim who hailed from Assam, denied him the city where he lived, made connections, and lost his life. Such simplified renditions of reality are akin to recognizing the victory of the shrillest voice in the mob that demanded his blood. To recognize Farid Khan as a

foreigner and label him as solely belonging to Assam ... is to oppose the
choices of thousands of people who choose to settle down in Dimapur and
call it their home.

Dimapur is a city of migrants. People from different communities have
settled here seeking work, opportunities, and refuge, and on postings
in the armed forces, government, and with religious organizations.
Khan's fate brings to forefront the tensions between the migrant city
and the tribal territory; tensions that are exacerbated when there are
violations of the city's spatial order. As discussed in the 'Introduction',
it is an in-between space, a zone, an enclave, an experiment that is at
once exceptional and that foreshadows urban futures in other parts
of the frontier.

In this chapter, we use this lynching as an entry point into the
tensions between the migrant city and tribal territory. We do not take
these tensions to be problematic per se; rather, we consider them
as fundamental for analysing Dimapur as a frontier constellation.
These tensions shape Dimapur as a city and as more than a city—a
zone, an enclave. To explore this, the first section focuses on place-
making in Dimapur—the ways in which different communities
from within and outside Nagaland create a sense of belonging. In
the second section, we focus on the ways in which communities
have created a sense of belonging through religious buildings,
gates, architecture, naming, memorials, and various other material
and ideational tools. A city with minimal planning (until recently),
communities have built it in patches, creating an urban fabric that is
uneven but vernacular in its form. As a city of migrants searching for
opportunities, refuge, and hope, place-making is integral to life in
the city and staying connected to home, provided that people remain
in their place. In the third section, we play with the idea of Dimapur
as a city 'off the map'. Despite its size and commercial importance
Dimapur is 'unseen' in the cultural production of Nagaland as a
tribal state. This both reflects and enables the production of Dimapur
as an enclave or zone: part of a tribal state but not subject to strict
enforcement of its rules and laws, which in turn makes it attractive
for migrants. However, being part of a tribal territory does matter,
even if the form varies from other parts of Nagaland. In the fourth
section, we examine the edges of the city where urban space and

tribal territory intersect. In some areas, such as the northwest of the city, the tactics of place-making are not simply about belonging to the city but extending the city and, in turn, the tribal land. In others, such as Lahorijan, there is a 'line' between Dimapur and Assam that marks not just different states, legal regimes, and forms of authority, but different perceptions of morality; perceptions that reverse the assumptions of savagery discussed following the lynching. We end the chapter with a brief conclusion and argue that the migrant city and tribal territory produce and reflect a spatial order particular to Dimapur. This order appears cosmopolitan, though, as the lynching showed, it can also be fragile.

Belonging in the Migrant City

Dimapur draws migrants from all over the frontier, India, and across international borders, making it a place of contact, encounter, and belonging and exclusion. While incidents like the lynching suggest the failure of Dimapur's cosmopolitanism, when one considers the contentious politics of identity that take place in the city and in the territories it rubs up against, the history of armed conflict embedded in the city, and the multiple forms of authority and law that control space, the persistence of everyday civility—and mutual dependency—between different communities suggests a more robust urban fabric. We explore this urban fabric by exploring the ways in which different communities establish a sense of place in the city: an integral part of the city's spatial order. In the absence of effective urban planning, communities create the city's urban fabric and—in some cases—destroy it.

Dimapur does not have a public history: There is no city museum, no old photos mounted in a public square, and few monumental objects narrating an official version of the city's past. There is no public repository of when the area was first occupied, by whom, and what happened after. During fieldwork, both authors called on various government departments searching for maps, settlement information, and photographs, with limited success. In one case, we were asked to bring anything we find back to the bureaucrat, as they also wanted the information to better administer the city.

Accounts of Dimapur's past usually begin with the Dimasa/ Kachari community—a now-majority Hindu tribal community living in Assam and Nagaland—and their fortified garrison that existed on the site until the sixteenth century (see Guite 2015; Ramirez 2007). The ruins (as seen in the front cover of this book) are accessible in central Dimapur near the banks of the Dhansiri River and wedged between a paramilitary headquarters (MGAR, Maintenance Group for the Assam Rifles), Super Market, and a government high school. The ruins have been renovated in recent years and are now frequented by visitors and residents who picnic, socialize, and even study in one of the few public green spaces in the city—albeit in full view of the paramilitary barracks. There are other ruins in the city, mostly tanks, and they have given names to different localities such as Padampukhuri in the city's east. There are fragments of settlement in contemporary place names. For instance, Duncan Bosti is named after S.J. Duncan, the deputy commissioner of the erstwhile Naga Hills (1949–52) who encouraged settlement in the hills. Early settlers ended up becoming powerful landowners and in turn have their names reproduced in areas and roads in the city, such as the Nyamo Lotha Road. Achumi notes that Jain communities began migrating to Dimapur in the 1880s. She writes, 'the contributions of Jains in the making of Dimapur as early migrants and settlers is evident today in the business expansions made by Sethi and his brothers, S.D Jain Charitable hospital, the popular S.D Jain college and S.D Jain school in Dimapur' (Achumi 2019: 209). Similar traces are found in other commercial areas, such as the Marwari Patti, named after the Marwari merchant communities originally from Rajasthan; Hazi Park, with a large population of Bengali Muslims and a historic mosque; and Tibetan and Bhutia settlements around areas trading in clothes, such as the Shangri-La area.

Dimapur features in Assamese writing, especially the chronicles or *burunji*, and in various histories of Assam, especially of the Dimasa and Kachari communities, who still inhabit parts of Dimapur, though most of them are based in Assam (mostly in the Dima Hasao district). Dimapur has been of limited interest to scholars of the colonial frontier, though it does make appearances in accounts of the Kachari ruins and monoliths, accounts of routes and passes between Assam and Myanmar (Burma), information regarding frontier railways, and writings on the Second World War (Barpujari 1997; Hutton 1922; Maretina 1978). It also appears in accounts of the Naga tribes in the vicinity—especially Semas—though this reveals little about the environment of the settlement, as most accounts are village-based. The distant past is of little concern to those who call Dimapur home.

During the Second World War, the decades of the Naga insurgency during the 1950s to the 1990s, and the conflicts that fractured neighbouring polities (Manipur in particular), Dimapur was a major site for supplying different armed groups and militaries. This past is reflected in locality names such as the Burma Camp, Supply Colony, Sewak (a project of the Border Roads Association), Veterinary Colony, Railway Colony, Signal Bosti (and Signal Angami, named after the Angami tribe), and Firing Range. Other locality names reflect the communities that settled in different sites, such as the Nepali Bosti, Manipuri Colony, Ragailong Colony, and scores of names of different Naga villages and clans, some of which have suffixes like 'Old' and 'New', 'A' and 'B', and prefixes like 'Half' and 'Full' to account for expansion. Other names identify the current and former sites of state-building (pre- and post-Nagaland), such as the Taxes Colony, Bank Colony, and NST (Nagaland State Transportation) Colony, while still others refer to the current and former sites of production—Sugar Mill Colony, Brick Kilns—as well as urbanization—Electrical Colony, Industrial Estate Colony, and Model Village.

Given that it is a city of migrants, a city that has grown tenfold in the 30 years between 1981 and 2011, the past that shapes the city is a relatively recent one, a vernacular one. What is perhaps far more relevant than a recounting of communities and kingdoms that passed through Dimapur centuries ago are the objects built by the nation state (India), the local state (Nagaland), and other groups such as churches, property developers, and customary authorities. Also relevant is that the monumental is dwarfed by the vernacular in much of the city, or at least covered up, defaced, juxtaposed with it, or countered by it (see Amin 2014). With this in mind, we are interested in the ways in which this vernacular can be gleaned from the landscape, objects, the built environment, symbols, and texts. Through these, we are able to trace Dimapur's past in its lived present and possible futures. In particular, we are interested in the place-making practices that have turned settlements into neighbourhoods and migrants into residents.

Place-making is an oft-used concept subject to debate and contention in different disciplines and interdisciplinary intersections (see Massey 1993; Merrifield 1993). The basic premise is a distinction between space and place, particularly in human and political geography, wherein space is rootless and shaped by external forces and place is rooted and shaped through human agency to produce and reproduce a social and moral meaning (Agnew 2011: 322). Thus, place is often aligned with community and, by extension, tradition: the counter to spatial hegemony. As such, place is seen as an arena of struggle against modernity, against the soulless demolition of place, of community, especially in urban areas. Oakes has provoked this bifurcation by arguing that place and modernity are not antithetical. He encourages us to engage with the 'sense of ambivalence, contradiction, and paradox with which people continue to engage with the changes swirling around them' (Oakes 1997: 510). For Oakes (1997: 520), place is not solely a 'progressive counterpoint to some vague placeless modernity'; rather places are where the paradoxes of modernity play out and where people struggle to create identities, belonging, and a sense of their world. Indeed, place-making can be a way to become modern and escape tradition, or at least dull its effect.

In this chapter, and also in the stories that follow in Part II of the book, we adopt Friedmann's use of place and place-making as an entry point to explore belonging, exclusion, and boundaries in Dimapur. Friedmann defines places as 'small spaces' of a city. Place-making occurs when a material space is inhabited and allows patterns and rhythms of life to develop. Based on his work in China and Taiwan, Friedmann (2007: 272) arrives at seven propositions for understanding place-making, and it is worth discussing them and their relevance for our context. First, place-making is a social process characterized by contestation. Place is not granted but made through social practices that often invoke competing claims over material space. Once created, places are not fixed but subject to continued contestation. Second, habitation of material space leads to patterns of everyday life centred on places of encounter where rituals of life are performed (such as parks, markets, churches, restaurants, and houses). Third, places are impermanent and undergo changes over time. Fourth, the rituals of everyday life offer a sense of security and stability. Fifth, the autonomy of place is illusory and subject to regulation, which in Dimapur includes actions and rules of the state, armed forces, customary bodies, underground groups, and the local municipal authorities. Sixth, commonality and solidarity among a community in a particular place should not always be assumed, and the state (and in the case of Dimapur non-state and state-like actors listed in the previous point) can divide communities over certain issues. Finally, as people, especially younger people, move away from the places they have carved out, their sense of place can diminish. In Dimapur, there are two elements to this. Some people move away from villages and ancestral homes to be in the city permanently, and some of the rituals and fabric of everyday life are lost in that movement, though there are concerted efforts to reproduce home, especially the village, in the city. People also move away from Dimapur temporarily, especially young people, usually to larger metropolitan cities elsewhere in India or abroad. Many return, especially in the post-ceasefire era, and while some of them readjust without difficulties, find their place and networks once again, others struggle to reconnect with the city and with an ancestral village they may never have lived in.

While we are very conscious of the concept's limitations, we see value in place-making as a way to come to terms with the city's diversity and with the visible and invisible lines that denote belonging and exclusion which shape the city's spatial order. Belonging and exclusion can be read through the visual culture and built environment, through what is consumed and peddled, and through the stories of those living in the city (see Part II). The possibilities for identifying place are almost limitless. Here we focus on sites that we feel capture Dimapur's urban fabric and reflect the dynamics of militarism, capitalism, and urbanism that have driven the city's growth and capture its diversity: (*i*) churches and places of worship; (*ii*) urban villages and village urbanism; (*iii*) memorials; (*iv*) belonging on the margins; and (*v*) banal militarism.

Churches and Place of Worship

Perhaps the most telling examples of place-making in Dimapur are places of worship. This is true for both Christian and non-Christian communities, and arguably, it is even more significant for the latter.

The number of churches in Dimapur is staggering and there is little consistency in their appearance. They tower above localities as grand displays of ultra-modern architectural expression, as pastiche of foreign church forms, and in neighbourhoods as modest cement and bamboo buildings behind brick-and-wire fences and concealed in houses and commercial buildings. Many churches include the name of the tribal or ethnic community that constructed them, and in some cases, the language or languages of worship are mentioned as well, including non-Naga languages like Nepali, English, and Hindi.

Churches show belonging. They mark an established presence. They also mark power: the power of particular communities (tribes), denominations, and the networks and circuits that contribute to building and maintaining churches. Some of these circuits are close by, villages and towns in the hills; others are farther away, in south India, USA, and Italy. These churches also generate circuits of faith. Missionaries and seminarians train in these churches and associated colleges and travel to other parts of the frontier for activities like planting churches in Karbi Anglong in Assam, heading congregations of Northeast migrants in other parts of India, or working as missionaries abroad. Upon their return, some clergy start new churches or strengthen the existing ones in Dimapur, adding to their reputation and centrality in community life.

The power reflected in spectacular church architecture representing dominant-faith communities, tribes, and denominations is contrasted with more modest churches suggesting marginality in the city or, at the very least, a more subdued presence. Churches of smaller communities tell stories of migration, settlement, and place-making. For instance, the small Kuki church in Half Nagarjan (central Dimapur) was established in 1983 as one of many Kuki churches in the city (Image 1.1); a non-Naga community of the larger Chin/Kuki/Mizo tribes mostly found in southern Manipur, Mizoram, and Myanmar. In a small brick, timber, and cement building behind a brick wall hugging the roadway, this church is dwarfed by the other enormous churches within a hundred metres, including the six-floor pyramid-style Yimchungrü Baptist Church (Yimchunger), a simple three-floor Tangkhul Baptist Church on large grounds, the Ao Baptist Arogo in a multi-floor velodrome-like structure, and the Ao Christian Revival

Image 1.1   Kuki Baptist Church, Half Nagarjan

Source: Duncan McDuie-Ra

Church featuring an elegant three-floor spire connected to a sloping triangular block (Images 1.2 and 1.3). Walking this strip of churches makes one aware of the communities of different sizes, resources, and presence in the locality. If you continue walking north, past the Christian Revival Church, the organized laneways open to a wasteland of dust and mud, depending on the season. In the wasteland are a row

Image 1.2   Yimchungrü Baptist Church, Half Nagarjan

Source: Duncan McDuie-Ra

of new houses under construction, a few small shacks, and layers of debris. Standing alone on the narrow dirt track—a shortcut through to the Civil Hospital Colony—is a small Kali Mandir, suggesting an even greater degree of marginality for the Hindu communities in this site, but also demonstrating the importance of making place, of marking the landscape with a place of worship, signifying belonging and presence.

Image 1.3 Ao Baptist Arogo, Half Nagarjan

Source: Duncan McDuie-Ra

A place of worship is also a sign of making it in the city, of getting a foothold in a community, a village, or a clan. In Supply Colony, a fascinating neighbourhood where government housing has been transformed into private residences through occupation, a small Phom church was built over a few months in late 2016 and early 2017 (Images 1.4 and 1.5). There are a number of Phom churches in the city, including a large Baptist church on the banks of the Dhansiri River near the highway to Kohima, located far from Supply Colony. With a growing Phom community, a new church was constructed on a small patch of land using timber, bamboo, and sheet metal. This church denotes the presence of the community in this part of the city and connects the new arrivals to the rest of the community, village to city. As is typical of Dimapur's diversity, the new church is adjacent to a madrassa in a private residence.

The commercial areas of Dimapur are marked with places of worship for other communities, such as the Jame Masjid in Hazi Park (part of the main bazaar) established in 1906; the cluster of mandirs, a gurdwara, and a Jain temple around the Kalibari road near the train station and Railway High School; and altars and shrines in the houses of Tibetan and Bhutanese merchants, all of which denote longevity of settlement of railway workers, administrators, and traders in the city.

Image 1.4   Construction in progress for the neighbourhood church for the Phom community, Supply Colony

Source: Duncan McDuie-Ra

There are countless more examples, but the point stands: Places of worship are crucial for belonging, for marking place, and can be read as projections of power, domination, and marginality, which vacillate from neighbourhood to neighbourhood, almost corner to corner, in the city.

Image 1.5 Completed structure of the neighbourhood church for the Phom community, Supply Colony

Source: Duncan McDuie-Ra

Urban Villages, Village Urbanism

If churches are symbols of tribal modernity, then gates are symbols of tradition, and of the recalibration of customary authority in an urban area. Gates mark a locality for a particular community, a particular customary authority. Here the urban form mimics the village, and during times of heightened tension (and mourning) in the city, gates can serve the same function, closing off the locality to outsiders. Not all localities have gates, even where the majority of the population belongs to one tribal community or a community with a shared place of origin. In some areas, gates have come later, after long periods of settlement, after one community has ascended, or after enough money has been raised. Some of the more recent gates found around the city have plaques commemorating their opening by a politician, which also reflects the standing of the community and the networks of patronage that bond customary and state powerbrokers. The form varies a great deal from simple concrete arches with faded motifs to combinations of timber, bamboo, and brick.

One of the most striking gates in Dimapur is at Chekiye, a Sümi village now part of the urban sprawl close to the airport. A shining plaque notes that the gate was opened by the Nagaland parliamentary secretary for Irrigation and Flood Control in December 2016. The names of the village council members are chiselled onto another plaque, and even a casual passer-by can see that the parliamentary secretary shares the same clan name as the majority of the council. The gate features a tiled roof under a cement gable, resembling the prolonged bamboo beams that rise out of traditional dwellings at the front resembling horns (*tenhaku ki* in Sema language) or found on a village gate. Under a four-sided, tiled roof, the pillars feature glass cases. Inside these cases are life-sized fibreglass mannequins dressed in Sümi traditional dresses. Behind the figures are photographs of hills, fields, and the sky. It is difficult to know what to make of the gate. It is a clear expression of power, connections, and standing in the community. The mannequins in the pillars are likely a statement of pride in traditions and narrate a transformation from agrarian life to urban life. Yet they also mirror the colonial and postcolonial reification of tribals—as frozen in time—displayed in museums throughout India, images many tribals struggle to repudiate in their everyday lives (Kikon 2009a). However, it also suggests that a community is in control of how its image is presented. Perhaps what makes the mannequins even stranger is that they face the main Dimapur–Kohima highway, a route that passes from the plains into the hills and on to Manipur, making it the main thoroughfare for goods, passengers, and the military travelling to and from the rest of Nagaland and Manipur. They also face the slick four-floor Cherith Centre. With a façade of mirrored blue glass, the centre hosts a famous music school and recording studio, a gym, and a training school for migrants in the hospitality industry. Behind this is a training ground for the Assam Rifles Paramilitary. The mannequins representing the past gazing at capitalist and military modernity is poignant, as well as eerie and somewhat comical.

Foundation stones function in a similar way to gates, marking longevity in a location and the legitimacy of the authority exercised in the particular site. On the one hand, while Duncan Bosti is marked with a simple concrete slab and crude inscription, likely decades old, hidden amongst debris and barely visible on a street corner; Kuda Village on the other hand has invested in two large foundation stones facing one another on opposite sides of Half Nagarjan Road. The first one dates from 2009 and celebrates the establishment of the village in 1941. It names the founder (Pehielie Sekhose) and the first settlers (Khriehulie Kirel, Deliezhu Angami, and Suonguhie Kerhuo), and adds 'Later, by the grace of God and through hard work of the inhabitants, the village progressed and developed to what it is today'. This is a settler's narrative. Pioneering migrants turned the settlement into place, into 'what it is today'. Across the road is an even more recent celebration stone (though it is made from cement), inaugurated in December 2016 by the then-chief minister of Nagaland, T.R. Zeliang. In ornate lettering, the stone celebrates the Platinum Jubilee (75 years) of the 1941 founding, notes the inauguration by the chief minister, the dedication by the Pastor of nearby Kuda Village Baptist Church, and lists 39 'Founding Fathers and Pioneers', including the 4 listed on the 2009 stone. The stone is placed in front of the Kuda Village multi-purpose commercial building, opened by the chief minister on the same day. The three-storeyed building in functional style features five shopfronts on the lower floor and more on the upper levels with balconies. It also has the requisite iron rods shooting into the air from

Image 1.6   Lotha Hoho, Duncan Bosti

Source: Duncan McDuie-Ra

the top floor. Here the settler narrative is extended to more pioneers, the most notable of all secular patrons (the chief minister) and non-secular (the pastor from the church), but it also incorporates the longevity of the village with the opening of the commercial building, a journey from pioneering settlement to urban capitalism.

Customary authority is materialized in buildings for tribal councils, often in cement reproductions of traditional architecture (Image 1.6). These buildings stand out in a landscape of cottages and concrete boxes, and much like churches, they provoke a mixture of fear and awe as sites where rules, mores, and morals are debated and judged by those bestowed with authority.

Memorials

In a city that has been witness to extraordinary levels of violence, memorials mark the landscape. Mitchell (2003: 443) argues that 'both memory, and its corollary, forgetting, are hegemonically produced and maintained, never seamlessly or completely, but formidably and powerfully nonetheless'. In other words, they are part of the monumental, with public projections of power by various actors: state, non-state, and state-like. Yet memorials can also be part of the vernacular, part of the fabric of place. Memorials thus serve as 'texts' that can reveal the interests, actors, and histories behind their creation; as 'arenas' where different groups debate and contest the meaning of the past and the future; and as 'performance', places where rituals, festivals, civic ceremonies, and public dramas are enacted and, at times, subverted (Dwyer and Alderman 2008: 166). The tactics of producing identity out of memory and place are often similar whether enacted from above or below. As Hoelscher and Alderman (2004: 349) put it, 'what subaltern and dominant groups share in their efforts to utilise the past is the near universal activity of anchoring their divergent memories in place'. In Dimapur, like in other frontier cities where sovereign power is fragmented between state, non-state, and state-like actors, there is not always a clear distinction between 'public' memorials as the products of state attempts to utilize the past (the monumental) and subaltern attempts to utilize the past 'from below' (the vernacular). Such distinctions are particularly unstable in Dimapur and this varies from place-to-place depending on which actors dominate a particular area. With multiple loci of power producing urban space, the location, condition, and permanence of a memorial suggest a position in relation to dominant narratives of the past and present in that site, in that locality, neighbourhood, or patch of the city.

Memorials take various material forms. Stones, much like the foundation stones discussed earlier, mark sites where locals were killed by the armed forces, in factional killings and public assassinations. On Duncan Road, in Duncan Bosti, is an approximately three-metre-high stone memorial mounted on a tiered platform in memory of Chalie Kevichüsa (see Images 1.7 and 1.8). Kevichüsa, a journalist and editor of the *Ura Mail*, was assassinated on that spot in 1992. The memorial features a crucifix, two Bible verses (Lamentations 3:52 and Job 16:18,19), and a dedication by 'those who loved him'. The memorial is poignant as it acknowledges the senselessness of Kevichüsa's death—Lamentations 3:52 reads, 'Those who were my enemies hunted me without cause', while not naming those responsible. This is a common dilemma for those fighting the

Image 1.7   Chalie Kevichüsa memorial

Source: Duncan McDuie-Ra

violence that wrecked the city and society prior to (and to some extent after) the 1997 ceasefire. In the localities of the city—even among a particular tribal or linguistic community hailing from a particular village or area—the networks, affiliations, and sympathies of relatives and neighbours are not always known, and memorializing violence necessitates careful manoeuvring. How to condemn the violence

Image 1.8 Chalie Kevichüsa memorial detailing

Source: Duncan McDuie-Ra

without naming the perpetrators? In some cases, naming is not necessary. The implications are chilling. To name would be to distance the perpetrators from the community—easier when the perpetrators are the Indian Armed Forces. Not naming the perpetrators reflects the nature of violence in the city in the 1990s, yet is defiant in the face of that violence. In a poem dedicated to Kevichüsa, Monalisa Changkija captures the dilemmas of showing defiance without naming. The poem 'Not Be Dead' was published in the *Ura Mail* following Kevichüsa's assassination and has been reproduced in various anthologies since (Changkija 2013: 142–3). In the poem the narrator speaks of living on even after being 'riddled with bullets', as their words cannot be 'defeated and silenced'. Indeed, to be killed for reporting, writing, and speaking is a sign of:

> the capitulation
> of those who
> cannot think
> beyond the AK-47.

It is these unnamed but clearly known perpetrators who have shown weakness, unable to tolerate voices that question. The Kevichüsa memorial captures defiance, which serves as a kind of belonging, a claiming of space, of a refusal to capitulate to the power of the armed forces or underground groups.

The Kevichüsa memorial captures a violent episode in a tumultuous period in Dimapur. There are other memorials that celebrate lives lived with power and influence, and also lives cut short. Some are located on the street marking a particular spot, while others are in the grounds of private residences. Memorials are also common indoors as photographs and small altars. There are memorials built as schools, or schools built as memorials, and as buildings, often donated to a church or a community group. For the very powerful and influential, there are forms that blur the line between public and private, as with private memorials found inside family compounds, discussed in Chapter 5.

While class is clearly a factor—the wealthy and influential have entire parks dedicated in their memory while the poor end up as photos hung on the wall and carted from one rental house to another—Dimapur's memorials are also gendered. With the exception of the city's (crowded) cemeteries, there are very few memorials and monuments dedicated to women despite their prominent roles and unprecedented suffering during decades of conflict. Indeed, the only visible representations of women 'on the street' are in advertising, usually highly sexualized, and in the posters for the doomed municipal elections discussed in Chapter 2.

Belonging on the Margins

Almost all the place-making tactics discussed so far are related to tribal communities. While many have a recent settler past, they have a sense of legitimacy in the city that begets belonging. Dimapur is a tribal territory, even if the city is open to migrants from outside the state. Non-tribal communities also make their own place; they create sites of belonging symbolizing longevity, and in some cases recent arrival. Non-tribal communities are diverse in faith, language, and tenure in the city. Some individuals spend their entire lives in Dimapur and their families have lived here for generations. Non-tribals in Dimapur include traders and financiers, though since the ceasefire, there has been a huge increase in tribal capital and investment in the city, including from returnees who have spent time in other parts of India and abroad and are now returning to Dimapur to start businesses like clothing boutiques, music studios, and hairdressing salons. Despite these recent changes, Dimapur, like other cities (and towns) in the frontier, spatializes ethnicity into tribal (non-commercial, administrative) and non-tribal (commercial), reflecting a division between public sector work (tribal) and commercial enterprise (with a diverse labour force of non-tribals), many of whom are recent migrants. Some stay. Some come and go. Some never return. Some live and work in the teeming bazaars around G.S. Road, M.P. Road, and Bata Lines. Others move about the city performing labour tasks but usually return to specific areas or clusters of housing on the edge of tribal localities when the workday is over. Despite this diversity there are certain zones within the city where non-tribals have a sense of place, a sense of belonging, or at the very least a sense of 'flexible place', to adopt the phrase used by Roberts (2016) in her study of the Chinese community in Rangoon. Roberts argues that as a community that is restricted in property ownership, has limited political opportunities, and is treated with suspicion by the state and the rest of the population alike, Rangoon's Chinese have created places 'that are meaningful and sustainable without threatening the state through

claims of permanent territorial boundaries'. As such, the location
of Rangoon's Chinese in the city's social order is 'unstable and
unbounded but not ungrounded' (Roberts 2016: 9). This resonates
with the experiences of non-tribals in Dimapur, especially since the
formation of Nagaland in 1963, when it became a tribal territory, and
following the ceasefire in 1997, when economic competition from
tribals increased. However, a major difference is that it is not just
threats from the state that affect place-making: customary authorities,
underground groups, and student organizations all play a similar
role. Indeed, one could argue that the state is the least of the concerns
of non-tribal communities.

Non-tribals have established businesses, places of worship, hotels,
and houses in the main commercial areas, where new arrivals often
end up looking for work and accommodation on arrival. The form
of these areas is distinct from tribal neighbourhoods, in that they
are often densely populated, high-rise, and a mix of commercial and
residential. These areas rarely exclude based on ethnicity, as market
relationships in Dimapur depend upon ease of interaction between
ethnic communities and networks of supply, sale, consumption,
tax, extortion, and protection that cut across ethnic lines and also
(imagined) lines between civilian, government, customary, and
underground groups. Dimapur's building boom since the ceasefire,
visible in rows of high-rise buildings as well as additional floors added
to older properties, provides rental accommodation to migrants,
both tribal and non-tribal, though non-tribals tend to stick closer
to areas where they feel safe, areas where there are other migrants
with similar backgrounds. While the spatial order between tribal and
non-tribal space is seemingly fixed, non-tribals move throughout the
city for work. During the day, they enter different localities for day
labour, to peddle goods, to provide transport, and also as residents,
and wives, husbands, and relatives through marriage. Marriage
between tribals and non-tribals causes anxiety among ethno-
nationalist groups and is integral to the narrative around Syed Farid
Khan's belonging, or lack thereof, in Dimapur. There are clusters of
smaller non-tribal businesses on main roads and within localities,
such as kiosks, tea stalls, food vendors (fruit and poultry) as well as
warehouses, but here, the presence of non-tribals is more muted, in
contrast with the physical, aural, visual, and olfactory effect on space

in the commercial areas and other established non-tribal places (see Low 2013).

Banal Militarism

If belonging inscribes the place where communities feel included, the presence of the armed forces creates spatial exclusions that are both fixed and mobile. Spatial distinctions between tribal and non-tribal intersect with the spatial distinctions between civilian and military—distinctions that hold firm at certain times and dissolve at others. During the Naga independence movement, Dimapur was also—and is still—a place where members of Naga independence organizations operated. Consequently, it was also a place where counter-insurgency forces and military intelligence sought out members of the NSCN-IM and other Naga armed groups and under the protection of the Armed Forces Special Powers Act 1958 (AFPSA), an extraordinary law still in place in the city, brutalized the population. The AFSPA operates in all disturbed areas in the frontier, permitting any member of the Indian military and paramilitary (armed forces hereafter) to fire—'even to the causing of death'—upon individuals acting in contravention of any law or order, carrying weapons (or anything capable of being used as a weapon), or assembling in a group of five or more. Suspected persons can be detained for 24 hours, with unlimited extensions/renewals, and members of the armed forces are permitted to enter any premises without a warrant. Most significantly, the AFSPA provides legal protection (in the form of both de facto and de jure impunity) to members of the armed forces operating in a disturbed area (see Amnesty International 2013; HRW 2008; Mathur 2012). For our purposes, here we will explore the impact of the law on space, place, and power in the city. Twenty years after the ceasefire, Indian Armed Forces still occupy the city (and the state and much of the frontier) and are still protected by the AFSPA. They can move around the city and enter any premises without warrant or pretext, leaving a sense of place fragile, even in the most robust communities.

With such a long-term presence in the city, the armed forces have also become part of its ecology and economy, involved in everything from timber trade to the recycling of vehicle engines. Particularly striking are the juxtapositions of infrastructure—military, state, and community—that coexistent but rarely comingle, producing and reflecting fractured publics and pockets of functionality and dysfunctionality. Though these overlap from time to time, the overlap is uneven—the military enters civilian space, but the reverse also happens. Firing Range and Hill View Colony are adjacent localities split by the main highway in the western part of the city. Firing Range hosts the Assam Rifles and Hill View Colony, the Central Reserve Police Force (CRPF); both paramilitary forces are under central command and protected by the AFSPA. The barracks are behind high walls topped with barbed wire, vehicles are routinely stopped out front, and a housing complex sits outside the walled compound. There is a post office and an ATM in the Assam Rifles compound, and a school and park in the CRPF area. Military housing sits between the two as yellow three-storeyed and four-storeyed complexes of rendered concrete. Dispersed among these complexes are private residences, schools, churches, and shops, which have filled the patches of land around the military infrastructure as the city has expanded towards the border with Assam. It is not the presence of military barracks, firing ranges, housing, and micro-urban environments within the city that is striking; it is the difficulty in distinguishing between military and non-military space in some of these sites that exemplifies both the challenges of making place in Dimapur and the banality of militarized urban life.

Tribal Territory

Despite its diversity, there is a tension between the city as a migrant space and the city as part of tribal territory under Article 371A. Dimapur is, perhaps intentionally and perhaps not, an enclave that functions as an 'in-between' space suspended between Nagaland and Assam, making it a particular type of urban zone. It is a city, to be sure, and one that is ostensibly Naga, but it is something more: an enclave, an exception, a constellation. Due to this political geography—part of Nagaland jutting into Assam—and because of the infrastructure connecting Dimapur to Assam and beyond to the other parts of India, the city itself has been a kind of frontier, an outpost, and the last enclave in the plains before the climb into the hills.

The cultural production of Nagaland through colonial and postcolonial periods has been analysed at length by scholars in several disciplines. Central to the production of knowledge of Nagas are images, especially photographs. In his detailed account of the entwined ethnography and photography of Nagas, von Stockhausen (2014: 40) notes that '[g]iven the parallel histories of photography, colonisation, and anthropology in India, it is not surprising that in the Naga Hills, visuality also played an important role within the context of colonial history, rule and the creation of various Naga "tribes"'. Longkumer notes the persistence of these tropes through colonial and postcolonial eras. He argues that the colonial representation of Nagas 'generally leans towards "exoticism"' that used 'descriptive and visual media to depict them (savages, head-hunters, warriors) that have had [sic] a lasting impact on the perception of the Nagas' (Longkumer 2015: 52). These tropes have persisted through the postcolonial era and 'retained a certain image of the Nagas in the Western mind, reinforced in more recent times through cultural reproductions of the Nagas in museums, tourist brochures, and "ethnic" clothes and jewelry as a form of "imperialist nostalgia"' (Longkumer 2015: 52). He goes on to argue that the production of Naga culture is a performance, and a 'two-way' process between the observer and the observed. Indeed, Nagas control, at least in part, their contemporary culture, and the economy created around it, especially with regard to the Hornbill Festival.

In the last decade and a half, the production of Naga culture—especially for external consumption—has coalesced around the Hornbill Festival, held annually at the Naga Heritage Village in Kisama outside the state capital Kohima. Hornbill is an amalgam of various festivals of different tribal communities, and it also features music concerts, fashion shows, and beauty pageants. Typifying the coverage of the festival by visitors, Rawat (2017) writing in the mainstream newspaper *The Hindu* recounts her visit to the Hornbill Festival in 'a land lost in time'. She endures the 'shamefully bad road', meets 'happy people' but skips the 'pork and dog meat buffet', instead purchasing handicrafts before describing the costumes and beauty of the Naga women, and closes with regret about how her busy life in Delhi will resume as 'life can't be all song and dance, especially if you are not a Naga', suggesting that the happy tribals will keep on dancing even as she returns to her serious metropolitan existence. Aside from references to selfies and airports, this account varies little from colonial-era writing, particularly the combination of a tourist and military gaze. And perhaps this is the point. This is what Hornbill is trying to create.

The festival would not be possible without the ceasefire (Kikon 2005) and is an exemplar of the ceasefire capitalism that we discuss throughout the book. The festival is a huge draw for tourists and corporate sponsors, and has become a focal point of public expenditure at the state level, drawing anger in recent years as teachers and other civil servants have not been paid salaries while the budget for the festival increases (see Jamir 2015). For critics, Hornbill has become a smokescreen for government ineptitude and corruption yet remains central to internal and external projections of Nagas and Nagaland.

Not all contemporary images of exotic and wild Nagaland and Nagas come directly from Hornbill, but most are Hornbill-like in their aesthetics and intent. This is countered by images of Nagas and other Northeast communities made and circulated in other ways. As McDuie-Ra (2012b: 87–98) argued in his work on Northeast migrants, the Northeast tribal is understood as a generic exotic subject, often highly sexualized, in the malls, spas, hotels, and airline industry throughout India; even so, the Hornbill-like images are crucial to the cultural production of Nagaland as a territory in the hills, on the border, where the past can be discovered (and delivered). It also helps to locate the Nagas within a pantheon of 'colourful tribes' of *Incredible India*. This is more than just a novel by-product of the tourist gaze. During his visit to Nagaland in 2014, Prime Minister Narendra Modi spoke of gender equity, 'sport-loving' people, the importance of both biodiversity and 'tapping' the 'Natural Economic Zone', and the importance of the tourism sector, which itself could be the subject of detailed analysis, though beyond the scope of this book. Other Indian leaders, ministers, and negotiators have done the same, donning a Naga shawl or necklace during public appearances in the state or at peace talks, yet the sight of Modi dressed as a 'Naga warrior' making a speech about integration in a territory that has resisted Indian rule for seven decades to a crowd of adoring public and festival performers wearing their own tribal costumes was rich in hyper-nationalist overtones.

Dimapur is excluded from this form of cultural production. It has undergone decades of conflict and ceasefire because of military presence, migration, commercial expansion, and investing the spoils of conflict, resources, and statehood into the built environment. Dimapur is the antithesis of the Nagaland constructed through tourism and promoted domestically and globally as a site of exotic tribes, festivals, and 'otherworldliness', and is kept separate from this space entirely; a spurious and inauthentic adjunct to Nagaland.

Dimapur is effectively 'off the map' of Nagaland despite being its largest city. It is not an accident that the Welcome to Nagaland gate that greets visitors, replete with carvings of hornbills, spears, and buffalo motifs, is located outside the city, after passing Chumukedima and crossing the Chathe River. Here the landscape climbs up through the foothills and patches of trees are interspersed with *jhumming* fields. This is the Nagaland of the hills, of colourful tribes, of the Hornbill Festival, even though all the communities living in the hills also exist in substantial numbers in Dimapur. It is the realm of 'inner-sovereignty' (Chatterjee 1993), embedded in the village, tribe, and hilly landscape; authentic Naga space, free from Indian control and modern influences. Hill states like Nagaland view the higher elevations of the hills and hilltop villages as 'places of purity and authentic Naga culture' (Kikon 2019: 79). Only after passing through Dimapur and leaving it behind do you enter authentic space. As the cultural production of Nagaland coalesces around Hornbill and Hornbill-like images with pristine elevated mountains as backdrop, Dimapur expands unplanned and unseen as a site where residents seek modern aspirations and lament their failure to manifest these aspirations. Dimapur will continue to expand until the problems of being a growing city under multiple socio-legal regimes and loci of authority require intervention.

Edges and Intersections

While the road leading out of Dimapur into the hills suggests the city as an in-between space, not quite Naga enough, the peri-urban fringes on other edges of the town reinforce the notion of a tribal space: an enclave, a zone, a constellation. Dimapur may not be a part of the cultural production of Nagaland, but extending its edges—especially those that border Assam, a non-tribal space for argument's sake—means extending tribal territory. We will give two brief examples here to show the ways in which Dimapur and 'tribal' have become mutually constitutive spatial categories on the edges of the city. The first is the ambiguous boundaries on the western edge of the city, and in the second, we identify the firmer boundary in the commercial area of Lahorijan, a boundary marked by distinctions between commodities and moralities available on either side.

Heading to Indisen on the western edge of the city, one passes a raised signboard suspended over the road welcoming visitors, an unusual sight in most (but not all) urban localities in Dimapur. Indisen road peels off the main highway and through a gate featuring four pillars, benches to wait undercover, a neo-traditional Naga roof, a beautiful green-and-white patterned bamboo thatch ceiling, and motifs along angular timber-roof edging and the timber slabs that form the roof frame. It is striking, even in a city featuring scores of similar gates. An engraved plaque on the gate attributes construction to the adjacent Kashiram Ao Village Council, parts of which can be reached by the same road, suggesting an expansion of an older settlement into Indisen as per an established village authority as per Ao customary law. The gate was completed in 2007. However, such a claim is not uncontroversial, especially here where Dimapur shares its border with Assam—a border that has been a flashpoint for violence, militarization, and inter-state conflict at various sites along its length in the last 50 years. The area around the gate has several other interesting features. A plaque on the ground commemorates the opening of the Indisen Village Road by the parliamentary secretary for rural development at the state level, and notes funding through the Mahatma Gandhi National Rural Employment Guarantee Act, a national scheme to provide employment on local infrastructure in rural areas. An adjacent public toilet block advertises funding under the same scheme. This is not unusual in Dimapur, as areas throughout the city, especially away from the commercial centre and old public sector housing colonies, have accessed funding for rural development at the state and national levels, often to create or mend urban infrastructure. Two less elaborate signs announce the prohibition of peddlers (specifically scrap metal and scrap peddlers) and heavy vehicles on

Sundays, demonstrating the particular spatial control exercised at the neighbourhood level.

After entering the gate, the first main building is the Indisen Baptist Church, established in 1984, with a concrete foundation and thatched bamboo walls under a corrugated iron roof. The locality is organized with well-established plots behind brick walls, a wide walking path on the side of the road, and a mix of large three-storeyed and four-storeyed houses, single-storeyed cottages, hostels, and signs featuring proverbs hung on trees and against walls at ground level, one of which reads 'Education makes people easy to lead, Difficult to drive: Easy to govern, but impossible to enslave', and another, 'People who know little are usually Great Talkers: But people who know much Say Little'. The signs reflect the aspirations common in the region around morality, education, and community. The neighbourhood has a strong sense of place, it *feels* like a hill village. Moving along one of the roads heading away from the main neighbourhood the land breaks up and the houses are more dispersed. Two enormous telecommunications towers occupy the high ground, along with a large four-storeyed house with deep blue tiles and new white paint, and an orphanage on a promontory (Image 1.9). On the lower reaches are small thatch houses, animal shelters—mostly for pigs—and wells and fruit trees. After the towers, the road ends abruptly. Among the low trees and shrubs, a group of labourers are building a house on a flattened patch of land overlooking Assam, or in Assam. It is difficult to know, given the ambiguity of the boundary. The land juts out over what looks like a bumpy wasteland; an Assam Police Post can be seen in one direction under a small clump of trees. As the bell in the orphanage compound rings to signal dinner and dusk descends, the labourers start packing up, while their guard, a member of one of the Nagaland police forces, stands vigil looking out into the wasteland.

Tribal communities are extending the edges of the city into Assam by occupying the villages latched on to the city, by virtue extending the state of Nagaland and the tribal territory. Some of these localities, like Indisen, are orderly and secure resources from the state to build community infrastructure. Some have a more do-it-yourself ethic, with community-built roads and pathways funded internally. Others, like the one we will call Netho—a settlement dating from 1991 formed between a bend in the highway and tracts of the wasteland

Image 1.9   Looking towards Assam from Indisen

Source: Duncan McDuie-Ra

and forest—have uneven sections, organized patches closer to the main road and more ad hoc streets and buildings closer to the edge of the settlement—an edge that is being pushed further and further into unsettled land. These are places for new arrivals from villages of shared ancestry and, in some of the areas we visited, for settlers with few ties to the city.

For some of the families living here, the edge of the city is the attraction. During our time in Netho, we met a network of hunters, mostly from the Lotha community, about whom we will talk in further detail in Chapter 4. For the hunters who were of different ages and had 'day jobs', Netho was an ideal place to settle as it was close to the hunting grounds located on the Assam side of the border and also had plenty of wildlife around. The settlement is in proximity to the state police forces (Assam and Nagaland) and the Indian Armed Forces who have barracks at Firing Range a few kilometres away and at checkposts along the highway. Furthermore, various insurgent groups operate nearby in the ambiguous zone on the city's edge. Residents take pride in living on the edge of the city and being able to navigate legality, illegality, and risks posed by human and non-human actors in the area.

As Harms (2011: 84) writes in the case of Saigon, 'There is no real edge to the city, no point where the city stops, and the countryside begins. But the categories of country and city and inside and outside themselves seem to demand such a strict division.' The edge of Dimapur too demands such a division because here the edge of the city is the edge of tribal territory. However, as Harms (2011: 84) adds, 'people cannot readily define the edge of a city in practice, while ideal conceptual categories lead them to expect that such an edge exists'. In this part of Dimapur, there is ambiguity over where the city ends, where Nagaland ends, and thus where tribal land and the constitutional protections inscribed by the category end. Harms (2011: 84) states: 'The potential power these categories offer softens the threat of dispossession, and people often play into the reproduction of imperiling ideals that ultimately relegate them to the margins of the city'; this 'social edginess', as he calls it, can 'represent the cutting edge of possibility or the edge that cuts, the possibility of social advancement or the sharp edge of social marginalization' (Harms 2011: 85).

If the boundaries in the western stretch of Dimapur are ambiguous and encroachment the norm, the boundary along Highway 129 between Dimapur and Golaghat in Assam at Lahorijan makes the most of different legal and moral orders between the two territories. On the Dimapur side, the highway is crammed with businesses— hardware, construction materials, wholesale food supplies, eggs and poultry, an enormous flourmill, and mechanics and panel beaters. On the Assam side, there are similar shops along with scores of bars and hotels, many with car parking out front. And while there are checkposts for the various state police forces, it is the sudden public availability of alcohol, or the sudden disappearance, that really marks the movement between territories. Alcohol is banned from being sold in public in Nagaland, though it continues to be sold clandestinely (and not so clandestinely); however, a short trip to the northeastern edge of the city eliminates the hassle. Even recent national laws to stop the sale of alcohol at highways and roadsides is unlikely to make a significant dent in this area, given the experience of traders in the movement of the licit, illicit, and semi-licit along this corridor. The stretch also features mosques and *mandirs* of various kinds for the trading communities, and noticeably few churches compared to the other parts of Dimapur, demonstrating the commercial power of non-tribal businesses in this zone. Juxtaposed with the places of worship are brothels, usually nameless or labelled 'hotel', which cater to the truck drivers moving along this stretch from lower Assam through Nagaland to Manipur (and on to Myanmar), and to Dimapur residents who cross the border seeking booze and sex. Thus, the Assam side of the border has a reputation for vice, sleaze, and infidelity. As such, the border here operates somewhat as a moral line between the alcohol-'free', majority Christian, piousness of Dimapur—and by extension Nagaland—and the hedonism across the border. Despite Dimapur having many establishments that offer the same services, the distinction holds and appears important for how many residents of Dimapur construct their own sense of belonging as part of a tribal state, albeit one that is 'off the map'.

It is this urban enclave with both firm and ambiguous edges, unseen in the cultural production of Nagaland, unplanned in its growth and much of its development, where attempts to produce legible urban space have taken place in the 2010s, especially following changes at the national level from 2015. And it is from these that the recent history of Dimapur is informative for urbanization in other parts of the Northeast frontier.

Popular Cosmopolitanism

Dimapur's urban fabric, its vernacular urbanism, produces a kind of popular cosmopolitanism. On the surface, the city adheres to a cosmopolitan vision of multiple tribes, ethnic groups, denominations, faiths, and affiliations living in a dynamic and often dysfunctional 'in-between' space. Dimapur's appeal is that it is a city that does not really belong to anyone—a recent creation, an enclave where pioneering settlers start villages that become localities, traders start stores that sustain generations, and itinerant peddlers traverse. This is not cosmopolitanism understood as universal humanism or even one that challenges narrowly conceived ethnic, tribal, and—in some cases—national identities. It is a more complex interplay between ethnic, national, and worldly components in grounded social contexts (Calhoun 2003; Darieva 2011; Pollock et al. 2000; Robbins 1998). As Schiller et al. (2011: 400) argue, rootedness and openness to external influences need not be seen as oppositional. It is more than just coexistence, but perhaps less than a shared set of values and aspirations attached to place. In a migrant city, this cosmopolitan veneer rubs up against tribal territory. Despite Dimapur's distance from the cultural production of contemporary Naga culture, and the uneven way in which rules and regimes enforced elsewhere in Nagaland are enacted and subverted in the city, Dimapur is still part of tribal territory; its edges, both firm and fluid, are the edges of tribal space.

In this in-between space, different communities, families, and individuals find ways to belong, to make place. They claim it, mark it, order it, celebrate it, and occupy it. There is mobility through the city's multi-ethnic patchwork, but a certain spatial order holds. Patches of belonging and exclusion hold Dimapur together: patches watched over by the armed forces and directed by underground groups. It is the perforations in that order that produce crises, crises like the lynching of Syed Farid Khan in 2015. Perhaps as a lived experience, Dimapur's cosmopolitanism is closer to what Cheah (2006: 486) calls 'a form of consciousness without a mass base'. It is a veneer that is swiftly torn down when an individual violates the spatial order, when the tensions between a migrant city and tribal territory escalate.

Perhaps this overstates the fragility of Dimapur's spatial order. The lynching has had limited impact on Dimapur's diversity, or at least whatever impact it had is almost impossible to measure. Established migrant communities still dominate Dimapur's commercial areas, migrants still arrive looking for work, and Nagas still hire migrant labourers to fix their houses, cars, and pedal them around the city on rickshaws. Different tribal communities still coexist, building churches on adjacent plots. Supporters of the NSCN still live next door to veterans of the Naga Regiment (infantry regiment of the Indian Army) who served in Chhattisgarh. Home owners still add extra floors to their houses to take in paying guests, relatives from ancestral villages, or unknown tenants. Capitalists still pour money into multi-storeyed housing. Everyone still complains about the lack of housing supply. The lynching of Syed Farid Khan and the alleged sexual violence that preceded it was a horrific event, but it does not seem to have diminished the appeal of Dimapur as a place to live.

Certainly, the lynching perpetuated fear and anxiety among the city's non-tribal residents. Yet the city has always produced fear and anxiety. Non-tribal communities have survived bomb blasts in markets, fires in businesses, extortion, kidnapping, and blackmail—so have all the residents of Dimapur. Everyone has lived with killings, violence, harassment, and surveillance. Yet the city grows. Existing areas become denser, areas on the edges capture new territory, and the wealthy occupy new swathes of land for their mansions.

Characterizing Dimapur as cosmopolitan may be a stretch, but in a frontier where social and political life has been dominated by what van Schendel calls (2011: 32) 'the exclusionary politics of belonging', massively popular in the Northeast 'as a political project of aspiring regional elites and as an administrative solution to law and order problems', it is as close as it gets, especially in a tribal state under protective constitutional provisions. Dimapur's in-betweenness is both a product and an enabler of its peculiar cosmopolitanism. The migrant city/tribal territory duality may appear as an exception, but it may also be a prototype of urban development in the frontier. Cities in the Northeast, especially the hills states, are unlikely to be solely populated by communities indigenous to the territories in question. The spread of domestic and transnational capital, the continued transfer of funds directly to cities and indirectly through their appropriation and reinvestment in housing and other commercial ventures, the ongoing need to supply and service the military, the diminishing appeal of agrarian livelihoods, and the aspirations for urban lives draw migrants from within and beyond the tribal states. As these cities grow, they are under internal and external pressure from the public and the state—local and national—to be more urban, to be governed as urban space. And it was the attempt to transform Dimapur into a legible urban space that led to the next major crisis in the city: the municipal elections of 2017.

2

Producing Urban Space

In early 2017, Dimapur was brought to a standstill for almost a month due to a *bandh* (an enforced strike) that shut down businesses, schools, and government offices, and blocked roads in and out of the city. Bandhs have had a major impact on other cities in the frontier, especially Imphal in neighbouring Manipur. In Dimapur, trading communities and tribal associations have called for bandhs in the past to protest against extortion, corruption, and state violence. The 2017 bandh was unique because it was called by various Naga organizations, mostly representing tribal authorities under the agglomerate Naga Tribes Action Committee and Joint Action Committee, and enforced by their members and a group of citizens with various tribal affiliations. They blocked roads, toured commercial areas and neighbourhoods, and engaged in skirmishes with the police and armed forces. There were reported incidents of property damage, arson, and injuries, and two youths were killed when a group tried to enter the chief minister's office and was fired upon by the police. The two youths, Khriesavizo Metha and Bendangnungsang Longkumer, were martyred in the defence of Naga traditions, customary law, and by extension Nagaland and a prospective Nagalim; the Naga people associate their lives and bodies with sacrifice. For a period in late February and early March, posters featuring their headshots were seen at a few spots in the city. Photo portraits of the two were sent up into the sky on white balloons from a memorial service in Diphupar in the city's east (*Tir Yimyim* 2017). Large posters featuring Khriesavizo's and Bendangnungsang's photos were hung from a row of steel billboard frames atop four-storeyed and two-storeyed buildings facing the City Tower, the first junction reached when entering from Assam via Golaghat Road—a showpiece intersection for advertising and a rapid induction into the spatial context. Here, next to a billboard for Pizza Hut's pork pepperoni pan pizza, a flight attendant school, and a Kung Fu tournament, and on top of rows of migrant housing and paint suppliers, Khriesavizo's and Bendangnungsang's faces gradually disintegrated until they were just strips of vinyl blowing in the fierce winds. By late April, the poster was gone.

Over the same period posters of candidates contesting in the municipal election—the event that triggered the bandh and a change

of chief minister, and pitted self-declared defenders of traditions operating since 'time immemorial' against reformers (and 'feminists') intent on undermining these traditions—remained on walls, doors, pillars, posts, and gates (Image 2.1). Some were ripped, some defaced with mischievous additions (such as beards and moustaches on the faces of candidates), some were covered in red spittle from betel nut, some were pasted over with other notices, and some had just decayed (Images 2.2 and 2.3).

Image 2.1 Election Posters I: Various locations

Source: Duncan McDuie-Ra

In the days following the end of

Image 2.2 Election Posters II: Various locations

Source: Duncan McDuie-Ra

the bandh, the posters were haunting. Life on the streets was slowly recovering and the city lacked its usual bustle. The posters were a reminder of an election that would likely never be held and the violence that shook the city. The faces of the candidates in the various wards

Image 2.3   Election Posters III: Various locations

Source: Duncan McDuie-Ra

representing major parties, such as the ruling Naga People's Front
(NPF) and the Bharatiya Janata Party (BJP), along with independent
candidates from each ward, looked out on the city with uniform expressions of sternness, perhaps the only variation being a 'Namaste' pose
among BJP candidates and a few other candidates standing in wards
with many non-tribal voters, mimicking the standard political gesture
in other parts of India. A few had slogans such as, 'give me the privilege

to serve you', 'let me be the change you need'. An extraordinary number of candidates were women as party members and as independents. The municipal election was to have 33 per cent seats reserved for women, reflecting systems in place in other parts of India (Pisharoty 2017). Opposition to the election galvanized around this issue, seen as undermining customary law.

The posters of women candidates seemed destined for special treatment. This was more obvious in the backstreets of residential areas where the walls are cleaner and have few other posters of advertisements. One of the candidates in Ward 9 used a white background for her posters and these attracted wads of red spittle covering her face. Some posters remained fully intact but had the eyes and mouths of candidates ripped out or drawn over. Others had been plastered over with 'Don't Kill Nagacracy'. Most of the posters had just been ripped. Whether male or female, party-dependent or independent, Dimapur was covered in ripped posters of election candidates. The act of ripping them off the walls was a manifestation of disgust and contempt for what many saw as an imposition on an existing system of rule.

By early May, three months after the height of the bandh, there were still posters all over the city. Campaigning had been going for weeks before things turned violent and there were just too many posters in too many places that it was impossible to take them all down. It mattered, and parties and individuals were invested heavily in it. Every now and again, pristine posters were seen in hard-to-reach places—above doorways or on bamboo thatches—and on walls where 20 or 30 posters had been stuck, and whoever was ripping them down probably grew tired and just left some of them to dissolve on their own. Also, they seemed very difficult to remove, even if people wanted them gone. By now the posters were no longer haunting. Tensions had subsided. The posters were now part of the visual culture of the city, part of the fabric of the built environment, the layers of text and image that adorn almost every vertical surface of Dimapur. And they are a tempting metaphor for the politics that played out in the city during those months. Municipal elections and gender reservations are, like the election posters, unlikely to go away as the city grows and locality-specific authority and barely visible municipal council can no longer address its problems.

The abandoned election and the bandh received wide coverage in national and international media. Debates about customary law and gender were also a staple in editorials, blogs, and social media for weeks, with various scholars and experts weighing in on the issue but also on who has the right to even debate it or discuss it. This took a predictably nativist turn, except in cases when outsiders celebrated customary law, and debate fizzled when the voices of the status quo drowned out the rest. Allusions to a crisis of democracy, modernity, masculinity (which we discuss in Chapter 3) circulated—all legitimate readings of what took place. Yet this was also an urban crisis. The election and the 2016 amendment to the Municipal Act that heralded it are responses to the pressures and incentives in India to produce legible urban space under standardized systems of rule.

This chapter explores the production of Dimapur *as a city*. In particular, we focus on the visions, projects, and experiments intended to make Dimapur more 'city-like'. Producing legible urban space from the collection of settlements, villages, barracks, commercial zones, ceasefire camps, encroached tracts, and wastelands under various socio-legal regimes is an immense challenge. It is not the result of a single act or campaign, nor simply of external or internal pressures. Here, Lefebvre's (1991) dialectical approach to the production of space is a useful starting point. For Lefebvre, the urban is a level between everyday life and the existing order—an order shaped within and beyond Dimapur, Lefebvre's 'near order' and 'far order' (Kipfer et al. 2013: 124). The urban is a space of 'encounter, assembly, simultaneity' (Lefebvre 2003: 118) and needs to be understood as a social force *and* the product of social forces produced through three connected dialectical processes (or 'moments'): spatial practice or perceived space, representations of space or conceived space, and spatial representations or lived space (Lefebvre 1991: 33–42). The first process refers to material structures reflecting the spatial manifestations of social and political power; the second is the abstraction of this power as ideology, knowledge, and language used for domination; and the third is the space of everyday experience where material and abstract power are lived. These three moments enable analysis of the material and symbolic elements of space, and how they are produced, challenged, and experienced.

In the following section, we first discuss attempts to put Dimapur 'on the map' by exploring the 'near order' attempts that aimed to make Dimapur more like a city. Second, we pay particular attention to the attempts made to impose order on the urban landscape. Third, we discuss the urban turn at the national level, the 'far order'. India's urban fixation is travelling to the Northeast. As one of the largest cities in the region, Dimapur has little choice but to find ways to make itself more urban. There are implications for the classification and reclassification of land as urban throughout India, but in tribal areas under various protective constitutional provisions—Article 371A in the case of Nagaland—intended to protect tribal lands, the idea of agglomerating localities and circles under a singular municipal authority challenges the interpretation of customary law. As the largest city in a tribal state, Dimapur is also an experiment in the production of legible urban space in areas with constitutional protection. Finally, this chapter discusses the revised Municipal Act and the culmination of attempts to produce legible urban space 'from above' and reform customary law 'from below', especially by activists seeking female representation. We argue that the city is a space to challenge and transgress customary law in ways unthinkable at the village level. However, transgression was a catalyst for the crisis discussed earlier; a crisis we return to in closing.

Big City Feel

Dimapur has many sites to analyse local attempts—public and private—at producing urban space that reflect local imaginations and imitations of how a city should look and function. Some are intended, others not. The absence of state taxes on land and buildings make Dimapur a perfect place to launder profits from armed conflict, extortion, extraction of natural resources like timber and coal, and 'black money' from all kinds of ventures into buildings and commercial enterprise. Some of these commercial enterprises have little pressure or incentive to turn a profit, though they contribute a veneer of development to the aesthetics of the city. Commercial buildings, hotels, billboards, and electrified advertisements along main roads give central Dimapur a 'big city' feel.

For many migrants who come to the city from the hills, Dimapur is distinguished from smaller towns and villages by its verticality, the density of settlement, and diversity of population. Striking too are the materials and surfaces used on some of the commercial buildings: reflective glass, coloured panelling, and decorated façades. These sit alongside neo-traditional tribal architecture for the various tribal council buildings, some of which are built and designed by architects from outside the state; spectacular churches, some of which tower above other multi-floor buildings; and countless reinforced concrete boxes, some with local adaptations discussed in Chapter 1. The heat, humidity, and rainfall of Dimapur are merciless on the concrete buildings. As Lowenthal (1975: 163) notes, 'concrete becomes more ugly every passing year, looking greasy if smooth, squalid if rough'. Parts of Dimapur that are classically urban in density and vibrancy look partially ruined, and along with continual construction, potholed roads, and waste-strewn streets and waterways, the 'big city' patches suffer from an aesthetic disorder. Many buildings feature steel reinforcement bars shooting into the sky, and 'incompletion becomes a permanent state ... symbols not of the past, but of a future, a future that may never arrive' (Forty 2012: 30). In short, the built environment that is most city-like also looks the most disorderly and the most incomplete, especially in contrast to the relative order of many neighbourhoods.

In order to look more like a city, to put Dimapur 'on the map', the state government has constructed several showcase development projects. We focus on these in this section as they can be traced to some intent, some infrastructural logics, and attempt to address a public(s). Showcase development projects include functional infrastructure, like the flyover that arches in a U-shape over the railway line. Despite taking decades to build and being embroiled in multiple scandals, the flyover does have a practical purpose. It is used as intended for vehicles to pass over the railway line, though in busy periods there are long traffic jams. The alcoves are used by labourers to rest, sheltered from the sun and rain. Residents and visitors take selfies from the flyover, with the city spreading out below in the background. Young couples spend their evenings sitting on parked motorbikes on the highest elevations of the flyover. Underneath the flyover on the railway tracks is a market where vendors and customers assemble between trains and visits by the local police. The market space occupies the pre-flyover pedestrian route between Walford and Hong Kong Market in the commercial centre. Tribal and non-tribal vendors sell food—including meat, produce from the hills (herbs, vegetables), and live animals (snails, frogs, eels)—along with clothes, buckets, and toys. The ramps that splay in two directions on the bazaar side of the flyover form an arc of concrete that fixed vendors use as shelter for their stalls, mostly dry goods and second-hand clothes extending out the back of Hong Kong Market. As the epitome of big city infrastructure, the flyover has become symbolic of modern Dimapur and plans to build additional flyovers are routine news items every year or two (see *Nagaland Post* 2013; *Eastern Mirror* 2016b).

Less practical projects are also worthy of exploration. And while they may appear as white elephants, they are ways of generating contracts, repaying favours, and securing patronage, as well as producing urban space out of the collection of settlements that make up the city. There are two contrasting sites that we feel epitomize the desire to put the city on the map, which have become symbols of different strains of the city's politics: City Tower (Image 2.4) and the Sovima Cricket Stadium.

Image 2.4   City Tower

Source: Duncan McDuie-Ra

City Tower is a steel tower in the middle of a traffic island, one of the few in the city. This forms the showpiece intersection discussed earlier, where banks, billboards, and the prized Pizza Hut and KFC face one another. The tower itself resembles a scaled-down Eiffel Tower. It is also known as 'Clock Tower' or 'City Clock Tower' in reference to the slim digital clock on the upper panels, replacing the original analogue clock face. City Tower is a landmark. Advertising hoardings hang on the tower along with banners announcing community events like faith healings and season's greetings at Christmas along with a few meek municipality signs asking people to keep the city clean. Residents gather here to celebrate New Year's Eve. The site has hosted music concerts, prayer meetings, and protests, and is where the mutilated body of rape accused Syed Farid Khan was hung (on the perimeter fence) after being dragged naked through the city in March 2015, as discussed in Chapter 1. Photographs of the night show locals, almost all men, climbing high up the tower and surrounding it, preventing the security forces from getting to the body. The site was likely chosen because of its centrality but also because of the statement that could be made, the image of the beaten body hanging from the fence, a reminder to residents of the fragility of Dimapur's urban order, something to consider every time one passes the tower.

Following the death of Isak Swu in mid-2016, the tower became a site of vigil with banners of Swu's photograph hanging down the sides of the tower and mounted on the fence surrounding it. Mourners brought candles to the site and placed them on the fence and the lower levels of the tower. The tower was transformed into a deeply spiritual site, reflecting the deep sense of loss among many people in Dimapur but also indicating the counter-sovereign claims being made in the city. Images of the vigil from the local press show a striking juxtaposition: the face of a life-long fighter for Naga independence next to an advertisement for an Indian mobile phone company. The vigils for Swu's death brought crowds to the City Tower once again, this time in remembrance of heroism and shared struggle—a cleansing of the tower and perhaps of the city's soul a year after the lynching.

Symbolic of a different kind of politics is the day–night cricket stadium at Sovima, the 'millionaire's row' or the 'Beverly Hills' of Dimapur. We walked around the site one late afternoon in December 2016 after wandering in through an open gate. The gates are an interpretation of a Naga village gate, made from concrete and bamboo with a black buffalo motif on a green background. The site was certainly impressive: 6 massive towers soared into the sky with around 60 spotlights on each. Stadium seating was being constructed on the northern edge of the ground, where a small group of labourers from Assam staying in the construction site were busy preparing their evening meal. Upon walking around the pitch, we noticed that the field was a bit misshapen and a little small but as neither of us were cricket experts, we just kept walking, wondering aloud to each other why there was a cricket stadium in a city desperately short of sporting facilities. The existing State Stadium in Oriental Colony was used more for learning to drive than exercise, and the Dimapur District Sports Council Stadium located along the Golaghat Road alternated as a sports venue and a site for political meetings and cultural events. Moreover, in Dimapur, cricket was far less popular than football, basketball, and just about any other sport imaginable.

At the southern end of the ground is a raised bamboo hut with a computer-printed sign on an A4 sheet 'Officials Only' (perhaps the only bamboo cricket officiating structure in India), cricket nets, and the Nagaland Cricket Academy housed in an incredible piece of architecture with a cement reference to a *morung*[1] entrance built in front of a three-floor glass and concrete box and connected by horizontal beams. A knee-high plaque informs visitors that the complex was opened in 2012 by the president of the Board of Control for Cricket in India (BCCI), who at the time was also the union minister for agriculture, in the presence of the then-chief minister of Nagaland Neiphiu Rio, who was also president of the Nagaland Cricket Association. There are various summations that can be drawn from this. Sport is a crucial part of integration tactics when it comes to the Northeast and sportspeople from the region are often held up as ideal northeasterners and proud Indians in comparison to deviant and anti-national counterparts (McDuie-Ra 2015b). The BCCI holds camps and trials in the Northeast and suggests that these camps held in the Northeast are the best way to 'integrate them [players] into the cricket mainstream' (Samyal 2016). In 2016, Rio appealed the BCCI to

[1] Morung refers to a men's dormitory or house with ornate carvings and a gabled roof.

pay more attention to Nagaland and a few months later the then-head of the BCCI visited Nagaland, praised Sovima, and promised to build another stadium (*Morung Express* 2016a). With the national body eager to promote the game in the frontier, there were opportunities to access funds, especially from an individual who headed both the state and the state cricket association. Here, we can also see the desire to enrol Dimapur in national and international circuits, in sporting events that, with any luck, might be televised and could put the city 'on the map'.

Yet the stadium also symbolizes the desire to be accepted as part of India, a hazardous position in Nagaland, though one that tends to be eased when it simply involves taking money from the centre. Perhaps it is the location of the stadium that best illustrates the worlds it straddles. Located at the edge of the 'millionaire's row', the 'Beverly Hills' of Nagaland, the stadium is nestled among the mansions of the political elite, many of whom have made their fortunes by appropriating state funds and through the conflict economy of the frontier; elites were likely buoyed by the idea of teams from India coming to play cricket in their backyard. Yet the stadium is also on the road to Camp Hebron, the ceasefire camp on the outskirts of the city. Former insurgents and their families who have fought against the Indian state have to pass by this structure—and its fawning gesture to Indian sporting and political cultures—on their way to and from Dimapur. Though perhaps the most ironic moment comes for officials visiting the stadium and returning to the city, as they pass through a gate several kilometres closer to the city that reads 'Kuknalim' (victory to the land), the rallying cry of the Naga movement.

Experiments in Order

An earlier precursor to creating space that is urban-like, as opposed to village-like, is the Super Market at Walford Junction. Built over 30 years ago as a formal retail space during the years of intense conflict and violence that engulfed the city, Super Market features long rows of two-storeyed concrete buildings with a wide paved thoroughfare in front, and a small plaza in the middle. The site is adjacent to the weekly market where goods from all over the hills and across the border are sold off bamboo stalls in the outdoor area behind, leading to the Kachari Ruins. The paved area is taken over by vendors—mostly tribal women and non-tribal men—peddling a few handicrafts, food, snacks, and animals every Wednesday. At the western end on the corner with Half Nagarjan Road is the Town Hall, locked up behind a gate with a thick steel grill. The Super Market is an archive of Dimapur from 1990s to 2010s.

Two of the oldest shops in the complex are coffins shops, Coffin? Yes Coffin and Omega Coffins. Adjacent to each other, the shops have become landmarks in the city. The coffin shops are also symptomatic of Dimapur's recent past. They started popping up in the city in the late 1990s and began to cater to tribal clients living in the city, an account we describe in Chapter 5. The establishment of the coffin shops in the city corresponds with the period of intense violence from factional killings within the Naga movement. A trip to the Naga Cemetery in Hill View Colony, where graves and memorials are layered on top of one another and any resemblance to a path has been long since buried, gives us a sense of the scale of death in the city, so do the memorials scattered about the streets and neighbourhoods. The growth of the city has also meant a growth in medical facilities. While not a medical hub on the level of Imphal in Manipur (see McDuie-Ra 2016), Dimapur hosts around 15–25 hospitals/clinics (depending on how one defines these facilities) ranging from the impressive facilities of Eden Medical Centre near the Sub-Jail area in Kashiram Colony to the semi-dilapidated District Civil Hospital. There are several public and private hospitals of various qualities and repute in between; some funded by religious organizations have come up across the city. With pitiful medical infrastructure in the hills, Dimapur is a site to seek care for serious diseases, terminal illnesses, and palliative care. As a consequence, Dimapur is a place where life ends and where arrangements for burial in the city or back in the village take place, as discussed in Chapter 5.

Sections of the Super Market feature faded signs from businesses that have moved on remaining above some shop-fronts: cassette sellers (part of the landscape of the audible city, as discussed in Chapter 3), an alcohol vendor, and cybercafés charting the consumer preferences and circuits of technology that have passed through the city. Current trade features handicrafts (some with a long presence at the site), bakeries, nutritional supplements, and baby clothing and accessories, reflecting changing tastes of the urban middle classes (Image 2.5).

Image 2.5   Super Market Complex

Source: Duncan McDuie-Ra

Many shops are empty, while several have taken to selling second-hand clothes, popular throughout the city (and region). In these shops, rather than dig among the bales, customers can browse clothes on hangers. Cafés and music venues have begun opening up, slowly since the ceasefire but more rapidly in recent years, including places that serve alcohol 'under the counter' as it were; the city providing the anonymity to transgress the moral order imposed on the state since the alcohol ban. The Super Market is also the centre of a more recent contestation between the municipal authorities and local vendors over the sale of dog meat, but one seemingly at odds with the imaginations of a modern urban society. This is discussed in detail in Chapter 4.

The drive for order also comes from below, from neighbourhoods and communities fatigued by urban dysfunction. Community infrastructure takes many forms: bamboo threshed into bridges to cover holes in the pavement (Images 2.6 and 2.7), timber flooring to patch up open drains, fines levied by tribal councils, and spatial control as shown in the Indisen case discussed in Chapter 1. Perhaps the most striking example can be seen in Duncan Bosti in the north-

Image 2.6   Community infrastructure I: Bamboo garbage platforms,
Duncan Bosti

Source: Duncan McDuie-Ra

Image 2.7   Community infrastructure II: Patching up the pavement,
Dhobinala Road

Source: Duncan McDuie-Ra

west of the city. At intervals, along all the main roads, are raised bamboo platforms where residents and vendors leave waste to protect it from being scattered by animals, rain, and wind. A private vehicle paid through contributions by residents and shops in the locality collects the rubbish, though it was difficult to find out exactly where and how it is disposed.

Regardless, community infrastructure operates as it would in a village. Yet there are limits too. Other sites in the city where tribal councils post notices banning waste dumping and announcing fines on defaulters are littered with high piles of rubbish. The existence of tribal authority does not necessarily equate to the respect of that authority in an urban context where so many bodies move through urban space—bodies that cannot all be identified, known, or punished unless caught in the act. The city is an assemblage of linked localities, which, even if governed as villages, have blurred boundaries, known and unknown residents, and constant traffic of people, vehicles, and animals.

Nonetheless, community infrastructure is a telling contrast to the showpiece infrastructure produced by municipal, district, and state governments. These local imaginations of what a city should look like, feel like, and be like, are layered with incentives and resources transferred from centre to state, core to periphery, and Delhi to Dimapur. The urban present and urban future of Dimapur are also shaped by national visions of what cities should look like, and most importantly, act like: how they should generate revenue, impose order, and become arenas where flagship government schemes can be enacted.

Dimapur in Urbanizing India

In his provocations into the 'urban turn' in India, Prakash (2002) explores the appeal of the city to the Indian developmental state, particularly Nehru, and its centrality in planning and modernization. The lived city, however, failed to live up to this promise and its appeal gradually unravelled, picked apart by 'the inability of its linear narrative to accommodate the spatiality of historical processes, the uncomfortable coexistence of the modern and the "obsolete", the intrusion of the rural in the urban, the combined emergence of official and unintended cities' (Prakash 2002: 5). While the mega city has dominated research and popular accounts of the spatiality of urban India, small or regional urbanism is becoming increasingly salient aṣ an arena for analysing 'uncomfortable coexistence' beyond 'metrocentricity' (Bunnell and Maringanti 2010). This echoes the agenda put forth by Bell and Jayne (2009: 689) to take small cities more seriously, a crucial task in developing countries where 'two-thirds of urban residents live in places of less than 1 million people'. They argue that 'if the role and nature of small urbanity is to be more fully understood, a number of "imaginative leaps" must be taken by theorists currently hung up on the notion that globalization of the city means globalization of the metropolis' (Bell and Jayne 2009: 690). The scholarly deficit is pertinent in India, where the mega city and the village dominate research. Like others, we argue that this focus overlooks some of the most significant sites of change in India (Bhattacharya and Sanyal 2011; Brown et al. 2017; Guin 2017, 2019; Jain 2018; Sircar 2017; van Duijne 2019). As Verstappen and Rutten (2015: 232) demonstrate in their study of Anand in Gujarat, towns and small cities function as 'node(s) of interconnection between rural urban and local global mobility'. India's urban story is broadening. Dimapur is integral to that urban story, weaving various national projects—what we group together as militarism, capitalism, and urbanism—into the city's landscape, producing a frontier urbanism that serves as an exemplar of the urban turn in the Northeast, especially given that categories of space, rural and urban in particular, are not fixed or even well-delineated.

Since the national electoral victory of the BJP in 2014, the urban turn has become accelerated, though there are certainly continuities with decades past (see Bhan 2009; Brosius 2012; Datta 2015; Gooptu 2015; Roy 2009; Sami 2013). Modi has inserted urban space—existing and new—into the national dream sequence as prime minister; a dream sequence shared with global networks in the diaspora and potential investors. Urban development is integral to Modi's 'hi-tech populism' as the 'Vikas Purush' (development man), narrated in promises to 'bring urban amenities to our rural areas' and building and retrofitting 100 smart cities (see Jaffrelot 2015: 152–3). Campaigns like 'Make in India', 'Swachh Bharat! (Clean India!)', and 'Digital India' (Doron 2016; Jeffrey 2015; Nielsen and Da Silva 2017) also connect to this urban vision, especially around infrastructure and the aesthetics of what Kuldova (2017: 39–42) calls the 'luxtopias' of contemporary Indian cities. Our concern here is locating the Northeast, and Dimapur more specifically, in this accelerated urbanism, in the dream sequence of urban modernity.

The Ministry of Urban Development (MUD) has a number of flagship schemes. From 2015, the Atal Mission for Rejuvenation and Urban Transformation (AMRUT) has transferred funds to state governments for urban infrastructure, primarily around water supply, drainage, sewage, and spatial reorganization, such as pedestrian areas, parking, public transport, and green space. The Mission has provided infrastructure funding to 500 cities in India, including Kohima and Dimapur, with Dimapur receiving a higher level of funds 'considering the gaps' in infrastructure and the higher proportion of urban poor in the city (AMRUT 2016: 12–14). States submit a State Annual Action Plan and the Government of India pays 90 per cent of the project costs. In return, cities are required to make a number of reforms under 11 themes around planning, taxation, levies, building codes, waste management, and creating green space, and a proportion of funds (10 per cent) is withheld to incentivize these reforms (AMRUT 2015). The AMRUT also seeks to build capacity for urban governance focussed on accountability, transparency, and empowering 'municipal functionaries' (AMRUT 2015: 5–6). The Mission promotes the use of consultants to oversee tendering and project management, what it calls Project Development and Management Consultants. There are provisions in the Mission to increase fund allocations annually if the number of municipal areas or the population under municipal authority increases during the period 2015–2020 (AMRUT 2015: 8).

There are other schemes that seek to boost urban development, yet Dimapur has been left out, even when other frontier cities have been included. The Smart Cities Mission (also from 2015) aims to 'promote cities that provide core infrastructure and give a decent quality of life to its citizens, a clean and sustainable environment and application of "Smart Solutions"' (MUD 2016: 2). The vagaries of the scheme have been heavily criticized (see Hoelscher 2016), however, the scheme, nonetheless, has appeal for local authorities seeking to put their city 'on the map' and gain from the swarm of consultants and contractors seeking the prized compulsory public–private partnerships. Yet Dimapur is not a part of this scheme, missing out to Kohima.

Furthermore, the MUD dedicates 10 per cent of its annual budget to the Northeast (as do other ministries) and explains: 'Given the difficult access to and remoteness of (the Northeast), the urban areas in the North Eastern States perform a much higher order function than those of similar size in India' (MUD 2016: 72). The Ministry had a North Eastern Region Urban Development Programme running from 2009 to 2019 supported by the Asian Development Bank, which along with infrastructure helped initiate reforms enacted by 'Institutional Development Consultants' to introduce user fees for various utilities and implement property taxes. The latter was a major controversy in the crisis of 2017. Indeed, in the Ministry's annual report of 2016–17, it is noted that in the case of Nagaland, 'Decision of the State on all other reforms including property tax is awaited' (MUD 2017: 71). Tax is a contentious issue, as members of scheduled tribes in the Northeast pay no income tax, but non-tribals do. In Nagaland, including Dimapur, as many as nine different groups run a system of parallel taxation on salaries, revenue, and transportation (Santoshini 2016). Property taxes paid directly to a municipal authority are seen as threatening the power of the state-like parallel system and undermining the rights of scheduled tribes.

Land reclassification in India does not have a single trajectory. Areas that were once classified as rural are reclassified as urban, but the reverse also takes place. Using data from Tamil Nadu, Denis et al. (2012: 58) argue that settlements 'change from urban to rural and back to urban at the pleasure of the state government'. The primary rationale is to have better access to funds and schemes. Dimapur receives funds earmarked for both urban and rural development for projects carried out in the city proper. In heavily dependent states like Nagaland, and with the dissolution of institutions like the Planning Commission that brought some stability to transfers from Delhi, reclassifying land as urban and increasing the size and reach of municipal authority in order to access urban development funds is tempting, but not straightforward. In Dimapur and other frontier cities located in tribal areas, the authority over space is more important than its classification.

As Karlsson demonstrates in the case of Shillong, 'tribal cities' in the Northeast under relatively strong constitutional land protection regimes—the Sixth Schedule in the case of Shillong (Meghalaya)—are facing difficult decisions around the customary authority in urban areas. He writes that for critics of customary law in urban settings, 'the headman usually lacks appropriate education and skills and ... financial and technical resources required for increasingly bureaucratic and complex urban administration, such as that relating to roads, power, water, sewage, education, health, policing and various other infrastructural arrangements that need to be in place' (Karlsson 2017: 33). The counter argument is that expanding municipal authority may alienate tribals from urban land and return frontier cities to economic and social relations characterized by domination by non-tribal communities and the armed forces, or as one of the customary bodies, the Ao Senden, puts it in response to amendments to the Municipal Act in Nagaland, taxation would force Nagas to become 'landless or slaves in [their] own land' (*Shillong Times* 2016).

The 'far order', the national drive to improve urban areas as sites for capital accumulation and generation, is catching up to the Northeast. Dimapur, despite being left out of the flagship Smart Cities scheme, is nonetheless subject to interventions from the centre intent on improving urban areas and reforming their systems of rule. Property taxes and elected representation are focal points of reform. Even when not subject to the specific solution—a specific formula for improvement—Dimapur is subject to the imagination of being urban, of being more like a city, exemplified in revisions to the Municipal Act in 2016, the precursor to the crisis.

Making a Municipality

Nagaland has had a Municipal Act since 2001, replacing the Assam Tribal Areas (Administration of Town Committees) Regulation 1950. The 2001 Act led to the formation of the Dimapur Municipal Council (DMC), replacing the township committee. The DMC consists of elected representatives from each of the 23 wards, ex-officio members—MLAs from constituencies that overlap the municipal area, and up to one-fifth (one-third in the 2006 amendment) of members nominated by the state government 'from amongst the persons having special knowledge or experiences in Municipal Administration' (Government of Nagaland 2001: Clause 9(4)). The urban sprawl of Dimapur extends beyond the 23 wards and includes Chumukedima and Medziphema, which have town councils. The term for each council is five years. Up until the recent crisis, instability in the DMC was internal, with 5 leadership changes between 2005 and 2015. These changes came from power struggles within the ruling NPF, which won 18 of 23 wards in the last municipal election in 2004. There were no municipal elections between 2004 and the abandoned 2017 election. Through 484 clauses, the 2001 Act is detailed on tolls, taxes, infrastructure, and prohibitions, but there is no explicit mention of Article 371A or the tax status of scheduled tribes, suggesting not only that much of the Act is imported from standard Indian municipal acts, but also that no one in Nagaland was too concerned about this until the measures to reserve seats for women came up in the first amendment. The 2001 Act just ignores the potential conflict between forms of authority and the inter-legalities—the complex, contentious, and constitutive relations between legal norms and processes—of the different regimes put into place, which we discussed in Chapter 1.

With the DMC formed and chugging along, there were several changes of note in the interim years that set the stage for the crisis. In 2011, the state-level Urban Development Department created the Municipal Affairs Cell to 'to fulfill the various reforms mandated under the 74th Constitutional Amendment Act' (Directorate of Urban Affairs 2017), referring to the 74th Amendment of the Indian Constitution in 1992, what Dupont (2007: 91) calls the 'cornerstone' of urban reforms 'that decentralizes the strategic level of government and promotes participatory democracy'. The cell became the Directorate of Urban Affairs in 2015, to be headed by the Urban Development Department at the state level. The list of responsibilities for the directorate aligns with those of the AMRUT at the national level around financial reforms, 'master plans', elections, 'rules', and '[t]ransfer of powers and functions to the Urban Local Bodies' (*Morung Express* 2015). Urban affairs have become serious business for Nagaland, too serious to be left to local-level authority and capacity. State-level bureaucracy is needed to steer urban reform, to produce urban space in the form stipulated by Delhi, or at the very least appear to do so. A shift in language towards Urban Local Body (ULB) can also be seen during this period, aligning with language at the centre and suggesting an equivalency between municipal and town councils as producers of urban space.

Perhaps the most crucial changes are to the Nagaland Municipal Act itself. The Nagaland Municipal (First Amendment) Act 2006 makes amendments to the functioning of the council, but most crucially it specifies reservations for scheduled castes, scheduled tribes, and women (Government of Nagaland 2006: 23A(1)). The Amendment called for those holding seats that were deemed reserved (to be deemed by November 2006) to vacate them and stated that they would be accommodated as single-person committees in the municipality (Government of Nagaland 2006: 23A(2,3,4,5)). The council elected in 2004 was not dissolved and, through a Cabinet decision, the state government postponed the election due for 2010 over fears of tensions and violence threatening the ceasefire. Members of the Naga Mothers Association, a respected collective of activists crucial in fighting factional killings within the Naga movement (see Manchanda 2001), acting as the Joint Action Committee for Women's Reservations (JACWR), petitioned the Gauhati High Court (Kohima Bench) in 2011 to end the postponement and hold elections according to the 2006 Amendment. They won. The High Court decreed that the '[i]ssue of reservation of seats for Women in Municipal Councils and Town Councils and the ongoing peace process in the State have, if at all, a tenuous link. There was no material before the Cabinet that if elections are held there will be break down of law and order in the State' (HRLN 2017).

The High Court decision was challenged in the Supreme Court by the Government of Nagaland, citing concerns about customary law and violence in the attempted town council elections in Mokokchung in 2011 as precedent. The Supreme Court deliberations further delayed the elections, while the existing council performed rounds of infighting and the state government sought greater control through its new directorate. In April 2016, as the Supreme Court converted the Special Leave Petition placed in front of it into a Civil Appeal, the deliberations within Nagaland picked up a new pace. The office of then-chief minister T.R. Zeliang released a statement in October 2016 making a clear link between the election funds from Delhi and development, saying Nagaland

> cannot receive grants from the Indian Government if there are no
> Municipal and Town Councils ... If we want development, we need to
> inculcate a progressive mindset and attitude.... We need an attitude of
> willingness to contribute our best towards our common developmental
> needs. Instead of asking what the new Town Council can do for you, please
> ask yourself what you can do for the new Town Council. Only then will the
> new Council be able to flourish. (*Eastern Mirror* 2016a)

In October 2016, he met with JACWR and other members of the Naga
Mothers Association and assured them that the election and the 33 per
cent reservations would go ahead; photos of the meeting were widely
circulated in the press (*Morung Express* 2016b). In late 2016, a Third
Amendment to the Municipal Act was passed, removing references
to Scheduled Caste Reservations, taxes on land and buildings, and
the provision for future municipal taxes as contravening Article
371A (*Morung Express* 2017a). The 2016 Amendment did not alter
reservations for women. It was interesting to note that in a press
release by the legal cell of the NPF, the party in power in the state,
they asserted that: 'the present government has in no way violated any
of the provisions enshrined in Article 371A of the Indian Constitution
for creating space for women to participate in ULBs' (cited in *Morung
Express* 2017a), under which they list the different functions of the
two kinds of authority. The NPF put up candidates in every ward
for the municipal election, including many women, and they had
much to gain by winning seats in a tier of government that had
become moribund but was now on the verge of resurrection; even
their own press release stresses that 'the role of ULBs will be crucial
and mandatory with the Smart City in the offing' (in *Morung Express*
2017a). Clearly, coexistence went against the wishes of many in the
city.

Preparations for the elections began in the following months.
Campaign posters were beginning to appear in Dimapur by January
2017 and by February could be seen in almost all wards. At the same
time, protests against the election were also starting to be organized
by the time both authors left the city in late January 2017. By this
time, the debate had bifurcated into pro-reservation/pro-election and
pro-customary law/anti-election. The anti-election position hinged on
the issue of Naga exceptionalism, captured in this statement by Naga
Hoho President Chuba Ozukum:

We have been urging the state government not to go ahead with the reservation in these elections because we strongly feel that it doesn't go with the special rules that the Naga society follows. We are allowed to follow our customary rules and laws by Article 371A of the constitution. So, we are different from other states and need not follow a certain rule simply because the other states are doing it. (Cited in Pisharoty 2017)

Issues around taxation and land were also raised, mostly as rumours of new taxes, but were relegated to the background or subsumed under the pro-customary position, which was also anti-taxation. Interestingly, both sides used the rhetoric of democracy in their positions, the pro-election side claiming that this was a path to a more representative government (and a way to address the urban problems common across the wards and townships) and the anti-election side claiming that Nagas have a unique democracy that should not be altered, and neologisms like 'Nagacracy' were plastered onto city walls (Image 2.8). Odd to us was the use of gender justice in the anti-election camp: Some of its members claimed that women are

Image 2.8   The Dimapur Municipal Council promoting urban sensibilities, MP Road

Source: Duncan McDuie-Ra

already 'equal' and 'well-treated' in Naga society and thus reservations are unnecessary and will only harm what already exists (see Dhillon 2017).

Events escalated in February 2017 after Naga tribal associations, including the apex Central Nagaland Tribal Council and the Joint Coordination Committee, called a bandh in Dimapur that would last for almost the entire month. Blockades went up all over the city, manned (they were usually only males) by youths, businesses were closed and monitored by yet more volunteers, and crowds of men and women came out in support of the bandh in different parts of the city on different days, wearing their best clothes or tribal dresses. In a poignant column in the Dimapur-based *Morung Express*, Aheli Moitra (2017) recounts the children in her neighbourhood playing 'bandh-bandh' imitating the blockades and referring to homespun traditional clothes as 'bandh dress'. As time went on, these positions became entrenched, with several attempts at mediation, most notably by interlocutors from the Nagaland Baptist Church Council. All manners of strange events took place in this period, including the killing of Khriesavizo Metha and Bendangnungsang Longkumer as well as a third death, Tsapise Sangtam's, at Longkhim in the east of the state; a move against Zeliang from within his party (he was ousted and replaced with Dr Shürhozelie Liezietsu); the mysterious flight of 49 MLAs to Assam, where they holed up in a resort; and the return of former Chief Minister Rio from Delhi amid speculation that he would take up the post of chief minister (he did not then, but did in 2018). Other events included the shutdown of the city, a curfew enforced by the armed forces, a period under Section 144 of the Indian Criminal Code banning unlawful assembly, several days with no internet, media censorship, arrests, property damage, violence, intimidation, threats to women's activists including original members of the JACWR and women running for office, and a collapse of urban order.

The crisis was also debated in the local media, in social media, and among scholars and the Naga diaspora in different parts of the world. These debates augmented the bifurcated positions, while also provoking accusations about voice and authenticity, especially in attempts to undermine voices critical of customary law. Pro-reservation/pro-election writers and activists were labelled 'anti-Naga' among other things, showing the convergence of customary law with a (imaginary) 'genuine' Naga. Kikon (2017a) was active in these debates and her work supporting the 33 per cent reservation has argued consistently that this goes well beyond municipal elections, and '[u]nless debates and dialogues for gender justice and Naga women's experiences of patriarchy, violence, and everyday humiliation are recognised, the movement for gender justice will remain a fragmented one'. Fieldwork in Dimapur in the months that followed brought the issue of women's reservation to the fore in almost every conversation, and while the bifurcated positions came up often, so did nuance, concern, and desire for change from people representing all walks of life—from fitness entrepreneurs to theologians in training to musicians. Perhaps most striking was the open disagreement on the issue between friends or colleagues in conversations, even conversations that started out about something else entirely.

Urbanism's Limits

While the bandh ended in late February, the election posters remained, haunting the city and slowly peeling away through the months that followed until life, it seemed, returned to 'normal'; always an unstable concept in Dimapur. What, then, does the municipal saga suggest about the production of urban space in Dimapur? First, and this perhaps has the most resonance for other cities in the Northeast, attempts at enrolling Dimapur into the urban 'far order' promoted by the current (and likely future) government in Delhi have their limitations. Urban forms on customary land have fuelled Dimapur's building boom, and yet governing this space *as urban* according to the reforms advocated in Delhi is destined for confrontation here and elsewhere in the region. Fascinating, thus, is the challenge for the state and municipal governments to produce legible urban space to satisfy the demands of the MUD and access funds—funds that are significant given the shifts towards urban development at the national level—without seeming to undermine the authority of customary institutions in urban areas. Perhaps this will result in more visible showpiece developments: infrastructure attempting to stitch together the various localities of the city to give a more urban veneer without changing what lies beneath.

Second, it is possible to read the crisis of 2017 as the resistance of a frontier polity to changes imposed by the centre, changes that seek to define what urban is and how it should be governed. In this reading, the defenders of customary law refuse to give in to attempts at enrolment, conjuring images of brave resistance of indigenous communities on the frontier to neocolonial control by the Indian state and the neoliberal agenda of the current government. While tempting, romantic, and surprisingly popular, this reading ignores the powerful gendered critique of the existing loci of power in Naga society, power that was capable of dissolving an election, ending the term of a chief minister, and shutting down a city for a month. If resistance of the municipal elections is resistance of neocolonialism, Naga resistance of India, then where do we locate local politics? Where do we place the acts of women standing for office, the acts of women and men challenging customary law, and the acts of voicing dissent against the cultural hegemony of conservative tribal bodies? The defaced posters of candidates contesting for the municipal election tell a powerful story of the courage to stand, campaign, and ultimately continue to live and work in a city and society after being demonized as anti-Naga, anti-tribal, and anti-customary law. This courage is erased from a crude resistance narrative.

A third reading is that producing urban space has hastened a masculine crisis, one building in tribal societies for some time (McDuie-Ra 2012c) and laid bare by the push to implement reservations at the municipal level. Urbanization and migration disrupt conventional masculine pathways, coming of age, and ascendency to customary authority. As Kikon (2017b) has argued,

> state organs and public offices in Nagaland are defunct, and Naga society is extremely militarised. Leaders who are heads of parliamentary political parties and hold important positions are accused of corruption and of instrumentalising the (armed) conflict (with India) for their political gains. Given the political instability, the tribal organisations have emerged as a powerful public forum.

Reservations threaten this power, and also highlight the expansive role of tribal organizations. In one of the few mentions of the urban nature of the issue during the crisis, Monalisa Changkija argues (2017), 'Naga male-dominated tribal bodies' opposition to women's reservations in ULBs is understandable—the fear is that women would finally have a say in how resources are used and shared in towns, which could then spill over to villages'. Villages matter, given that they are the sites where Naga cultural production is focused, even if they are not the source of revenue or even community that they were generations ago, especially with so much outmigration. Changkija (2017) adds, '[t]he opposition to women's reservation in ULBs not only underlines the badly bruised Naga male ego, but has critical economic connotations accentuating how their economic and political strongholds are perceived to be threatened'.

We will discuss masculinity further in Part II when we explore gendered space in Dimapur. For the moment, we posit that if the production of urban space, especially the 'far order' of reforms, taxes, and reserved seats in municipalities, can be implicated in a masculine crisis, then the challenge to this order by women activists is also an urban phenomenon. If, as many scholars of urbanism have argued (see Cresswell 1996; Doron 2010; Hubbard 1998; Lees 2004), cities are themselves sites of transgression, then urban space in a tribal land, even—and perhaps especially—an in-between space like Dimapur, makes the opportunity for transgression less possible in rural areas. In other words, challenging customary law and the gendered power dynamics of Naga society seems more possible and more likely in urban space. The (relatively) clean slate of the migrant city, the city 'off the map', adjacent to the inner sovereignty of the village, is perhaps the ideal site for transgressing powerful cultural norms. Assessing success or failure is premature; reservations will continue to be a political issue in Nagaland in the coming years, and the urban, the municipality, seems like the most likely arena where the issue will play out and where powerful norms will be transgressed.

Part II

Stories

3

Audible City

As we climbed the stairs of a freshly constructed building in Duncan Bosti, the sounds of drums and guitars, and a chorus of hymns greeted us. We were at The Jam Tree—Root in Branch Out, a music school and recording studio where sound mixers, musicians, and producers hung out. It was a Saturday afternoon and a music band occupied the recording studio, a vast hall with musical instruments and stools. They were members of a praise and worship group for a local ministry and were rehearsing their songs for the following Sunday. What appeared like background music as we entered The Jam Tree—Root in Branch Out captured an essence of Naga sociality in Dimapur. Music plays an integral role in bringing social groups together. Naga people across the spectrum—intergenerational, intertribal, interclan, inter-kin—have always found reasons to sing and jam together. As the largest city in Nagaland, Dimapur has attracted many tribal groups from across the state and beyond. Over the decades, they have settled down here. Thus, across the city and the ever-expanding localities, music and concerts bring together diverse groups of people. From choir practices and new music projects to new bands jamming together at local events, music builds communities and creates bonds in this city and beyond.

Musical Roots

A large generation of the Naga society considers that singing and being musically inclined is deeply rooted in Christianity. The virtues of singing and playing the guitar (or the keyboard) have always accompanied the sermon. Therefore, being musically sound as a singer or playing an instrument is perceived as an important quality that accompanies the life of a pious and modern Naga. This belief is deeply embedded in the Naga moral world so much so that many families aspiring to bring up a musically literate child do so with the aim of letting them perform at the local church and showcase their talent for the glory of God. This is also true of many church-based communities across Northeast India where faith and musicality intersect. Thus, many talented Naga musicians and singers grew up performing in the church choirs and with church bands. In Naga society, early on Naga armed groups also recognized the power of music and adopted it as part of their political mission across the Naga areas to sing about the armed struggle and liberation. Beginning from the era of the Naga National Council (NNC) in the early 1950s and continuing even in the ceasefire period, music has found its presence. Irrespective of the conflict, factional killings, and fights, all the factions of the National Socialist Council of Nagaland (NSCN) have choirs and musicians in their respective organizations. A substantial personal archive of music and images scattered across family albums as well as official dossiers, books, hymns, videos, and documentaries illustrate the history of the Naga nationalism and music.

Today, the sound of drums, guitars, and keyboards is not limited to Christian music only. Dimapur has become a hub of music and performances. This chapter focuses on the circulation of music, musicians, and music entrepreneurs in Dimapur and examines how music and performances produce a peculiar knowledge about militarized urbanism. With a crumbling infrastructure and a landscape dotted with ceasefire camps, posh-gated mansions, military barracks, and checkposts, the city of Dimapur is divided between state (Indian security forces and government organs) and non-state actors (Naga insurgents and smugglers). Everyday movement of goods and people are regulated and controlled by Naga insurgent groups (imposing taxation), the Indian security forces (carrying out routine patrol surveillance), and the Nagaland Armed Police (who oversee the law and order functions). Naga politicians and business families aspire to build their 'rest camp'/transit houses/retirement homes here. During the ceasefire period, the mansions with swimming pools in a city without basic civic amenities like water supply highlight the life of wealthy tribal families as opposed to an increasing number of households who are unable to make ends meet.

Against this militarized background, many musicians and composers from Dimapur find ways of using their voice and music to engage with their audience.

We draw from Laura Kunreuther's (2018) work on voice and sound in Kathmandu to highlight how audible experiences connect the rational and the affective to a distinct practice of making music in Dimapur. Kunreuther's work is significant for us because it allows us to generate insights about the social and political experiences of musicians and their engagement with music, the audience, and listeners. Their songs, notes, and tunes offer us a fine-grained account of the changes taking place in a rapidly expanding urban hub. As musicians sing and speak from various stages and studios, they practice connecting affectively with the audience in Dimapur and beyond. The ceasefire city, we realized, is also experienced through its music and lyrics. We explore this connection between the musicians and the city by thinking about audibility and militarized urbanism. Thus, the concept of the 'audible city' that we propose in this chapter helps us highlight the experiences of urban life through voices (vocal and conversations) and sound (mechanical and vibrations). We employ the concept of audible city to talk about ways of hearing and discerning the history and memory of Dimapur through sound engineers, recording artists, and composers. Describing Dimapur as an audible city means understanding how local musicians describe their urban experiences to initiate social and political discussions about violence, infrastructure, unemployment, and community. We explore audibility, which refers to hearing and being heard, in connection with deliberations about urban experiences in militarized societies like Nagaland.

Second, we situate the conversations about frontier urbanism by linking the experiences and struggles of musicians in Dimapur. As a zone between a tribal and a non-tribal space, conversations with Naga musicians in Dimapur help us to understand how music and accounts of disenchantments (to be stuck with a rigid traditional musical past), and the lure of the market (to become professionals and adopt music as a livelihood option), produce new knowledge about frontier urbanism. Sensibilities and everyday practices in Dimapur are significantly framed by histories of militarization, capital, and violence. Musicians from militarized cities like Dimapur, therefore, not only inform us about the role of music and the audible repertoire in influencing its audience and the larger public, but also the new pathways and connections that emerge through the circulation of new tracks and tours across this frontier region. Thus, understanding the audible city is also mapping a landscape to recognize how new forms of Naga music, sounds, and movement reconfigure experiences of everyday politics and social engagement.

New studios in old buildings, bedrooms converted into jamming spaces, and music schools with classrooms to rehearse hymns and new songs. This chapter draws readers to these spaces and the diverse ways in which singers and songwriters describe the dynamisms of urbanization. Since the 1990s, an increasing number of children across the city have started taking music lessons. For middle-class Naga families, as a music teacher from Dimapur reminisced, it was a status symbol and a sign of seeking refined taste (founded in the church) to provide private music lessons to their children. While we are not dismissive of the music scene prior to the 1990s, the ceasefire period (post 1997) witnessed the rise of new bands, singer–songwriters, and artists.

Today, there is a new kind of energy and awareness about music and the music industry in Nagaland. But the ongoing consumption of music and the production of a musical taste can be traced back to, among other things, a larger social and political atmosphere. After the Indo-Naga Ceasefire Agreement in 1997, the expression of peace and development became a powerful political project. For the Government of Nagaland, music became a way to promote the state as a potential music and talent hub. Less than a decade after Naga armed groups and the Indian state signed the ceasefire agreement, the Government of Nagaland set up the Music Task Force (MTF) in 2006. By 2012, Nagaland became the only state in India to declare music as an 'industry' where the government developed programmes to train musicians and provide them with scholarships to buy musical equipment.

The MTF was an earnest effort by the state government, but this vision was not solely geared to nurture talent. Packaged as part of a livelihood and development scheme, the MTF was categorized alongside numerous skill/livelihood programmes launched during the ceasefire period. The MTF aimed at streamlining what was so far a 'hobby' into a 'profession'. By introducing terms like training, hard work, talent, stakeholder, and market, the MTF focused on young Naga musicians and encouraged them to take up music as a full-time career. It aimed to transform Naga society as a creative hub of talent and counter the dominant narrative of insurgency, violence, and conflict (Chisi, cited in *Homegrown* 2014). The MTF focused on producing 'market-friendly' Naga entrepreneurs who could produce and perform music to generate revenue and profit. The MTF promoted music as a powerful way of showcasing a post-conflict society, free of violence and conflict, while at the same time addressing the economic crisis of unemployment in Nagaland. In 2019, the Government of Nagaland rebranded the MTF as the Task Force for Music and Arts (TaFMA), to be more inclusive and include other forms of creativity like dancing and performances (Ambrocia 2019).

In Dimapur, there is a proliferation of music schools and recording studios. Some are small operations in existing commercial buildings and residences, while others are impressive stand-alone structures with state-of-the-art equipment and even accommodation for visiting musicians, such as Jam Studio 11 in Diphupar (see Image 3.1).

However, the world outside the aims and objectives of the MTF/ TaFMA is different. Musicians in Dimapur said they could not aim for Delhi, Mumbai, and Chennai alone (referring to performing in big cities). They required a home crowd. Such conversations drew us to reflect on the ground reality of what constitutes a home crowd and in what ways does making music sink into the audience in Dimapur. For instance, new cafés in Dimapur that showcase new bands and performers constantly shut down due to the erratic power supply and other kinds of logistical challenges. Performing outside the church, for example, in cafés, is a new concept. Alobo Naga, a renowned Naga musician, told us that local audiences initially did not warm up to the local bands from the city. They also refused to pay to watch musicians perform in cafés. But this gradually changed. In a *Rolling Stone India* piece on the music scene in Nagaland, Sarah Pongen and Nokcha Aier, founders of the Jumping Bean Café in Dimapur, said that local bands like Polar Lights and Avancer successfully managed to connect with the audience (Suhasini 2013). But there were always uncertainties about organizing gigs for local bands. The political atmosphere of militarization and the ceasefire are constantly present

Image 3.1   Jam Studio 11, Diphupar

Source: Duncan McDuie-Ra

as the city shuts down whenever there are army raids, factional shootings, or assassinations of traders and citizens. In a city where civilians, insurgents, and security forces share the public space, instances of shootouts, curfews, and attacks are not uncommon. But through it all, music continues to happen.[1]

Sound, text, and voice are connected to listening, techniques, and practices. Musicians in Dimapur helped us to draw these links. However, such nuances and reflections of artists are erased because there is a taken for granted perception, often a brash outlook, that 'music and dance' is integral to Naga culture. These practices, as we are aware, are clubbed together in tourism offices. Is there another way to understand Naga people's connection with music? Grounded in a history of church music and traditional folk and culture, music is often perceived as a natural and 'god given talent' that Naga people are born with (like many tribal communities in Northeast India). Many Naga musicians traced their initial musical journeys with their respective churches. We also came across a scattered history of short-lived bands that had performed covers of famous rock groups from the English-speaking world.[2] But there is a growing anxiety about

[1] Bands such as Purple Fusion and their original numbers like 'Ho Hey! You Came Along' and 'Tring – Marks of War' have found their place among the audience in Nagaland and beyond. See https://www.tourmyindia.com/states/ nagaland/dances.html. Also, Naga bands like Abiogenesis, Tetseo Sisters, and Rattle and Hum Band are some of the groups from Nagaland that have given visibility to the music scene. The rise of popular bands from Nagaland like Polar Lights with their original numbers like 'A Beautiful Life' gives us a glimpse of the innovations and creativity among artists from Nagaland. See http://www. abiogenesis.altpro.net/, https://tetseosisters.com/, http://morungexpress. com/rattle-hum-music-society-nagaland/, https://www.youtube.com/watch? v=ZpyC9wyX43s.

[2] Of course, there are exceptions to the story. Music initiatives like the Rattle and Hum Music Society from Nagaland have been on the scene for a long time. Today, they represent the Government of Nagaland and have become a model brand ambassador to showcase music and talent and promote the message of peace and harmony during the ceasefire period in Nagaland.

the pitfalls of copying from the West and the risks of drawing solely from Naga traditional music. Behind the efforts of the government to streamline the musical talent for the market like the MTF, now rebranded as TaFMA, musicians we met in the field reflected on the political realities and the techniques they could deploy to refine their skills. Their concerns and our conversations with them emanated from experiences of living in a militarized ceasefire society.

Sounds That Matter

Kevi Kiso, a musician in his mid-thirties from Dimapur, established a music school in 2014. The Jam Tree—Root in Branch Out is a popular music school located in a newly constructed building. As we entered the building, we noticed that the cement walls had a rough finish and the concrete was bereft of any paint. The rough texture of the staircase, just solid cakes of cement, indicated that the building was yet to be completed. When we met Kevi in his office, he said that music was his passion and not a profit venture (Image 3.2). He had been

Image 3.2   Kevi at The Jam Tree—Root in Branch Out

Source: Duncan McDuie-Ra

struggling to maintain the school since the last four years. 'I have not earned a penny from here. Sometimes, it is not even breaking even,' he said.[3] Sometimes, he picked up contracts for construction work, and at other times he rented out electronic equipment for concerts and public events. 'It needs courage. It is a struggle for me, but it is so much fun to be passionate about it without even calculating about it,' he reflected.

Like many Naga artists, Kevi is a self-taught musician. He briefly received a 3-month guitar course when he was 13 years old. Other than that, it was his elder brother who taught him how to play the guitar when he was a small boy. His childhood memory of falling in love with music started with a cassette called *Non-Stop Music*, an English music compilation that started in the early 1980s. Kevi continued, 'I had not yet gone to school but I remember climbing up on a chair and playing that cassette at home. I dropped it once. I pushed the play button and suddenly the tape recorder fell. The tape did not break, it is still working. They were built to last. That was my early stage of music.' Kevi shared his musical 'coming of age story' in Duncan Bosti, a suburb of Dimapur that connects the railway station to the Rangapahar military station. *Non-Stop Music* and the sounds of rolling army trucks, *Non-Stop Music* and the sounds of guns, *Non-Stop Music* and a young boy picking up the rhythm of music. We were fascinated non-stop as we listened to Kevi and his life as a musician in Dimapur.

'I am a huge fan of Chet Atkins today. But the first song I learnt to play on the guitar was a number by Four Non Blondes titled "What's Going On". And my uncle also played Eric Clapton and Jethro Tull at home,' Kevi reminisced. Growing up, Kevi was not the only one to fall in love with music. He was surrounded with music lovers across the locality. As teenagers, Kevi and his friends learnt music by 'hearing— by listening'. There were no music schools or music teachers in Duncan Bosti, the suburb where Kevi grew up. They learnt music from the tape recorder and cassettes. They came up with innovative ways to learn the songs. Kevi and his friends would hold down the

[3] All quotes by Kevi Keso in this chapter are from a personal interview held with him at The Jam Tree—Root in Branch Out, Duncan Bosti in Dimapur on 8 January 2017.

rubber roller on the tape recorder to slow down the number and learn the lyrics of the songs. 'So, all of us who played classic rock from the seventies and eighties, we all learnt from the tape that is for sure. This is how we really picked up music before we learnt music.'

For Kevi, the connection between learning by hearing meant developing one's ability to hear was an essential part of becoming a musician. Describing the quality of factory-made Chinese guitars that were available in music stores across Dimapur, he drew a connection between the availability of musical instruments such as Chinese guitars in Dimapur and how they taught him to sharpen his auditory ability. Dwelling on the quality of the Chinese guitars in Dimapur, he said, 'For us, we have developed our hearing, for them [the engineers who design the mass-produced factory guitars], they have developed their technicality. I think as musicians, hearing is very connected to your heart, your soul. Learning by book or from the internet does not bring that out.'

Kevi was not the first person who had made the connection between hearing and the heart. Anthropologist Charles Hirschkind (2006: 71), following the listening practices of pious Muslims in Cairo, highlights how the practices of listening produced ethical sensibilities and rearticulated a range of moral virtues and ethics to live a pious life to 'avoid moral transgressions'. Listening is not simply a process of disseminating sound, ideologies, or messages. For Hirschkind (2006: 2), an important feature of listening (to sermons) is its deep effect on the 'human sensorium, on the affects, sensibilities, and perceptual habits of its vast audience'. Thus, he notes, 'I want to think of ... listening as a practice predicated on the developability of the body as an auditory instrument' (Hirschkind 2006: 79).

To 'hear with the heart', a phrase that Kevi invoked during our conversation, was in relation to his experiences of listening and connecting with the sound of the mass-produced Chinese guitars available in Dimapur. Like many frontier cities in Northeast India, the bulk of trade and movement of goods comes from Indian cities. There is no overland organized trade with Myanmar, although it shares a border. Apart from small trade in food produce (which is made in Myanmar) and Chinese household goods like rice cookers and blankets that enter the region through Manipur, major trading networks for the region are routed via mainland India. Thus, the Chinese guitars come from Kolkata and Delhi in commercial trucks and goods trains. By the time these goods arrive in Dimapur, the cost of the instruments is often two-fold or more. For instance, a Chinese guitar that costs Rs 3,000 in Kolkata or Delhi can be priced at Rs 6,000 or more in Dimapur.

While musicians in Dimapur are aware of the design and 'technicality' of Chinese guitars available in the city, they improvise and experiment with them. They modify the guitars to connect with the 'sound' they are looking for. Jamming sessions and practicing new compositions on different strings and instruments means constantly adjusting and improvising. It means not only moving body parts like wrists and elbows to work out the motion and movement of various tempos, but also thinking about ways to produce the sound and continue their musical journey. This resonates with Hirschkind's (2006: 79) point where he notes that the process of listening means developing and shaping the body as an auditory instrument, one that involves 'the body in its entirety, as a complex synthesis of patterned moral reflexes'. Meeting and observing the movements of artists and the instruments they played (as an extension of their bodies) drew us to the range of sensory experiences in Dimapur, and the place came alive as an audible city through conversations with musicians. This began through the circulation of music and sounds produced by those who were employing their bodies and sensorial experience to highlight a distinct experience of urbanism.

Kevi explained that there were different kinds of Chinese-made guitars available in Dimapur. He said, 'Some of the factory-made instruments [guitars] are good. Maybe in a set of 100, 10 are great. But you must twig it, restring it, and maintain it. Then after a year or two, the sound becomes great. It is not like some [of the] American guitars. You feel like it has been played for a year as soon as you pick up a new one. I will not say the Chinese ones are bad. They are good; it depends on the piece.' New music shops opened in the city and the flow of guitars and other musical instruments increased in the post-ceasefire period after 1997. The proliferation of music cafés, music schools, and new bands in Dimapur was also a ceasefire development. But even though there was a vibrant music scene, musicians like Kevi were conscious of the challenges. He said:

It has been only 13–14 years that we have been exposed to instruments
and have access to different instruments. We have picked up music only in
the last 15 years. I feel the pace [at which] we are going now; we are doing
well. (But) we have skipped jazz. We have not listened to blues. Rock and
pop are easy for us to pick up. It has to do with the instruments. There is
no trumpet, there are no instruments like double bass. If we are given a
chance to hold any instrument, we pick it up.

Both the keyboard and the guitar were integral parts of the church
music in Nagaland. However, the affordability and availability of the
guitar meant that many more children and teenagers could learn
to play the instrument. For instance, the guitar was the only musical
instrument in Kevi's house when he was a child. This meant that Kevi,
his older brother, and his uncle took turns learning to tune and strum the
same instrument. As the youngest boy in the house, Kevi developed his
musical skills on a broken guitar. When McDuie-Ra enquired, 'How?',
Kevi said, 'I sat on the guitar and broke it. It was on the bed under the
blanket, I did not see it. My brother put a metal plate on the neck [of the
guitar] and pulled the strings on the other side of the box. Then he fitted
the tuners of the body. It was on that guitar [that] I learnt the chords.'
A local craftsman named Yanger made the first hand-crafted guitar
in Dimapur under the label Yahuya. Kevi bought his first custom-
made guitar from Yanger in 1996. It cost him Rs 1,600. 'I feel that
instrument taught me a lot too. But the arrival of Chinese goods
finished his business. Now he makes electric guitars on demand,' he
said. Kevi exemplified the lives of musicians seeking new range and
sounds in Dimapur. His knowledge about sound drove him to seek
out resources to enhance his skills. In the last few years, he began
visiting forests and plantations across Nagaland looking for trees,
tapping the barks, feeling the textures of the trees, and calculating
their age. These new ventures led him to start new conversations about
the lives of trees, lives of the villagers, and the ongoing deforestation
in the village commons. Over the years, he has developed a habit
of collecting guitar strings from Europe because an integral part of
producing the sound he is looking for comes from 'mixing up the
parts'. Elaborating on the process, he notes:

For example, I put German strings in a local guitar. The guitar wood is
from Khonoma village. It is called Elder Wood. It is the same wood that

is used for manufacturing the Fender guitar. So, after I bought the wood [from Khonoma village], I asked Yanger to make me guitars. He made quite a few pieces for me. He is cutting one piece now; it is walnut wood. The wood came from Burma. But one must know the tone of the wood. We do not get Maple here but there is local wood that has the character of Maple. Some woods are very bright in sound. When we tap the wood, we can hear a *ting ting*—higher frequency. For teak, it is *puk puk puk*—no resonance. So basically, it is about mixing a higher frequency and a lower frequency one to build a guitar, that will sound good.

Kevi and his friends in Dimapur shared notes and discussed their instruments and styles regularly. Some of them had played for bands that were short-lived, some played covers of famous rock bands, while others focused on creating original numbers. Yet, there was a sensorial and a spatial connection that brought them together. They were all based in Dimapur and saw themselves playing music in this city as part of their life. Through conversations about sound and their passion to seek out new techniques, a vibrant community of musicians in Dimapur and across Nagaland had begun to talk about innovation. All these conversations brought out the complexity of living as musicians in Dimapur and elsewhere: the expensive Chinese-made guitars, seeking wood in the forests, and their association with seeking improvised sounds. Most prominent among their anxieties was the feeling of being 'far behind' when it came to the range of technological innovations and genres taking place outside Nagaland.

The attitude of musicians in Dimapur who constantly sought to blend, improve, and collaborate stood in contrast to a Naga nationalist outlook of Naga-ness and Naga identity. Musicians, at least the ones we spoke to, unlike Naga nationalists, did not dwell on notions of uniqueness or exclusivity. Neither did they toe a nationalist line where Naga culture and heritage were incessantly glorified. New techniques and practices emerged from connecting with a range of experiences, be they social, political, or economic transformations that were taking place around them. Talking about his connection and conversations with the musician community in Dimapur, Kevi said:

We end up talking about music; it is about the same thing again and again! About gears, about workshops, about collaboration. When we meet musicians from Delhi, from the United States [who come to Dimapur to jam with them], it is not difficult to understand one another. But when they talk about genres we have not heard about, then there is a gap. Because for us [Nagas], whether it is in politics or education, we have skipped a lot, so there is a big gap. When one grows in one's musicality, then you feel this. I have reached my cap now; I need to venture out into this particular genre. One cannot impose it, but I feel that something is missing [when one is not aware of the different genres].

Music in Dimapur is produced by a myriad of social relations and connections, from the friendly relations among musicians in the city to new collaborations that come from cities like Delhi, Mumbai, and beyond. At the same time, it also comes from the aural texture of wood from the forests of Nagaland and German guitar strings from Europe. These practices and performances capture the exciting ideas and feelings of inadequacies about playing music in Dimapur.

Was anything 'missing' or was there a 'gap' in the music scene, we wondered? And then our conversations highlighted that it all came down to the question of what constituted Naga music. For instance, Kevi felt there was 'nothing that the world would recognize as Naga music'. When Kikon asked, 'What about folk?', he said he stayed away from Naga folk because he found it 'boring'. The existing music scene in Dimapur and across the state was geared towards promoting folk and traditional music. According to Kevi, the presence of a market for Naga folk and traditional music drove musicians to pick up this genre. This was a very specific market. Linking Naga culture and tradition to a form of folk music from the past was limiting for many artists because they did not 'feel' for it. As a result, young Naga musicians felt pressured. There was a tacit expectation that a Naga musician should/ought to know folk and traditional music. Kevi said, 'It is just like the Naga spear. I am confused. Should I develop the modern side of it [music] or go back and revive [Naga traditional music]? I have tried it [folk music] but I just don't feel it.'

What is real and authentic Naga music? Can improvised and original compositions from contemporary Naga artists be categorized as Naga music? Senti Toy, an ethnomusicologist and singer-songwriter, encountered similar questions when she examined the political effect of Naga acoustemology. According to Toy, voices, vibrations, or other musical expressions are all experiences that emerge from 'particular knowings' (Toy 2010: v). Situating 'particular knowings' is founded on experiences in the backdrop of social, political, and musical transformations. This was the case among musicians in Dimapur.

Theja Meru, a pioneer in the world of Naga gospel and rock music in Nagaland and a driving force behind the MTF/TaFMA, dwells on the topic of Naga expressions and singing. In a conversation with Senti Toy, Meru notes, 'We just can't sing like they used to anymore, I feel like the traditional music most youngsters perform today is just ... like some beautiful noise. It doesn't sound quite the same. Call it soul, feel, emotion whatever ... I can't really pinpoint what it is but it just sounds a bit different' (cited in Toy 2010: 30). Musicians in Dimapur absorb different kinds of music, sound, and ways of listening as they move in the urban surroundings and immerse themselves in the cosmopolitan world. Meru's poignant reflections about 'feeing' and 'emotion' are reiterated in the experiences of musicians in Dimapur. They 'feel' for the music they are making *now*, drawn from an intimate connection with strings, wood, body movement, and a passion to create something different, something new: a particular knowing about the age we live in—the expressions and sounds that are produced from the anxieties and hopes of living in the present times.

Knowing the city and being concerned about expressions, performances, and sensorial processes produces a distinct account of living in a ceasefire city. Musical expressions and feelings are linked with everyday experiences (about contemporary developments in the form of new musical genres) and also memories (about a Naga past in the form of folk). When such sensibilities are located in an urban setting like Dimapur, it can also mean balancing a Naga past and being ambitious to break through as a successful artist.

Performing Dimapur

On a January morning in 2017, we drove along the Asian Highway 1 (commonly known as AH1) moving away from the heart of the city and arrived at the southern fringes of Dimapur. The AH1 highway is the longest network of highways in Asia and runs through the city of Dimapur. This road links the city to the state capital Kohima and beyond. Alobo Naga, a successful and dynamic musician, entrepreneur, and performer, guided us through the complexities of living as a successful artist in a frontier city. People in Dimapur contend with the crumbling infrastructure and a militarized civic life where state and non-state actors vie for power and control every day. Musicians also live in the same space and negotiate the challenges. Yet, they write songs of love, hope, and fantasy to connect with their fans. Alobo sings in Sümi (his mother tongue), English, Hindi, and Nagamese (the lingua franca spoken in the foothills of Nagaland).

We crossed security check gates, navigated broken bridges, travelled on city streets full of potholes and dust, and saw overflowing drains and garbage piles. Through electricity failures and complaints about corruption and unemployment, we managed to remain excited about our fieldwork in Dimapur. Yet, the spirit and energy that Alobo possessed was phenomenal. The young Nagas we met in the city and across India spoke about Alobo Naga. We wondered what the city meant to his band and what was his experience as a musician living here. We met Alobo Naga at his music school, Musik-A (Image 3.3), in an area dotted with tribal localities, churches, and Nagaland's sole airport. Established in 2016, Musik-A is located on the second floor of a commercial building along the busy AH1.

Image 3.3   Alobo Naga at Musik-A

Source: Duncan McDuie-Ra

'I am starting a busking culture in Dimapur. Here, right outside the music school. We will not get any money initially but they [students] must learn how to play on the street,' Alobo said.[4] In Dimapur, the highway AH1 is also a city 'street' and an integral part of the city. Localities, shops, commercial ventures, and schools have come up along this highway. Alobo joins thousands of commuters every day in navigating through the crowded cars and trucks along the AH1, crossing localities, shops, and schools to arrive at his music school. Such experiences, ranging from organizing busking shows along AH1 and moving in crowded highways cutting across the city, highlight the dimensions of mobilities and spatial realities in frontier regions. By 2018, the highway construction project had expanded right to the doorstep of the music school, taking away any pedestrian space to busk, or even walk. The semi-completed road expansion churned out dust and fumes, making re-purposing by musicians impossible.

While residents of Dimapur often talked about the crumbling infrastructure of the city, musicians and performers connected with everyday challenges that were not limited to power failures, load shedding, and unemployment, but also with experiences of finding love and/or encountering heartache in the city. And then there is always a grim reminder that hovers over this vast and growing cityscape: the presence of two ceasefire camps in the peri-urban areas of the city where warring factions of Naga armed groups wait for a final political solution. As political negotiations continue, the fragile political reality comes to the forefront. As such, the city is not an easy place to navigate.

Since musicians like Alobo Naga sing and perform and connect with a home crowd, they are able to find a home across the city and beyond. Alobo's lyrics not only highlight the experiences and aspirations for peace and dignity, but they also invoke familiar landscapes of and dwellings in the city. Irrespective of the difficulties and challenges of living in Dimapur, people always find ways to celebrate the city. In 2016, *Morung Express*, a local English daily from the city, carried the reflections of a young college student. In an essay

---

[4] All quotes by Alobo Naga in this chapter are from a personal interview held with him at Musik-A, Alobo Naga School of Music in Dimapur on 5 January 2017.

titled 'Dimapur—Heaven or Hell?', Tsukhumla Yimchunger gave an account of things in the city that were broken. The state of disrepair in Dimapur, according to Yimchunger (2016), mirrored 'hell' on earth. In other words, Dimapur was urban hell on earth. However, the tone of the essay shifted once she began to list out the beauty of the city. From green parks in the outskirts of the city to the exciting Christmas celebrations, she described the fun of living in Dimapur and concluded her essay with an appeal that read, 'Dimapur is our home, and maybe it's time we all work together to create it into an ideal city, a city we would be proud to live in, a city which we would pass down to our future generations with much pride' (Yimchunger 2016).

As discussed in Part I, from the inception of Dimapur as a town in 1954, there was steady migration of people from the hills of Nagaland. Some of the oldest residents included the Kacharis, Nepalis, Naga settlers, and groups such as the Marwaris and Bengali clerks who came with the establishment of the Dimapur railways lines. Today, residential neighbourhoods are organized according to tribal groups or along ethnic lines. Tribal churches and traditional council offices built in the city also have signboards and totem pillars signifying their respective tribal affiliations. Across the class and ethnic spectrum, the notion of a community remains strongly rooted in tribal values. These practices intertwined with ethnic and tribal realities form an important vignette of urban lives in Dimapur. As we have noted, the visual culture, infrastructure, and consumption practices allow us to understand frontier urbanism. But musicians in Dimapur provide us access to a distinct emerging urban culture in the forms of lyrics and commentaries. They inform us about a transformative moment. Here, the initiatives of artists like Alobo Naga to start their own busking stages and their decision to sing in Nagamese go against the dominant notion of tribal collective spirit, where the tribal space is beyond the circle of a fireplace, traditional councils, or churches. Everything around us—including music, performances, and improvisations—is no longer a tribal or non-tribal thing. Through improvisation and musical notes, musicians encounter a tribal modernity that is mired in a history of violence, displacement, and disenchantment. Yet, the existing inefficiencies, ranging from urban governance, corruption, absence of infrastructure, and unemployment, provide musicians with materials to create music and aspire for changes. The overlapping spaces in Dimapur, where music studios are coming up next to traditional courts or cafés appearing in residential neighbourhoods, show us the influence of music in transforming urban life here.

In the years following the 1997 ceasefire agreement, new restaurants and cafés came up in Dimapur. These places quickly became hubs for musicians to promote their work. From the hip and cool Hiyo Café, an initiative of Naga entrepreneur Betoka Swu, to the high-end club Zephyr Lounge (on its decline now), these developments became models for a new beginning in the state where peace and economic development went hand in hand. By 2011, numerous cafés came up in the city, including fast food eateries that operated as clubs where local bands played in the evenings (*Morung Express* 2011). But, gradually, the café culture began to disappear.

Alobo Naga played in some of the famous hubs like Hiyo Café and encouraged young local artists to take up music. As a visible face in the Dimapur café music scene, he said that the café culture declined due to 'the market'. The connection between producing music to generate revenue and profit and the poor infrastructure in a militarized landscape is a reality. These developments highlight the struggles of producing 'market-friendly' music in Nagaland and the visions of the state government–driven programmes like the MTF/TaFMA as we highlighted earlier in this chapter. Erratic electricity, reluctance of customers to pay to listen to local bands, and declining footfall in the new cafés due to the local economy led to the decline of the café music scene in Dimapur. In addition, the increasing rate of unemployment, outmigration, and financial uncertainty kept people away from spending money for musical performances and eating out in cafés.

Irrespective of the economic precarities, musicians continue to make music. Singers and songwriters like Alobo Naga or artists like DJ Sumika, who performs electronic dance music shows, have come up with creative events like music competitions and charity events. In these events, the music community comes together to showcase their talent and connect with their audience. The musicians' performances for their audience resonate with Michel de Certeau's (1984: 98) description of walking as a 'spatial acting-out of the place'.

Walking and performing both follow a path and have followers and create a 'mobile organicity', establishing a form of communication. Performing in Dimapur requires an audience.

'I cannot write songs about New York City,' Alobo said as he described his aim be an 'original' artist. Since he won the Best India Act at the MTV Europe Music Awards in 2012, he has become a visible figure in the music scene in India, but his inspiration and compositions come from his surroundings. The city he calls 'home' determines his moods as a musician and performer.[5] Originality for Alobo means living and making music from Dimapur and finding ways to channel the social world of the city—from the violence, political rivalry, and hope for reconciliation—visible in his lyrics. Here, New York City can be taken as a metaphor: a place that invokes, what Lakoff and Johnson (1980: 3) refer to as a 'device of the poetic imagination'. Metaphors are more than characters of languages. They are part of our everyday lives and actions that drive our imaginations and help us to define what constitutes our realities. For Alobo Naga, his quest to be original means engaging with the realities of the city, both mundane and exceptional ones, that people encounter daily.

In 2010, Alobo composed a song titled 'Kumsujulo' (Live as One), a Sümi Naga number about peace and unity. Today, this song has become an encore number in his concerts. 'Kumsujulo' has been translated into English and sung in concerts across Nagaland and beyond. While describing music as a field that is 'changing and evolving', Alobo dwells on his number 'Kumsujulo'. He says this is a song 'about Nagas—that we are so divided. It is only love and God that will bring us together.' Naga society is still haunted by the fratricidal killings that took place during the long decades of armed conflict since India's Independence (Iralu 2003). In the ceasefire period post-1997, besides composing romantic songs and pop numbers, themes of reconciliation and peace have emerged in the music scene.

---

[5] See Tora Agarwala's (2018) article on Alobo Naga about 'why no amount of international love will make him move away from home' captures his love for the city.

Therefore, music during the time of ceasefire offers accounts of human experiences that are grounded in sorrow and loss because of the Naga armed conflict. Yet, these songs and performances go beyond a rigid framework of nationalism or ideology of armed groups. Alobo senses that 'Kumsujulo' resonates deeply with his audience. He notes, 'In my concerts, I don't sing that song. The crowd sings that song.' Naga musicians have found a way to articulate new messages that capture the voice and sentiments of a larger public in a militarized city. 'Kumsujulo' (Naga 2010), according to Alobo, highlights the mood of the Naga people. A verse from the song goes as follows:

Day after day, sadness comes around
Each night and day, filled with sorrows, sadness, and pain
Little children wail in agony, widows increasing in our land daily
When we think of those wonderful glorious years
Nagas lived in peace and unity
But alas who brought the partition/division among us?
Let us bring back the peace within us all
Come on everyone let us live as one.[6]

Alobo has also successfully adopted new technologies to produce his music. For instance, in 2017, he distributed his music album in a custom-made pen drive wristband. He labels his music as 'western music with Naga melody'. Yet, his lyrics focus on local issues in the city and help him connect with his expanding fan base. For instance, there is no direct reference to the armed conflict in 'Kumsujulo', but the sense of sorrow and the longing for reconciliation and peace reflects the Naga history of conflict, violence, and loss. Perhaps this is the best way to understand the concept of an 'audible city' where musicians produce the conversations and experiences of the people living under militarization. The yearning for a home crowd/audience among musicians in the city reveals the experiences of creativity and performance in a ceasefire city.

Given the militarization and political instability in a ceasefire city, the audience attending music concerts in the pre-ceasefire period were often perceived as unruly citizens. Scores of accounts about being slapped, beaten, and kicked by the Indian Armed Forces

---

[6] © Alobo Naga. Lyrics used with permission from Alobo Naga.

while returning from concerts came up. Breaking curfews and moving around in the city jamming with friends becomes an issue of law and order for the administration and the security forces. The home crowd/audience and the citizen in Dimapur are one and the same. Yet, the relationship that musicians and security forces seek to establish with them are distinct. The musicians aspire to create an audible relationship with them based on vibrations, emotions, sounds, chords, and words, while the armed forces seek to establish a regime of immobility, terror, injury, and harm.

Musicians' articulation of seeking out an audience, therefore, departs from the existing militaristic and bureaucratic approaches of defining residents of the ceasefire city as citizens who must be governed, put under surveillance, and controlled. This is a significant marker of living in a ceasefire city like Dimapur. For example, as the armed forces patrol the city and monitor the movement of people and vehicles after sunset, they cross paths with children returning from choir practices or music lessons or young people heading out for band practice. In the pre-ceasefire period, mundane activities where young people desired to participate in jamming sessions after dark became risky and invoked fear and anxiety in parents. Today, there is a sense of anxiety and insecurity, but one connected to the past—the pre-ceasefire period of the armed conflict. In reality, city centres have become vibrant social hubs after sunset. The City Tower junction and the Nyamo Lotha Road, which houses ice cream parlours and bakeries, are bustling with people shopping after dark or enjoying ice cream treats. There is a degree of security and shops remain open for longer hours, way past 5 p.m. The bright lights and bustle along the Nyamo Lotha Road, shrouded in darkness during the decades of armed conflict, stands as a transformative development of the ceasefire period. There is an emergence of leisure and public space in the city.

Only through conversations with musicians in Dimapur were we able to witness the audiences'/citizens' joy and excitement of exploring old and new spaces of the city during the ceasefire period. But there are also other developments. The increasing rate of unemployment and the construction boom are visible across Nagaland. In Dimapur, the large mansions and shopping malls attract conversations about wealth, employment, and other desires. During our fieldwork in 2017,

Alobo Naga released a Nagamese song titled 'Mistry Gaana' (Mason Song). His music video focused on construction sites in the city to match the spirit of the song. Naga youths carried sand and bricks in the music video, producing a visually rich performance about the dignity of labour and hardwork.

We had met Alobo in Dimapur around the time when the song was being recorded and he sang the chorus for us. The song was clearly marked to deliver a social message to the listeners. A translated version of the Nagamese song (Naga 2017) goes as follows:

Mom said study hard and become an officer
Dad wouldn't settle for anything less than doctor or engineer
All family members talk of civil service (NPSC) exams
Villagers say if it's not a government job, it's nothing
But if everyone becomes a government employee
Who will be the one to build/construct your house?

(Chorus) I am the construction worker who constructs your house
I make use of my hands and feet which God blessed me with
I am the construction worker who constructs your house
But I am happy today

From the biggest to the smallest
Everyone needs each other in this world
You need a construction worker to build a minister's house
But everyone says it is not a government job
So if everyone becomes a government employee
Who will be the one to build/construct your house?
We think electricians, plumbers, painters, carpenters are small jobs and are ashamed to take up these professions

But everywhere, yeah, everyone's constructing a house
Everyone's putting up a building
There is money in this profession
And outsiders come and work; and take away all the money
So if everyone becomes a government employee
Who will be the one to build/construct your house?[7]

---

[7] © Alobo Naga. Lyrics used with permission from Alobo Naga.

Since the ceasefire of 1997, new residential areas, markets, and commercial centres have come up. From mega churches, commercial malls, and hospitals, to schools and colleges, the city has witnessed rapid urbanism during the ceasefire period. Today, the city's landscape is dotted with construction projects. Alobo's song also captures the experiences of unemployment along with the construction boom in Dimapur.

Besides out-of-state migrants from Bihar, Assam, and West Bengal who come and work in the construction sites, the city has also witnessed an increase in inter-state migration. Families across the hill districts of Nagaland have arrived in Dimapur looking for opportunities. Even in the pre-ceasefire period, people from all social and economic backgrounds were attracted to this city. It was often an aspiration for many Naga families to build a home or buy a plot of land here. Government employees and businesspeople alike consider Dimapur as an ideal city to settle down. Despite the overcrowding, increasing traffic, and congestion, many Nagas prefer the urban lifestyle to their rural villages in the hills. One of our respondents shared with us that she loved Dimapur because it is a city where 'You get everything'.[8] The migration of people from rural areas of the state to the city means that people are constantly looking for employment and opportunities.

Yet, construction work does not fit into the traditional idea of work in Naga society. There is immense societal pressure to secure a 'department job', a reference to government employment. Even professional degree holders like doctors or engineers are not considered worthy, unless they are able to find employment with the state government. All the important institutions in the city, including clans in villages, tribal councils, church, and family members, place high importance on the priority and status (social capital and security) of government jobs. Securing a job with the state government is seen as a great achievement and is celebrated with community feasts and congratulatory advertisements in local dailies.

In this context, Alobo's song 'Mistry Gaana' offers a solution to address the frustration and anxieties of the youth in the city. He encourages the youth to consider the construction boom as an opportunity and recognize the dignity of labour. These are simple

[8] Personal interview with Respondent 1 in Dimapur on 15 July 2017.

messages at first glance. But the rhyme, lyrics, tempo, and Naga faces in the music video showcase a modern way of living in the city. Even the equipment in the video, such as wheelbarrows to carry bricks or safety helmets (which are actually never used by workers in the construction sites in Dimapur), highlights a modern life. The outfits and visuals of trendy construction workers offer us a vignette that is far removed from the life of subsistence agriculture, where Naga people are shown with baskets on their heads standing in the middle of green paddy fields in tourism brochures and government programmes. Alobo's music videos offer us a new vignette of urban life with modern aspirations for jobs and dignity. The rhythm and beat of the music ensure that 'Mistry Gaana' is a foot-tapping number. The construction boom and the theme 'dignity of labour' underline the moral aspect of work in the ceasefire period. The song presents a layered account of the urban transformation of a ceasefire city. Yet, it is a city broken at many levels.

City of Lights

Dimapur has an erratic power supply. During summers the temperature shoots upto 40°C, and the city experiences massive load shedding. It is common to have power only for 2 hours a day during the peak summer season spanning from May to August. When the heat becomes unbearable and the asphalt on the roads melts under the scorching sun, there are frantic calls to the grievance cell of the Power Department. We also heard stories about citizens, armed with sticks and stones, marching to the Power Department to protest against the city being plunged into darkness in the unbearable summer heat. In recent years, the Power Department in Dimapur has begun to announce power shutdowns in local dailies, naming the neighbourhoods. For instance, on 25 July 2018, the Power Department shared a chart that displayed a week-long routine of power shutdowns in Dimapur (Table 3.1).

It is obvious to visitors and residents alike that the living conditions here are challenging. The crumbling infrastructure, such as the broken roads, erratic power supply, overflowing sewages, and absence of water supply, captures the lack of civic responsibility. In many ways these conditions also capture how militarized and

Date 04:00 AM to 08:00 AM	Locality/Colony
26th & 27th July 2018	Ganeshnagar, Doyapur, Dhansiripar, Razhaphe & Rangapahar Army Cantonment.
28th & 29th July 2018	Kuda, Walford, Rajbari & Adjoining Areas.
30th & 31st July 2018	Metha, Thahekhu, [Dhobinala], PWD, Forest, Duncan, Town Area, signal
1st & 2nd August 2018	Industrial Estate, Sub Jail, Referral, Lengrijan, DC Court, Chekiye, Naharbari, [Thilixu], Full Nagarjan, Power Grid.

Table 3.1　Schedule for power shutdown in Dimapur

Source: Reproduced from *Morung Express* (2018c)

dysfunctional systems in conflict zones have led to the establishment of new institutions and collectives. Competing actors, both state and non-state, such as the armed groups, business communities, church members, and tribal bodies show their loyalties to their respective groups. Activities and engagements to clean the roads and drains and repair the roads are routinely organized by cultural groups and other youth organizations.

These everyday practices reiterate what we refer to as 'community infrastructure' (Chapter 1). In the absence of state organs overseeing the everyday functioning of the city, residents come together and raise funds to create designated sites for community garbage collection or put up signposts that provide directions to shops and important landmarks. These can also be projects to beautify one's neighbourhood. Musicians in Dimapur actively participate in these civic activities and call upon the civic bodies to improve the governance and lives of people here. For instance, Alobo Naga is one of the brand ambassadors of *Swachh Bharat Abhiyan* (Clean India Campaign), a national cleanliness drive organized by the Government of India.

For Tali Angh, a prominent singer from the city, the focus is on addressing a different kind of challenge: not of the material kind, but the assurance of finding hope and belonging in a ceasefire city. He calls his audience to embrace a path of faith and love. His song 'I Am a Revivalist' (Angh 2016) calls for healing and transformation.

Sharing his experiences of living in the city, he admitted, 'it is a hard place to do business'.[9] He explained:

> I am mostly invited to church music festivals. We all have our target groups. I am not invited to places where Alobo is invited. That is his place, where he shines. My area of influence is mostly churches and the mainstream—but not as much as I am recognized in the church. My unique struggle is that I cannot deal professionally with churches and ministries. They do not come to me like an NGO [Some NGOs are commissioning artists to sing for their projects and pay them for their work]. They do not come to me to sign a contract. They just invite, and we cannot make a deal. They just expect [free performances]. But in the last four to five years, people are realizing that music has its own sphere of influence. So, people pay and invest in music. Now, I do get paid for most of my shows. But if there are 50 shows I do in a year, 25 are purely charity shows, but it helps me grow as an artist. I am self-motivated and am making new songs. I can see progress, so I am not stuck.

Today, music is well received by Naga audiences, but the music scene predominantly remains a community initiative. The practice of signing music bands and legal contracts is still uncommon. Musicians are expected to contribute towards various projects like supporting orphans, education, scholarships, and raising awareness for mental health, and so on. For example, during the devastating floods in Kerala (South India) in 2018, a Naga music society from the state called Rattle and Hum Music Society raised funds for the flood victims (*Eastern Mirror* 2018b).

Churches encourage volunteerism and this means paying musicians like Tali for their service is often disregarded. The music industry in Nagaland, as Tali described, is still in its 'infancy' and is riddled with challenges. Music is perceived as a 'co-operative' initiative. This means that the lines between payments and professional contracts are often blurry. Thus, musicians in Dimapur and elsewhere in the state end up doing charity shows. These events are important forums to connect with the audience, but the performers are not paid for these gigs.

[9] All quotes by Tali Angh in this chapter are from a personal interview held with him at Fellowship Colony in Dimapur on 8 January 2017.

Image 3.4   Tali Angh at Fellowship Colony

Source: Duncan McDuie-Ra

Pursuing music is a difficult passion. In Dimapur, many musicians take up part time employment to sustain their music careers. Many musicians and music studios have side business such as renting out sound systems for events, working as event managers, selling musical instruments, providing music classes, or earning money as contractors in the construction business. Many of them seek to promote and showcase their talents simultaneously. Generally, the experiences of the city or the urban do not feature as a prominent theme for songwriters. The Naga past—villages, forests, rivers, and mountains—continues to dominate Naga lyrics/songs/images, portraying a Naga sense of belonging and identity.

Yet, the reality is something else: broken bridges, overflowing drains, non-existent water supply, and erratic electricity. Then, there is a fear of the ceasefire negotiations breaking down. This fear is real. Two months after we sat down for a conversation with Tali Angh in Fellowship Colony (Image 3.4), a locality in Dimapur, there was a factional shoot-out in the city. The *Indian Express* (2018b), a national Indian daily, reported that 15 people were killed in a conflict between the two groups of the National Socialist Council of Nagaland (NSCN), the NSCN-U and the NSCN-IM. This led to the closing down of the Asian Highway 1 that connects Dimapur to Kohima, and the city coming to a standstill. Something else is visible in the city: the anxieties and depression of living in a ceasefire city.

Tali Angh's (2018) song 'City of Lights' showcases Dimapur as a site of creativity and suffering. When Kikon asked him, 'How did you write this song?', Tali responded:

This song was inspired not so much by the city but by the people. I see city as people. And some of the instances you see every day when you go to the town or city; you will see that people are so busy. People hardly smile. Some are filled with insecurity, some are filled with brokenness, fear, you just name it. They are carrying all these things and trying to live their lives. That is what I see in the town. [But] I try to see beneath their faces.[10] If someone is arrogant then maybe something is leading him to that kind of arrogance. So, it is basically compassion and a love-driven kind of song. Looking at people and how they struggle.

It is inspired by two stories. My cousin, he was a very talented singer but he committed suicide. I had such big dreams for him but he just ... that was quite shocking for me. All of a sudden, he ended his life in Dimapur. And another person from Dimapur, I will not name her, but she has been through a lot. That is why the song starts with 'She wants to sleep, night seems long'.

But there is a line that I borrowed from a scene I saw in Longleng [a district in Nagaland]. I was sitting at the balcony and suddenly I saw an ambulance right at the main road. I saw my neighbour, a mother who was very ill, being taken to Dimapur [for medical treatment]. Doctors gave up hope. She was taken out on a stretcher from the ambulance. All her children, five of them, all their hands were on the stretcher pushing their mom towards their home. So that scene really helped me write the line, 'Hands will guide you home'.

As a singer and composer from Dimapur, he described how urban experiences and social conditions of the people inspired him. Musicians like Alobo Naga and Tali Angh go beyond the framework of glorifying Naga culture and tradition. Their present surroundings—the city, brokenness, depression, and civic responsibilities—inspire them to be productive artists. Music of aspiration and brokenness in Dimapur highlights the intimate lives and experiences of its residents, a theme that remains invisible in the larger story of political negotiations and conflict in Naga society. These are immediate concerns—aspirations for employment and opportunities and breaking of dreams and the spirit—that dominate the lives of residents in Dimapur. To understand the meaning of city life, Tali Angh reflects:

[10] The artist was mindful about the struggles and hardship of living in the city and expressed how he tried to see the real emotions to feel the city and reach out.

There is a lot of brokenness in the city, in people. But in spite of all of these—bad roads, bad drainage systems, corruption, you just name it—I am positive and prophetically declaring and dreaming of a city where when we look at each other we light up one another.

And there is a sense of security in our city; you don't have to be scared of walking around in your own city. So, I have this ideal picture of a city where we can all celebrate life. So that is how the song came up. We are all designed that way deep down inside. Doing research, doing music; I think it is because we long for that kind of connection.

Everyday experiences of loneliness and anxiety emerge from the transformation of the place. Of course, the experiences of urbanization in Dimapur cannot be used to represent all the urban places in Nagaland. But there are strong factors—expanding neighbourhoods, increased population, new buildings, challenges of urban governance—and other aspects of development that highlight the experiences of urbanization. What is distinct, though, as we have reiterated earlier, is the militarization and the element of uncertainty in a ceasefire city. Musicians' tunes and lyrics draw from the social and political transformation and interrogate the dominant imagination of tribal people (in Nagaland and elsewhere) as living in villages and remote places.

During our fieldwork in Dimapur, upon hearing that we were conducting research and working towards writing a book on Dimapur, many informants (musicians in this context) were excited. They said that they were 'relieved' to not talk about Naga culture, politics, or history for once. Not that they disrespected these topics, but as Kevi shared, 'It is as if there is nothing else happening in our lives.' And then he said, 'It is refreshing. For a change we will read a book that is about our lives; a life we are able to connect with.' Musicians were improvising and adopting new techniques irrespective of the dominant social and cultural pressure to stick to a single genre. Many more musicians were composing new numbers or organizing cultural events with fusion music. Young musicians too were absorbing from different genres—dance, instruments, beats—and delivering messages about belonging and survival.

Tali's music and songs offer a philosophy of responsibility and accountability towards one another in a militarized city. How do we practice humanity in a ceasefire city? What is the meaning of home for migrants who come to Dimapur? Is there any space for compassion and hope? These questions are important not because they emerge from a ceasefire city, but because they direct our attention towards themes of suffering and surviving in the city. They inform us how it is inherently human to dream about security, love, and connection.

These are not connections that people seek in vacuum. They are situated in a city where people, according to Tali, are constantly dealing with brokenness and seeking hope at the same time. Collating experiences, composing beats, and pondering about the inescapabilty of city life and being left behind, Tali's performances and reflections, like the conversions with Kevi and Alobo, are about a city that is seldom celebrated.

The Nagas' nostalgia about culture, tradition, and a glorified past is always elsewhere, beyond the ceasefire city. It is in the hills and not in the urban bustling neighbourhoods or in the peri-urban areas of the city with ceasefire camps and Indian military stations. Generations of Naga families have grown up in Dimapur since the formation of the state in 1963. The tribal associations and the traditional bodies that are spread across the city are created and governed by tribal members who are city dwellers.

Dimapur is seldom identified as a place that has value or a site that inspires artistry or fondness. Since the ceasefire of 1997, wealth has poured into this city. New shopping malls, commercial buildings, mansions, and educational institutions have come up. Thousands of families and businesspeople across Nagaland prefer to shop and build their houses in Dimapur. The biggest business enterprises have their base in this city. Yet, as a place that has been long connected as the urban hub of Nagaland, Dimapur remains peripheral as a city in the imagination of Naga people. Given this history, we asked Tali how he coped as a musician. He said:

We have started really late. There are 10–15 of us who are trying to do something on our own, without the assurance of any returns.

There are parts of a music industry: studios, musicians, and sound venues in Dimapur. But there is no night culture here. So, there are small parts, the production values are really high and impressive. The pieces are there, but how they come together to sustain careers is a question. It remains unclear.

We have woken up late, but it is not too late yet. We are standing on a
threshold where it is not about creating a pool of talent but something
that promises us a long-term sustenance in terms of recognition and
livelihood. I think we have realized this.

Tali's anxieties about being left behind in the music scene (as
compared to the metropolitan cities in India) came up during our
conversation. Dimapur has come up as a hub to feed and serve the
state of Nagaland, but the militarized culture of surveillance, curfew,
and counter-insurgency operations are also an integral part of this
urban life. Being left behind is an anxiety that is attached to the
dominant discourse about progress and development in the ceasefire
period. The establishment of the MTF in the state is also pitched in
the language of 'catching up'. It is not our argument that Naga music
should remain outside the ambit of the music industry or that Naga
musicians should refrain from taking up projects that are designed
as profit-making ventures. But the lives of musicians in Dimapur
provide an insight about urban experiences and transformation
during the time of ceasefire. Naga musicians in Dimapur show us
how performances, sounds, and lyrics shape, and are shaped by, the
city and its imagining as a music hub.

4

Huntingscape

Today the community fishing meant for 500 is attended by 10,000 people or so. Imagine the rush. The villagers often return empty-handed because they give away the fish they catch to their relatives and kin groups from urban areas. Many people from the village who have [now] settled down in the urban areas return to the village for these community events. So, when people from the village meet their relatives living in the towns—it may be after five years or six years—they give them these fish.

Urban people end up with all the fish and their kin members from the village return home empty-handed. Whenever such events are announced, people from the town make sure they attend such community events. It is overwhelming. They arrive in cars and come unprepared for the fishing [no implements or skills]. Even though aquatic life has depleted, the population of our community has gone up, and everyone wants to be part of these community fishing events.

This story was narrated by a hunter from Netho (pseudonym), a settlement in Dimapur near the border with Assam.[1] He described how growing up in the village meant learning to light a fire on the mountaintop to signal to the neighbouring villages about the commencement of community fishing season. If the neighbouring villages reciprocated by lighting a fire, then the following week, *everyone* descended on the rivers and streams, but women were meant to follow the men (the hunters) and pick up the fish. In these community fishing stories, *everyone* meant men who possessed the traditional birth right

---

[1] All the quotes by hunters in this chapter are from personal interviews with them that took place between December 2016 and January 2017.

to organize and shape the social order of these community fishing activities. From fetching roots from the forest (used in community fishing) to organizing fishing activity in clans and dividing the catch, the story of tribal masculinity and leadership emerged as an important foundation of tribal fishing. But many accounts of community hunting have a strong resonance with urban residents.

This chapter explores the ways in which Naga hunting traditions are recast in the city as a place-making strategy, and highlights the inter-species relationships that persevere in the urban environment. As discussed in Chapter 1, Dimapur is an enclave surrounded by Assam, and most of the remaining forest in proximity to Dimapur is on the Assam side. Hunting expeditions bring hunters from the city into Assam's territory, where they come into contact with different security forces, other hunters, insurgents, and otherworldly spirits. This boundary crossing is not trivial, as the border between the states also designates a border between tribal and non-tribal land and the limits of customary authority. Intergenerational change, out-migration from Naga territories, and urbanization have reduced the popularity of hunting. For many urban residents, hunting maintains their connection to the village and, in the process, blurs urban and rural boundaries, especially on the city's edge. However, even the popular illicit hunting grounds in the border area are disappearing due to deforestation within and beyond tribal territory. Meanwhile, within the city, the debate on selling dog meat has reconfigured human–animal relationships in a different way. The pressure to ban the sale of dog meat and make Dimapur more city-like has been met with both opposition and approval. This debate reiterates our point that the fringes (where hunters live) and the centre (of trade and market) are both founded on tribal authority and identity, with the urban landscape taking form around these.

The urban hunters from Dimapur offer us new ways of thinking about tribal communities often categorized as 'foragers' and 'subsistence farmers' living in remote villages. It also helps us to think about a city where hunters create a sense of belonging as rapid urbanization takes place. Many young hunters from Netho said they learnt how to hunt in Dimapur after migrating from their villages to the city. In that context, we ask what is the 'right' place to hunt? What constitutes hunting? What are the contestations when animals from the Assam Forest cross over to the fringes of Dimapur? What about the aquatic animals that enter the water bodies that operate as boundaries between the Assam Forest and the city limits of Dimapur? Dimapur is one of the fastest-growing cities in Northeast India, but there is seldom a discussion about urban policies and governance with regard to this city.

Here, we examine stories of hunting from the fringes of Dimapur as processes of bonding and establishing a relationship with the city. As noted earlier, we refer to this as 'huntingscape'—a way of understanding the symbolic, material, and spiritual values that are attached to hunting and the landscape. The movement of animals and practices of hunters in the urban fringes of Dimapur highlight the layered experiences of urbanization in Northeast India.

Many animals, such as porcupines, otters, birds, and wild cats, enter Netho and its neighbouring localities like Indisen and Kashiram. These suburbs share borders with Assam. These neighbourhoods are also a testament of tribal identity where tribal motifs and traditional designs on gates and tribal council buildings dominate the landscape. For instance, Indisen is regarded as an Ao suburb, while Netho is defined as a Lotha 'village'. In Dimapur, a village means a residential neighbourhood with a *gaonbura* (village headman), an official position under the jurisdiction of the civil administration of the city. These practices showcase how a tribal city produces different systems of authority where tribal cultures and practices overlap with the urban civic administration of the city. As discussed in Chapter 1, across Dimapur, scores of localities feature the word *bosti* in their names (meaning 'village' in Nagamese). These names give us an account of belonging and spatial control across neighbourhoods. Despite these markers, hunters' stories offer us an exceptional insight about crossing various boundaries.

The stories we present in the following section need to be read as place-making experiences between the city and the forest from the perspective of the hunters. We are aware of the trans-species (Kohn 2013) and inter-species frameworks (Govindrajan 2018; Narayanan 2017) in relation to human–animal encounters, but in this chapter, we focus on the political and cultural boundaries of the forest and the city in a frontier region. We use stories of tribal hunters to trace the urban landscape of Dimapur. As the expanding city meets the forest, we build on the conceptual theme of 'huntingscape' to highlight the transformative aspects of urban tribal city spaces in Northeast India.

Forest at the Edge of the City

Tribal communities settled in Dimapur consider community fishing activities in the village as reunion events with their kin groups. Some kin members meet after a decade, while others meet in these community events annually. As such, hunting stories that are presented as part of the Naga culture and tradition are also shaped by urban residents. Particularly, tribal communities living in urban areas invoke hunting as an example of Naga culture and also as a connection with a rural way of life. What is poignant in the story that opened this chapter is the villagers going home empty-handed (during community fishing activity) after giving away their share of the catch to visitors from the cities and towns. This calls for us to shift our focus. Hunting remains a central trope of Naga identity. Today, many residents from Dimapur return to the villages to hunt and assert their social and political identity as a way of compensating for a vacuum in city life where they cannot participate in these cultural activities. For people who dream and desire to live their lives as hunters in urban cities like Dimapur, where do they go? When we visited a suburb and stories of hunting unfolded, McDuie-Ra enquired, 'Who tries to stop hunting?', and a hunter responded, 'Assam police. After the last house it is Assam.'[2]

Our conversation with hunters in Netho, the edge of Dimapur's urban enclave, led to a discussion on different topics such as hunting, desire, dangers, and navigating lives in the city. Implicit in these stories that the hunters shared with us were their experiences of living at the edge of the city. Bamboo fences, barbed wires, and residential concrete walls in Netho function as the border between Nagaland and Assam. The land beyond the fences of Netho is known as the Assam Forest.[3]

[2] Personal interview with Walker (pseudonym) in Dimapur on 9 January 2017.

[3] The areas known as the Assam Forest come under the Karbi Anglong Autonomous Council in Assam, a tribal administrative area that enjoys territorial autonomy in relation to managing its natural resources and recognizing its customary laws and practices.

In this chapter, we tell stories about residents who live in the western fringes of Dimapur that share its border with Assam. Returning to Harms (2011) and the idea of spatial boundaries, discussed in the context of Indisen village in Chapter 1, there is no edge of the city. Instead, what exists is a social edginess, a way of highlighting the realities of the coexistence of an urban and a rural social life as rapid urbanization takes place on the fringes. While it is an ambiguous task to define the edge of the city in everyday lives, in Dimapur, the edge resonates both as a spatial and a social perimeter. We apply the concept of edge/edginess to focus on huntingscape in order to understand how urban residents living on the fringes of Dimapur navigate and mark out the topography of the city and the forest. We focus on the terrains in which they hunt, the physical features they define as natural forests where animals inhabit, which in turn becomes an ideal spot for hunters. Hunting is restricted in the Assam Forest that stretches outside Netho. There are Assam police check gates at the entrance to the Assam Forest to monitor the movement of vehicles and people from Dimapur and beyond. This is where, a hunter said, 'the dangerous and wild things' take place.[4] In the Assam Forest, wild animals, spirits, insurgents, and security forces encounter one another and try to establish power and authority over the forest. These stories about the Assam Forest are narrated by people sitting in their living rooms and kitchens in Dimapur.

The topography of Dimapur plays a significant role in creating these connections between the hunters from Dimapur and the Assam Forest. The city is located along the foothills of Nagaland. It shares a border with Assam. The north, east, and west parts of the city hug the Assam Forest. Assam police checkposts mark the territorial demarcation of the city here. On the southern side, the city of Dimapur ends after the Chumukedima Bridge; from here, the winding national highway leads to Kohima, the state's capital and seat of power. A giant traditional signpost made of concrete that announces 'Welcome to Nagaland: The Land of Festivals' stands here. This sign, a few yards away from the Nagaland Armed Police checkpost, reiterates the obvious. Nagaland— the cultural state where tribalness and festivity is abound—only begins

---

[4] Personal interview with Walker (pseudonym) in Dimapur on 9 January 2017.

after the city of Dimapur ends. The edge of the city is both a jurisdictional and a cultural one simultaneously. Police checkposts, ceasefire camps, cultural billboard signs, and the Indian Army barracks are the symbols and authorities that mark the edges of the city.

Not everyone who lives in Netho is a hunter. Yet, experiences of hunters from this neighbourhood highlight how the boundaries between the Assam Forest and the urban landscape of Dimapur are produced. This is an 'off the map' practice; an illegal activity that nonetheless reflects how place-making occurs. Hunting, in this regard, helps us to highlight the different legal and political justifications and the urban ecology of a frontier city, especially the experiences of unprecedented urbanization and migration in Dimapur and the absence of an infrastructure to take care of its citizens, including animals who cross over from the Assam Forest. Stories of hunters also highlight accounts of bravery, masculinity, and Naga tradition in an urban setting. These adventurous encounters inside the Assam Forest invoke a sense of excitement and connection to a forest for the Naga hunters. Based on their experiences with animals and state agencies like the Assam Forest guards, they iterate hunting and eating game meat as a tribal way of life.

The Assam Forest is a place where young hunters from the fringes of the city learn the secrets of becoming good hunters, and seasoned hunters try to make sense of their inchoate experiences with strange entities. It is a place where the presence of spirits and the encounters of wilderness and nature, deeply founded in Naga legends about value and sociality, are brought to life. As such, hunting accounts in the Assam Forest capture important aspects of an urban conception of tribal modernity. Hunting tales from Dimapur are neither framed as a way of life that is integral for the survival of Naga culture, nor are they portrayed as a practice that is linked to livelihood (to secure a steady income). These accounts, perhaps, can be understood only in conjunction with the larger urbanization process of Dimapur that presents the city as a cluster of multiple tribal suburbs.

Spirits

These stories were told around a fireplace on a chilly January night in 2017. Earlier that day, driving to the tip of the western edges of Dimapur to meet the hunters, we noticed how the landscape transformed in this part of the city. The air was cooler, there was more greenery, and the terrain became elevated. We walked around the boundary of the village with some hunters who pointed towards the forest and said, 'That is Assam'. The word 'Assam' was synonymous with the forest that was visible from the edge of this neighbourhood. To say 'I will go to Assam' usually meant a trip to the forest. On that January night, stories about encounters with wild animals and spirits overlapped. Some of these animals were killed and consumed while others were set free or sold off. But there was a third kind who lived in the Assam Forest that could neither be killed nor set free. These were the spirits who took the form of humans, animals, and birds.

For Arhomo, it is this aspect of the spirit world inside the Assam Forest that continues to fascinate him. He is a confident hunter from Netho who comprehends the different aspects of urban living and associates his tribalness with a cosmopolitan setting in the city. He moved to Dimapur from his village (in the hills) in the early 1980s. His memory of his village is distant, and he is quick to identify himself as a city person. He receives a small pension from the government, and supplements his household income by picking mushrooms from the Assam Forest and selling them in Dimapur.

One day, Arhomo encountered a spirit inside the Assam Forest. The spirit took the form of an Adivasi man. When the Adivasi appeared in front of him, Arhomo sensed that he was not a human. Suddenly, the figure started making loud sounds like an elephant and started hitting Arhomo with a stick. Arhomo tried to shoot the spirit-man but the trigger was locked, so he threw the gun away and jumped at the spirit-man. They wrestled for a long time in the middle of the forest. Around midnight, they were both exhausted and stopped fighting. The spirit-man walked away. Eager to communicate with him, Arhomo followed the spirit-man, speaking to him in Hindi, Nagamese, and Assamese, but got no response. But after some time, the figure said, 'Bullets cannot hurt me', and walked away. In the morning, Arhomo returned to the site where they had wrestled the previous night. The ground and the area appeared pristine and untouched. Not long after that event, he met another forest spirit. This time, the spirit took the form of a dwarf. The spirit-dwarf was naked and carried a red purse and an umbrella. Once he started whistling, all the animals and birds retreated deep into the forest. After that encounter, Arhomo missed all his targets and was unable to hunt that day. He realized that the dwarf was the spirit manager of the animals' souls in the Assam Forest.

Such stories profoundly shape the sensibilities of hunters in Netho. One day, another hunter, Yisemo (pseudonym), was returning from the Assam Forest around sunset, when he noticed a deer jumping around a bush. When the deer saw him, it started laughing like a human being and began to tease him. The deer would stand and smile at the hunter, then walk off to a distance. Again, it would turn around and smile at the hunter. Yisemo aimed his gun at the deer and started shooting, but the animal was unharmed. Suddenly, a deep exhaustion set upon him. He struggled to keep his eyes open. Then it dawned on him that this was not a deer but a spirit in the form of a deer. The hunter put away his gun and left the forest.

A few months later, Yisemo returned to the same spot. It was a dark moonless night and the forest was pitch dark. When he pointed the flashlight above him, he saw a wild cat perched on a tree. He pulled the trigger and the animal fell on the ground with a thump. But something else happened. According to Yisemo, the spirit of the tree was also injured. 'There was a loud scream. It was a human voice. As though a human being had been injured,' he said.[5] The spirit of the tree scurried away to the neighbouring tree with a roaring sound. 'A sound *ahaahahaah* echoed across the forest,' he said. Yisemo realized what he had done and quickly left the forest in fear.

The belief about the presence of spirits in the Assam Forest cuts across ethnic lines. Karbi, Dimasa, Adivasi, and Naga hunters who frequent the Assam Forest also have their share of encounters with the spirits. Samuel from Netho village narrated a famous story about a Karbi hunter's experience. One day, a Karbi hunter entered the Assam Forest and shot a wild boar, but the injured animal managed to escape into the deep forest. In pursuit of the animal, the hunter found himself in a place that looked like a big village. When he entered the village gate, he came across a man who looked worried and asked, 'Where is my boar? Where is my boar?' Someone next to him said,

---

[5] All quotes by Yisemo (pseudonym) in this chapter are from a personal interview held with him in Dimapur on 9 January 2017.

'Here it is. Here is your wild boar. Oh, but it looks like he has been shot.' The Karbi hunter thought to himself, 'What have I done? I have shot someone's animal.' The villagers cooked the animal and invited the Karbi hunter to eat with them. After the feast was over, the villagers told him, 'It is time for you to go. But as you leave, do not turn back.' When the hunter left, he turned around for a last glimpse of the village, but all he saw was a thick forest behind him. There was no sign of a village or human beings in the vicinity. When he looked ahead, there was no path ahead of him. He was trapped in the middle of a thick bush in the deep forest. The Karbi hunter realized that he had entered a spirit village and the wild boar belonged to a spirit-man.

Samuel said that all the animals in the forest belonged to different spirit-owners, but there were instances when the spirits also teased hunters. On a hunting trip to the Assam Forest recently, Samuel and his friends sought shelter in an abandoned inspection bungalow inside the Assam Forest. Around 2 a.m., they woke up in fear and sensed that someone was watching them. Samuel was not sure what kind of spirits were hunting them, but he heard human voices calling out their names. The voices were coming from the deep forest. There were two Karbi hunters in the group and they appeared extremely terrified. When Samuel asked them about the voices, they said it was just birds. Samuel knew that was not the case. He had a feeling that they were non-human voices and sensed that they were being hunted. When they took out their guns and fired in the air, the voices stopped. The following morning, the Karbi hunters confessed. They said that the voices were spirits of the forest and they had encountered these voices on several occasions in the past.

These forest spirits were mischievous. They would also tease cultivators and foragers, calling them by their names. Sometimes, these voices were accompanied by loud trampling sounds on the ground, as though herds of animals were charging towards them. Sometimes, hunters saw animals and shot them, but they disappeared, and at other times, when they shot animals and went to the spot to collect the body, they did not find anything there: no bullet, no blood, no footprints, no signs of any creature. 'How can that be?' Kikon enquired as she and McDuie-Ra listened to these accounts. Samuel responded, 'We follow trails. Animals leave behind their trails. But spirits disappear without any traces.'

Hunters in Netho are either retired government employees or college students. None of them depend on hunting for sustenance, and almost all of them are fearful of the Assam Police. But there was something about male bonding, masculinity, and hunting that powerfully shaped their identities as urban dwellers in Dimapur. When McDuie-Ra asked a young man, 'How did you decide to become a hunter?', he said:

> I do not have the experiences of the elders, but my body itches. I want to go to the forest and spend time there with friends. I want to eat there. The forest calls me. The elders tell me that I am becoming a hunter. I was interested in birds initially. My desire to go to the forest is that even if you eat 500 grams of rice at home with meat, you eat one kilogram of rice in the forest just licking salt.[6] It is the desire for that experience again and again. Your taste buds change as you enter the forest. That is why you go to the forest.

And then an old hunter added:

> It is all about the game, how to fill the bag, how to carry it back from the forest. There are bad days. And then we tell ourselves, 'Forget it. I am never hunting again.' But once we go to bed, we start dreaming about hunting. The desire to go back is so strong that in the morning we wake up and head back to the forest. Once we are in the forest, we are only half breathing because we fear that the animals will hear us. We have to be still. We have to control our feet and our steps and our breathing. We cannot take full steps; we have to tiptoe. Sometimes for two or three nights we hunt continuously. And the moment we kill, our body feels light. But if we do not kill anything, we are exhausted.

There are concerns about the depletion of animals and birds, but these hunting trips to the Assam Forest are considered as masculine leisure trips and a way to experience nature and wilderness. These experiences draw our attention to new spatial relations and the constitution of the urban city life in Dimapur. Particularly, the different

---

[6] It means that that there is something enchanting about the forest where the body and mind connect to even the basic necessity of life (rice and salt) in a heightened manner.

experiences of the urban space and sensory claims in Dimapur. With the rapid urbanization and absence of any effective urban planning, map, or any vibrant conversations about the experiences of city life, accounts of hunting highlight how tribal groups living in cities define nature and wilderness.

As the tribal population define themselves as urban dwellers in Dimapur, conversations about hunting, the legality of these activities, what kinds of animals should be eaten, and how do we regulate stray animals (like dogs) within the city have come up in recent times. These developments, along with the stories of spirits in the Assam Forest, provide us with new accounts of governance, interventions, and surveillance. As humans and animals cross over to the other side demarcated as 'urban' (Dimapur) or 'wild' (Assam Forest), they allow us to see the routine conflicts and power to claim territories and boundaries.

Huntingscape

Hunting sensibilities and navigation, such as tracing, tracking, footsteps, and walking, offer us the different kinds of scales (neighbourhoods, municipal areas, city limits, and the region) and frameworks (audibility, mobility, and movement) of frontier urbanism. Hunting in the fringes of the city means continuously negotiating the estranged spatial relation established in opposition to animals, so much so that animals from the Assam Forest who cross over to the neighbourhoods along the western fringes of the city are called 'stupid'. Animals who do not escape upon seeing human beings are categorized as 'dumb'. One of the hunters described the nature of wild cats as follows:

> They are not bothered that hunters are around. They are stupid. So, it is easy to hunt them. But the only time you cannot hunt wild cats is during full moon nights because they think it is day light—so they are hiding and do not come out.

These experiences highlight the tensions that emerge from the distinctions about who belongs and does not belong in the city. Hunters and animals are both categorized as trespassers once they cross the spatial and ecological boundaries assigned to them along the fringes of Dimapur city and the Assam Forest. While suburbs like Netho mark the topography and limits of the city and the forest, characteristics of animals (as stupid) and the residents (as adventurers) are also produced in relation to these urban–wilderness boundaries. The physical body and mobility highlight the relations of hope (as successful masculine tribal hunters in an urban space), anxieties (of being caught as tribal trespassers), and citizens (as urban habitants of Dimapur). There are two ways to perceive this process of huntingscape.

First, the concept of 'edge effect' in ecology allows us to understand the ongoing changes as developments when two adjacent ecosystems intersect. Urbanization along the boundary of the Assam Forest is considered as an expansion of frontier infrastructure (in opposition to ruination, dilapidation, and rubbles), and highlights the material developments and urban habitation. Such developments create a 'tension zone' (Barton and Hewitt 1989) where one witnesses changes in the community structure and population of species. Examples of tension zones are common across Northeast India, like the impact due to the urbanization around Deepor Beel (a freshwater body) in Guwahati (Assam). We can also see the conflict around the Ntangki National Park in the outskirts of Dimapur where Naga armed groups and villages from the vicinity have claimed part of the forest (Bera 2015). In both instances, the establishment of residences and human habitation have threatened birds, animals, and aquatic life (see Basistha 2016).

Second, looking at cities as trans-species spaces, Yamini Narayanan's work (2017) challenges us to reverse the conversation about keeping stray/street animals out of cities. She calls for new approaches to urban theory that allow for an inclusive non-violent relation that includes recognizing 'animal citizenship' and anthropocentric framework adopted in urban development and planning. Keeping the animal/human binary, as Narayanan argues, denies animals from all rights-related issues in structures of urban governance. Zones of tension and animal citizenship both invoke different physical spaces that are based on urbanism.

Along the fringes of Dimapur, water bodies and forests are sites of development: new localities, memorial parks, and highways. But the western fringes of the city along the Assam Forest reveal the complex intersection of cultural practice (where hunting is defined as a trait from the past that nonetheless runs in the blood of Naga people) and jurisdictional processes (where urban hunters are arrested as trespassers in the Assam Forest). This is an important characteristic of frontier urbanism.

The concept of huntingscape—a way of navigating and marking out the topography of the city and forest—offers new ways of tracing everyday infrastructure, a physically distinct system of facilitating 'matter that enable the movement of other matter' (Larkin 2013: 329). In this context, the movement and experiences of hunters following the trails of birds and animals within and outside the limits of the city inform us about the urban ecologies and the tenuousness of the urban and wild boundaries.

The comparison of taste and seasons became an important topic during our fieldwork with hunters. When McDuie-Ra enquired (referring to wild cat meat), 'Is it tasty? How do you feel when you eat it?', Mhatung (pseudonym) said:

Strong and light. It is different from other meat. It has fats but unlike pork fat where we get fed up and nauseated, wild cat meat and its fat is smooth and nice. We want to continue eating. It is the best kind of fat. You get addicted to it.... During February and March, the windy season, all the fat will vanish from the cat's body. So, when the cat crosses the jungle it leaves a trail of smell, like the aroma of the rice from the first harvest. Then we know that the wild cat has passed *this place*.[7]

Mhatung went on to describe the mood swings and emotions his friends experienced as the hunting season came to an end. The hunters discovered how living on the edge of the city and the contact with animals from the Assam Forest meant there is no single definition of what constitutes urban 'nature'. The boundaries between the city and the forest dictate their moods, emotions, and senses. Beyond emotions, hunters said that wild animals who cross over to the city taste different. Animals, once they left the Assam Forest, began to transform. Something happened to their corporeal bodies. During

[7] All quotes by Mhatung (pseudonym) in this chapter are from a personal interview held with him in Dimapur on 9 January 2017.

a conversation with a hunter, he explained how he got sick eating animals who lived in the urban fringes of Dimapur. He said:

> So, I ate the porcupine one day. It was fat. After that I got a terrible headache. But in the evening, we went hunting again. We killed a civet cat and I ate that animal too. Then I knew I was going to fall ill. I started throwing up. In the hills, we eat the porcupine, but in Dimapur we fall ill when we eat this animal. We get headache and throw up. There is no forest in the city, so they eat seeds and whatever they find. Thieves [wood cutters/loggers] have stolen the forest. They have chopped it down.

As forests are fast disappearing, so are the seeds and fruits that animals and birds consume. Therefore, accounts of eating animals and falling ill also show the changes in dietary patterns of the creatures. Stories about eating animals and throwing up highlight how rapid urbanization creates a chain reaction. As Dimapur urbanizes rapidly, animals from the Assam Forest also seek out new homes and there is a change in the old ways of hunting and consuming animals. This also means new taboos like refraining from eating porcupines found in the urban neighbourhoods, and also new imaginations.

An old hunter said animals from the Assam Forest have developed a 'map' of Dimapur to avoid the dangerous city (referring to the common practice of hunting small animals like birds). The image of birds using a 'map' of Dimapur, given that there are no city maps for tourists or visitors alike, was poignant. Navigating the meaning of map or mapping one's movement in this case is founded on a relation and understanding of a place or location. The imagination of hunters, in the absence of any existing maps of the city, tells us how residents develop geographical expressions to describe the location of the city. They also draw our attention to the absence of urban governance and conservation guidelines.

Yamini Narayanan (2017) argues that Indian cities lack urban policy to protect animals. Perceived as trespassers, animals (and birds) are constantly evicted and culled from urban spaces. The Dimapur Municipal Corporation (DMC) does not have an integrated scheme for stray/street animals like many Indian cities. As the fastest-growing urban centre and the largest city in Nagaland, the absence of strict urban laws has posed a series of challenges for urban governance. Newspaper headlines such as 'Dimapur: The Garbage

Capital of Nagaland' (*Eastern Mirror* 2013) or 'Dimapur City Grapples with Mounting Garbage Problems' (*Nagaland Post* 2018) routinely made it to the pages of news dailies. In 2018, the Dimapur Municipal Corporation employed 14 trucks and 2 back hoes to collect garbage from 96 colonies within the city (*Nagaland Post* 2018).

The juxtaposition of a dysfunctional yet rapidly expanding city and hyper wealth in the hands of an exclusive tribal elite is a ceasefire development. Just like the growth of neighbourhoods in the fringes of Dimapur, the exceptional growth of the city centre is also unplanned, without attention to zoning and municipal regulations. In the ceasefire period, trading rights and licenses are monopolized by contractors and business families who had close ties with Naga insurgents and key political parties in the state. One of the most visible signs of growth has been the real estate boom in Dimapur. The mutual dependence on the conflict economy—where state and non-state actors enter into trading and political alliances—has led to the rise of new suburbs and townships in the peri-urban areas of Dimapur. Here, the experiences of the hunters highlight what constitutes a tribal culture and a traditional past as they seek to establish their 'city' identities while sustaining connections with their roots in the villages.

Urban Cultures and Rural Taboos

An old hunter named John invited us to his home. We sat on teak couches in a living room with lace curtains in a suburb along the fringes of Dimapur. The teak cabinet showcased a line of souvenirs and stacks of magazines. He offered us tea and showed us a fishing equipment he invented a few years ago. It was an electric box that could be strapped on to his back like a backpack. The box was connected to a metal rod (Image 4.1). In order to demonstrate the electric fishing equipment, he said, 'Imagine we are on the banks of a river.' He strapped the equipment to his body and began to tap the marble floor with his metal rod. We imagined the marble floor as water, our chairs as rocks beside a river, and the aquatic life in the river being electrocuted. Sitting in John's living room with a cabinet filled with souvenirs from his travels, we were transfixed by the fishing demonstration unfolding in front of our eyes. After the demonstration, he told us stories of hunting in his hilltop village in Wokha district.

Image 4.1   Ad hoc hunting and fishing innovations
Source: Duncan McDuie-Ra

According to John, hunting was carried out in accordance with strict rules of taboos and transgressions in his village (up in the hills). When he was growing up, hunting was not done for commercial purposes. Instead, social relations, taboos, and an equitable distribution system were strictly followed in hunting activities. This meant keeping the complex social relations in the village and the ecology of the place as well. Unlike the absence of taboos while hunting in the Assam Forest, there were taboos when hunting on the community land in the village. For instance, young hunters were prohibited to hunt slow-moving animals like anteaters. Slow-moving animals were left for old people in the village who were slow and unable to hunt in deep forest.

Game meat was distributed, and portions of the meat were given to the aged and households who were unable to hunt. In addition, firewood and old fences of the *jhum* (slash and burn cultivation) fields near the villages were left for the aged. The young and the able-bodied from the village were required to collect wood and other resources from forest areas that were further away from the village. A curse came upon a person who took away resources like wood and slow-moving animals meant for the aged, such as trembling knees while crossing bridges and streams in the mountains, and losing their balance.

These hunting practices and taboos no longer applied in urban spaces like Dimapur. Among other things, the rapid urbanization of the city transformed the relationship between humans and animals. Here, the connection of the hunters and their relationship with the animals/the game developed in an urban setting. These conversations opened new insights.

First, they allowed us to trace a Naga tribal past in the villages where hunting was carried out while keeping in mind a larger socio-ecology. However, there was a disconnect between these stories and the everyday lives of Nagas living in the urban areas. In inheriting these stories, what was absent was the complex world of reciprocity, labour, communal spirit, and the season. Now, hunting was generally perceived as a combination of a masculine leisure activity and an inherent part of Naga culture in an urban setting. As larger numbers of Naga families migrated to urban areas like Kohima, Dimapur, and Mokokchung, access to forest and the dependency on hunting to sustain a community way of living declined.

Second, John's account sheds light on the lives and memories of hunters themselves and how an account of hunting represents what is eaten and protected. Yet, the values that were inherently built in hunting activities were missing among urban hunters. In this aspect, the expansion of urbanization in Dimapur seemed like a zone without any taboos or regulations. By reiterating a dominant wilderness/urban settlement binary, hunters in Dimapur operated on a normative logic where animal and human habitats were demarcated and territorialized by urban authorities and state actors. Animals, by this logic, belonged to Assam while the hunters lived in Nagaland.

Finally, accounts of a hunting past highlighted mobility and migration from the rural to urban places, and encounters with state agencies in the Assam Forest. Stories of the aged in the fringes of the city are unlike their counterparts in the village who were dependent on hunting.

In recent years, Naga communities have started local initiatives to restrict hunting and call it a practice that is unsustainable and ecologically damaging (Image 4.2). What used to be considered 'a tradition and way of life' (*BBC* 2018) is no longer perceived that way. Yet, the propagation of a Naga past and glory founded on hunting continues to hold sway. In this narrative, Naga identity is predominantly constructed through eating meat and indiscriminate hunting. This meat-hunting tradition is increasingly tied to a modern narrative of a Naga culture that propagates Naga masculinity and Naga cuisine. Dominant imagination portrays Naga people as a proud carnivore community, as if Naga food and, by that account, Naga

Image 4.2   'Stop Wildlife Crime', near North Angami Colony Gate

Source: Duncan McDuie-Ra

culture, is centrally about eating meat. This logic is linked, among other things, to a masculine account of eating meat and retaining strength and stamina. The notion of eating meat and masculine personhood is deeply conditioned. Thus, when male members in a household demand meat on days when there is no meat, female members tell them off by saying, 'Even tigers eat grass sometimes! Just deal with it.' This show how tribalness and social practices continue to thrive in Dimapur.

The hunting accounts highlight the ramifications of adopting a romantic tribal imagination about the past. Tales of hunters and the absence of urban planning in Dimapur show that tribal people can also destroy, construct, and actively produce an urban environment that is irreverent to any frameworks of sustainability. In Dimapur, authority and power networks are driven by the conflict economy that includes rich tribal landlords, migrant traders, and insurgents. Each party violates the urban regulations of the city, creating tensions and conflicts.

Huntingscape, in this context, forces us to shift our focus away from dominant imageries of urban activities such as clubbing, shopping, or dining, and recognize how cultural practices (from the past) are performed and re-enacted in Dimapur. Performances of harvest songs and hunting rituals in tribal festivals across the city reveal how tribal cultural performances are out of place and in place simultaneously. It is such edgy moments that allow us to see tribal communities claim the spatial environment as a tribal space while embracing the urban experiences as an integral part of their lives.

When our informant, Achini Lotha, invited us for a community feast on 31 December 2016, we arrived at a large compound in Walford Colony towards the southern part of Dimapur. We found ourselves in a schoolyard with a festive atmosphere. After we were introduced to the community elders, we witnessed the celebration. It was an advance Christmas celebration by a tribal community. The celebration depicted a community who were confident and modern citizens of a city, and were perfectly at ease connecting with their cultural past. Young people and elders dressed in their traditional outfits walked around to a Bon Jovi song coming from a boom box. Red balloons tied to the bamboo poles, a colourful tent covering the school ground, and an elevated stage with a carpet for the chief guest were all set for the celebration. The anticipation for such cultural events and the hunters, who were volunteering as chefs for the event, showcased the importance of belonging and community (see Image 4.3). This kind of urbanism was visible across Dimapur. However, this kind of

Image 4.3   Community feast as an urban experience

Source: Duncan McDuie-Ra

sensorial and spatial experience, among the hunters, went beyond these community gatherings. The Assam Forest played an important role in shaping what constituted an urban experience.

Inside the Forest

Stretching from Golaghat district all the way to the Karbi Anglong Autonomous areas, Assam police and the forest guards patrol the Assam Forest. These security guards arrest Naga hunters and seize hunted animals and birds at regular intervals. When McDuie-Ra asked, 'Why do you hunt if it is unsafe?', a hunter said, 'It is always about the anticipation of what will happen next.' In Dimapur, hunting in the Assam Forest is a way to escape the vacuum caused by urban life, and experience a wilderness that is different from the city life. Here, emphasis on urbanity, hunting, and the sensorial allows us to appreciate what Low (2013: 226) refers to as 'sensescapes', amongst which 'everyday experiences of the senses take on an emotional character, where heightened feelings become apparent in the encounter between sensory selves and sensory others'.

Whether it is about relations or hunting for animals and birds, the desire for a sensorial experience is there. John, the hunter, said:

One day we went hunting. This was in the early days. My friend and I climbed a tree; he was on a lower branch and I climbed up higher and found a strong branch to sit on. Then I saw a deer; my first deer sighting in the Assam Forest. I was excited and very restless. My friend shot the deer and made me carry it on my head. It was very heavy, and at times I felt my skull was going to crack. But I had to navigate the forest. I kept falling and stumbling. I was very tired. How I struggled. I learnt that hunters do not care about their friends. They just walk ahead searching for the next game. We are good friends in Dimapur but when we are in the Assam Forest, he becomes the hunter and I become his helper.

But we learn to share inside the forest. When we meet Karbi hunters, we share our food and the game meat. We believe that the forest game meats do not belong to us. So, from our forefathers' time, when we meet people—even strangers—while returning home after hunting, our grandparents would cut off a piece of meat and share it with them. In the same way, in the Assam Forest too, when we meet the Karbi people, we also do the same. This is about sharing. No one carries utensils, so the Karbi hunters we meet inside the forest also share their food with us. That is the way in the forest.

And then we learnt that sharing went beyond game meat. John continued:

> One day, we met a Karbi man sitting in the forest with a bottle of rum. He had entered the forest searching for firewood with a bottle of rum. He was a stranger, but we took out the intestines of the deer we had just killed and cooked a meal together. We were carrying a bottle of rum too. After we ate and drank together, the hunter from my village and the Karbi man started talking in English. I was so tired and went off to sleep. But the Karbi man and the hunter did not let me sleep. Both never attended school, but they pretended to talk in English. They had no idea what the other person was saying. Forget about going to school, they had never even heard the sound of a school bell. They were that illiterate! The Naga hunter said, 'I am a master,' and the Karbi man nodded his head and said, 'Yes, yes, school master.' And the hunter replied, 'No, I am a karate master.' The Karbi man was drunk but ran away to the village when he heard that. Maybe he understood it. Who knows?

Other ethnic communities like the Dimasas, Karbis, Adivasis, and Nepalis also enter the Assam Forest adjoining Dimapur. But the most feared group are the Assam police and members of the ethnic armed groups. These groups carry their weapons openly and roam around in the forest. The images of people inside the forest with guns, axes, baskets, and food add to the story of spatializing authority and power beyond the ethnic village or the urban city. Here, the Assam Forest is a place where residents from Dimapur enter to experience adventure, nature, and wilderness, and to fulfil their masculine desires. Of all the stories we heard about hunting inside the Assam Forest, a story about meeting armed groups inside the forest highlights hunters' encounters with power and authority. Vandan, a hunter from Dimapur, said:

> One day I met an underground person [soldier from an ethnic armed group] in the forest.[8] He took away my gun. I went hunting again with my

---

[8] They are called 'underground people' because they go into hiding, and work in secret for a set political agenda that the state authorities consider as subversive and anti-state activities.

friends a few weeks later. We did not find anything that day. We returned to
the camp and cooked rice and made some chutney. But it was impossible
to eat the dry rice. We wanted some vegetables, so we went foraging. Then
we saw five underground soldiers. They were Dimasa armed soldiers.
They were carrying guns and ammunition. Some of my friends escaped
but two of us were caught. The Dimasa armed soldiers tied us up and
blindfolded us. Then they whipped us and asked us what we were doing
in the forest. We said we came for a stroll from Dimapur. I had hidden my
gun inside a bamboo groove, but they found it and took it away.[9]

The experiences of the hunter with the armed Dimasa insurgents
are illustrative of the ethnic tensions and suspicion. Hunting and
adventure in the Assam Forest can turn into unpleasant encounters.
This story shows us how the city and the forest are produced as ethnic
spaces, where human activities and movement are spatialized along
ethnic lines. This reality connects the lives in Dimapur to the new
conditions of illegality, danger, and encounters in the fringes of urban
spaces. A conversation between McDuie-Ra and Vandan (the hunter)
lingered on the topic of danger:

Vandan: The forest is a dangerous place. There are Assam police and
underground [people].

McDuie-Ra: Nowadays, where do people go for hunting?

Vandan: In Assam. But these days, there is nothing in the forest. Only
underground [people] and police.

McDuie-Ra: Do younger men go hunting?

Vandan: They are also going. To the Assam side.

McDuie-Ra: If you kill an animal in the Assam side, do you bring it back?

Vandan: Yes, yes. To Dimapur.

During the conversation, the hunter also narrated stories about thieves
in the Assam Forest who chopped down the trees. Different kinds of
activities took place in the Assam Forest, from hunting to logging—
all illegal operations. Talking about danger, hunters in Netho said
that elephants from the Assam Forest came to the neighbourhood
in Dimapur and ate fruits and whatever they could find. But this

[9] All the quotes by Vandan in this chapter are from a personal interview
held in Dimapur on 9 January 2017.

same story also applied to the hunters who entered the forest. They also ate *anything* they could find. Once a group of hunters went to the Assam Forest for a picnic. There they came upon a large log and found seven large pythons. 'We killed all of them and carried them back to Dimapur in a jeep,' the hunter said. When McDuie-Ra asked him, 'Why? To eat?', he replied, 'We went to the local wine joints in Eros Line and sold them. We also cooked some of the meat. We also eat the [snake] skin, so we sold it separately. We burn the skins and eat it; it is a medicine, a cure for all ailments.'

The conversation that transpired from the python story involved eating different body parts of animals. The hunter continued:

> The gall bladder of a dog is medicinal, an antidote to malaria. We swallow it. A porcupine's stomach is also medicinal because they eat only a particular kind of mud. We dry its stomach and store it. When we have tummy ache, we soak a piece of the dried porcupine stomach and drink that water. If you eat otters, you receive a gift of helping people. My wife ate an otter that I killed outside our house. From that day onwards, whenever people have bones stuck in their throat, she gently massages and scratches the neck area, and people feel better.

The list of organs points to accounts of consumption and personhood in urban spaces. Indian cities lack policy frameworks that recognize urban spaces as 'biodiverse spaces' that humans and animals inhabit simultaneously (Narayanan 2017: 477). In Dimapur, tribal communities living in the city construct meanings, symbols, and practices that enable them to oscillate their identities between the village and the city. For instance, names of localities and suburbs in Dimapur often end with the word *bosti* or village. These localities are also adorned with gates with intricate tribal motifs such as spears, totemic animals, and warriors. Usually erected in villages, these traditional gates across the city show how a sense of tribal identity or tribalness is visible in Dimapur. While animals hunted on the fringes of the city mark the boundary between the city (in Nagaland) and the forest (in Assam), these spatial and cultural forms, when linked with stories of hunting in the fringes of the city, reflect how identities (Naga-ness), spaces (forest), and practices (tradition) become boundaries of the rural/urban/wilderness.

Today, many traditional councils impose a seasonal hunting ban between March and October across many villages in Nagaland. Villagers who breach the law have to pay a fine to the village councils. According to Lansothung Shitiri, an officer with the Nagaland Forest Department, the seasonal ban is unhelpful because the rates of hunting during the winter months are high and, hence, they are unable to protect the species that are disappearing. Only a few villages have policies that completely ban hunting.[10] During his tenure as a range officer in Fakim, a Naga village along the Indo-Burma border of Nagaland, Lansothung played an important role in encouraging villagers to give up hunting and turn the community land into a conservation zone. Known as the Fakim Village Tragopan Reserve, the village council prohibits hunting in the community land that has become a wildlife sanctuary (Capila 2018).

In a state where 88 per cent of the land is categorized as community land, there is a dominant perception, according to Lansothung, that 'everything belongs to us'. This logic also follows when hunting on community lands in Nagaland. It is assumed that everything is fair game for everyone (see *Indian Express* 2018a). In this context, state laws such as the Wildlife (Protection) Act 1972 are applicable only to the 12 per cent of land that belongs to the Nagaland Forest Department. Therefore, the state continues to appeal to the traditional bodies and councils to cooperate with the state departments (*Morung Express* 2017c). According to Lansothung, the areas between the villages (which allow hunting) and the Forest Department in Nagaland are considered as the fringe zones. These sites are extremely contentious. For the Forest Department of Nagaland, animals on the fringes come from the forest and not from the village or urban spaces. For this reason, forest officials monitoring game meat at the Assam–Nagaland areas consider the fringes of the city and the Assam Forest as sensitive and high priority zones.

It is true that not everyone in Dimapur hunts in the Assam Forest or visits the fringes of the city. For hunters living along the fringes of the city, the notion of community land as in the rural areas of Nagaland does not apply since it is an urban zone under the municipal council governing the city. Yet the geographical boundary between

---

[10] Telephonic interview with Lansothung on 16 January 2019.

the city and the forest becomes most visible when Naga hunters are arrested with animals and birds inside the Assam Forest. Such stories involve experiences of spending time in prison or in police custody in Assam. These accounts also contain intimate details about arrest and punishment. During a conversation, Peter described his experiences of being apprehended by security forces inside the Assam Forest:

One day, three of us were caught. The Assam police tied us up with ropes and loaded us in a truck. We were taken to the Bokajan police station. When we arrived, I thought they will give us food. We were waiting for food. An Assamese police officer said, 'What were you guys doing in the forest? You will go to prison for that.' Then he left the room. But I thought they will have compassion and give us some food. I was hungry. But they sent us to the Manja police station. By now it was getting dark. The sub-inspector came to the station and told us to come out of the lock up. We thought we were going to be released. I was hungry. But we were loaded in a truck. It was night by now and we had no idea where we were going.

We were in Diphu the next morning. We had neither eaten nor slept for two days. When we saw the sunlight and the restaurants, our stomach starting churning. We were very hungry. But we were taken to the Diphu police station. The sub-inspector said that there was no place for us. So, we were taken to the Diphu Sub-Jail in the outskirts of the town. On the way, we met with an accident and the truck overturned. But we did not think about escaping because we were starving. Eventually, a police van came and took us to the jail. We were falling asleep.

When we got off from the truck, we saw a signboard: 'District Jail Diphu'. We realized we were inside a prison, and sleep left us immediately. We were given a blanket, one plate, and one cup. The warden told us if we lost the items, we would pay with our life. One of the hunters, still unaware they were being sent to prison, asked, 'But why are they not feeding us?' The other hunter responded, 'Maybe we are a big number, so they are still cooking the food.'

We waited for dinner but went to bed without food. In the morning, at around 9:30 a.m., the prisoners were asked to make a line. We got breakfast; one roti and one cup of red tea. The officers called out, 'Where are the Naga prisoners?' Then he informed us that there was no food for us. It seems the authority has not sanctioned food for us. It was the fourth day, we could not talk anymore. Around 11:30 a.m., it was lunch time and we were given half a cup of rice. We had suffered injuries and were very tired by now. We were kept in the Diphu jail for 28 days. This incident took place in 1992.[11]

The hunter's memories about prison capture the punishment and violence attached to hunting in the Assam Forest. Once arrested, the visibility of law and order including the punishment takes place outside the Assam Forest. The punishment meted out to the hunters and the places they are transported to—the Assam Police Station, the vehicles carrying the prisoners, and the hunters as urban inhabitants of Dimapur—demonstrate how the boundaries (of the forest, animals, humans, and the city) are produced and interpreted by state authorities and law-enforcing agencies. With the rapid urbanization, municipal bodies in Dimapur are unable to regulate legislation around hunting or killing animals, or wild animals entering the city's jurisdiction from the Assam Forest. There is a general perception among hunters in the fringes of Dimapur that hunting is part of Naga culture. John, a hunter living in the fringes of the city, said, 'Hunting is in our blood.' We wondered: 'How about eating? Eating contentious animals like dogs?'

The Dog Meat Debate

In 2016, a petition about the welfare of animals in the city, particularly the selling of dog meat, set in motion a series of events, declarations, and actions that laid bare the structure of municipal governance and the construction of the city in Naga identity politics. Once cultural practices were in question, the city began to disappear and Naga concepts of space as boundless and timeless became apparent.

Unlike hunting, which engages humans and animals on the fringes of the city, the dog meat debate was about what constitutes urban space and respectable urban behaviour in Dimapur and beyond. The Humane Society International (HSI) in India released a report, images, and video of the dog meat trade and sale in Kohima and Dimapur, dubbing the phenomenon as 'Nagaland Nightmare' (HSI 2016) (Image 4.4).

[11] Personal interview with Peter (pseudonym) in Dimapur on 9 January 2017.

Image 4.4   Local meat for sale in the open air in Duncan Bosti

Source: Duncan McDuie-Ra

The HSI (2016) wrote to the then-chief minister of Nagaland, T.R. Zeliang, requesting authorities to 'implement the existing [national] ban on dog meat consumption, patrol trade routes and shut down markets'. Despite agreement among government officials that Article 371A, the Constitutional provision protecting customary practices from interference by Indian parliamentary laws, holds in this case, responsibility for curbing the trade was passed from the Government of Nagaland to the Directorate of Municipal Affairs in May (*Indian Express* 2016). The directive included the phrase: 'to give wide publicity and issue an order to stop capture of dogs for the purpose of slaughter and meat, to stop the bazaars meant for selling dogs or dog meat and to treat animals with care and love' (see Pisharoty 2016).

Immediately, the Municipal Affairs Department of Nagaland sent official notices to all the urban local bodies (ULBs) in Dimapur to investigate the matter. Soon, the debate about eating dog meat and the dog meat trade appeared in newspapers and social media across India and beyond. Kikon (2017a) shows how the reports were centred on eating dog meat and condemned it as an inhumane practice. Highlighting the categorization of dogs as pets and a danger to human society as grounded in a larger story of urban development and governance in India, Kikon illustrates the role of municipal bodies across cities in India to cull dogs. Yet, unlike the national debates about dog meat one witnessed in 2016, the matter highlighted the anxieties of urban governance in a ceasefire city. Once the state government requested the urban bodies in Dimapur to oversee matters about the dog meat trade, the municipal body emerged as a dysfunctional structure struggling to govern a city.

The issue of governing a tribal space versus an urban space was at the heart of the dog meat debate. The dog meat blurred culinary, citizenship, and geographical lines. When politicians from Punjab expressed that stray dogs from the state should be sent to Nagaland, Mizoram, and China for 'whatever they do with them' (*Outlook India* 2012), a caste and moral framework became clear. Yet, the dog meat debate extends our point that the fringes (where hunters live) and the centre (of trade and market) are both founded on tribal authority and identity.

Connecting the prevailing condition of the urban administration during the 2016 dog meat debate, Kikon (2017a) writes:

> There has been no municipal election in the state of Nagaland since 2006. Therefore, officials overseeing the municipal functions in Dimapur with a population of 400,000 people are ad-hoc political appointees. They struggle to keep up with basic functions like garbage collection and maintenance of the sewage system and are barely able to manage the crumbling infrastructure such as water supply, drainage, and the increasing cases of land encroachments by land mafia, the municipality had little time and few resources to spend on animal welfare.

What were the reasons for postponing the municipal elections in Dimapur since 2006? As discussed in Chapter 2, unlike other states in India, the traditional bodies headed by males opposed a constitutional provision that provides 33 per cent reservation for women candidates in municipal and local body elections across India. Invoking that Naga people are bound by their own customary laws and regulations as per Article 371A of the Indian Constitution, a provision that recognizes the rights of the Naga people over land and natural resources including the right to practice their own customs, the 33 per cent reservation for women in municipal elections was suspended in Nagaland. In Nagaland, the groups opposing the 33 per cent reservation called for the recognition of Naga culture. By this patriarchal logic, urban governance to look at management of sewage and garbage would be considered as compromising on Naga values and identity unless they followed tribal customs (Kikon 2017b). These constructions of identity and space as boundless and at the same time continuously being governed according to patriarchal traditional practices played out on the city streets and centres (*The Hindu* 2017).

The dog meat debate highlighted how the tribal claims over urban spaces in Dimapur created a seamless connection between the rural and the urban. Even though Dimapur is a migrant city—a place that has witnessed waves of tribal groups across Nagaland settling down and reproducing a nostalgic past—its accounts, unlike those of Guwahati or even Shillong, do not include an urban narrative. The City Tower, an imitation of the Eiffel Tower in Paris, adds to the architectural imagination of the city. A city with traditional Naga gates alongside a copy of the Eiffel Tower speaks of its attempt to present itself as a place with global imaginations. Yet, these monuments are routinely covered with nationalist messages from Naga armed groups like the NSCN, billboards advising people to keep the city clean, or Christian revival meetings.

On 14 July 2016, Kikon arrived at the Dimapur Municipal Council office to enquire about the dog meat debate and the role of municipal bodies. She met a member of the Society for the Prevention of Cruelty against Animals (SPCA) (Nagaland Unit) and an administrator from the Dimapur Municipal Council (DMC). A conversation about the dog meat debate and Naga culture unfolded. According to the member of the SPCA (Nagaland Unit), Naga people ate dog meat for the following reasons:

> Medicinal purpose. It [eating dog meat] is not taught at the school or church, but it is [a] cultural [practice]. We have become habituated to eating dogs. This is very unlucky. So, at this juncture, animal activists at SPCA are campaigning against it.

Since the ULBs focused on the dog meat trade in Dimapur, the conversation was predominantly about managing dog slaughter. However, dog meat is sold in the open—in shacks beside the streets or on the ground in pen markets. Therefore, the 2016 dog meat debate in Dimapur generated multiple conversations about the source of these consumer spaces within the city. From issues about taxation and regulation imposed by state bodies and non-state actors to the experiences of tribal traders selling dog meat, the complexity of the city as a tribal space inscribed with histories of violence and militarization became apparent.

Unlike the story of the pythons from the Assam Forest sold in Dimapur that we discussed earlier, dogs are urban animals and belong to the city. They are killed and sold inside the city spaces and for that reason offend notions of what constitutes the urban. In Dimapur, there are no dog farms where animals are raised for food, but there are reports about dogs from Assam making their way as food into the local markets of Dimapur. Although there are no police reports, we came across stories of missing dogs from distraught owners in the city. Unlike Assam where it was common to spot stray dogs, it is rare to come across street dogs in Dimapur. Eager to capture images during our fieldwork, we requested a local researcher to help us with some pictures of street dogs. 'Every morning I sat beside a meat shop for several days, but I did not come across any street dogs', he told us. A few months later, he lost his pet dog.

The issue of legality concerning hunting for dogs in the city emerged. Unlike the community land (which generally allows hunting) and the protected areas that are under the state government such as forests (which prohibit hunting), the issue of regulating urban hunting is connected to the larger issues of governing urban spaces. The dominant perception that Dimapur is a tribal space where Naga customs and culture will prevail (at the cost of opposing affirmative policies for women in municipal body elections) shows new ways of redrawing spatial tribal power.

The 2016 dog meat debate and the measures taken thereafter to address the dog meat trade highlight how tribal spaces are deeply masculine, territorial, and boundless simultaneously. For instance, the dog meat debate became about cultural practices of consumption and fighting disease, and not about the environment (slaughterhouses and hygiene) and the regulations (laws) and policies (urban body acts) for hunting street dogs or stealing pets for consumption (Caisii 2012). 'Once ban on dog slaughter is imposed, then automatically there will be no meat there to eat', the SPCA member told Kikon at the municipal office in Dimapur. His argument that the ban on slaughter of dogs for meat will 'automatically' stop the consumption of dog meat ignored the cultural position. No rules and regulations will be applicable in the city if it prohibits people from carrying out or doing a 'Naga thing' on their own land. This tension between the fringes of the city and the urban centre unravelled the thin veneer of Dimapur's urban governance.

The topic of dog meat also opened a space to reflect about animals, cruelty, and interpreting culture in urban spaces (*Telegraph* 2016). The engagement departed from issues of governance, dog meat, or for that matter, hunting street dogs, and dwelt on 'controlling' and 'consuming' dogs. During a meeting with Kikon, an official of the DMC addressed the matter as a 'current crisis'. A conversation with local journalist Aheli Moitra, from *The Morung Express*, who was also present with the DMC officer and the SPCA (Nagaland Unit) unfolded as follows:

Moitra: What is being done now?

SPCA member: We are also trying our best to stop the cruelty towards animals. We are at the initial stage. We will find ways to look after the stray and injured dogs.

Moitra: So, stopping cruelty towards animals would be for animals and not only for dogs, right?

DMC officer (quickly interrupting): That depends on your interpretation.

SPCA member: For now, let us assume that it is only for dogs and not blow the matter out of proportion. Right now, we only have problems in controlling the issue of dogs, so why take the trouble to include all the animals? With the issue of cruelty, it is about the method of killing. It should be scientific. The animals should not be subjected to cruelty and pain.

Moitra: So, is there a way to kill dogs? Are there SPCA recommendations?

SPCA member: No, no. Who will recommend it?

Moitra: So how are the dogs being killed?

SPCA member: We will have to ask those who are killing it. It does not mean that we have to stop killing animals. But we have to stop the cruelty. Once people understand this, it is up to them to decide. Our duty is to prevent the cruelty.

Kikon: What is the connection between consuming dogs as food and for medicinal purposes?

SPCA member: When someone has malaria, they go for a black dog. They make soup [using dog meat] and drink it. For the detailed stories, we have to go to the interior areas and ask the elders. Dogs have high protein value.

Moitra: Do poor people eat dog meat more than the rich?

SPCA member: No, all Nagas eat dog meat. Those who see it as a delicacy eat it. Rich people and poor people both eat dog meat. It is not about rich or poor. Anyone can fall sick [and eat dog meat as a cure].

Moitra: No, I am asking this because I was told that in the interior areas where people cannot rear cattle like pigs and cows, but need protein to keep working, [they] consume dogs to get nourishment. So, I am just wondering.

SPCA member: I have not heard about rearing dogs for the sole purpose of consumption. So there is no case of farming dogs for consumption.

Moitra: Many people breed dogs to eat [them].

DMC officer: See, you came at the wrong time. I am quite busy. But government is directing us to institute a local committee to look into these issues. We are yet to do that. We do not know how this will shape up, but we will have a round of meetings with the government and the NGOs. Right now, I cannot give you a clear picture.

Kikon: And your designation?

DMC officer: Administrator, executive officer, or chief executive officer of the Dimapur Municipal Committee. [Laughs] I am all of these.[12]

The DMC officer abruptly ended the meeting. Although he looked officious and was escorted out of the DMC office by security guards, his peculiar response about his designation highlighted the status of urban governance in the city. What stood out in the conversation, among other things, was the reference to 'NGOs' and 'roundtable meetings'. These terms often came up during political meetings on the ceasefire between Naga armed groups and the Indian government, including dialogues between political interlocuters. They were used

[12] Personal interview with DMC officer in Dimapur on 14 July 2016. All quotes by the DMC officer in this chapter are from this meeting.

in the context of including NGOs for a roundtable meeting to find a long-lasting solution to the Indo-Naga conflict.

And for that reason, we wondered why the DMC official wanted to constitute a 'roundtable' consultation that included local NGOs to discuss the dog meat issue. These were matters for the urban bodies in the city to take up. But waste collection, sewage, or regulating constructions, given the inability of the DMC to manage urban issues, were often being taken up by neighbourhood committees or local NGOs in the city. For the DMC, the dog meat issue was centred on animal cruelty and the dietary habit of consuming dog meat. But as we went around the city and spoke to traders selling dog meat in Super Market and officers from the municipal corporation, the burden of urban governance, fragile networks (of state and non-state actors), and simmering tensions of governing a conflict city surfaced.

Life in a ceasefire city like Dimapur is associated with finding ways to survive and navigate the various power networks. What is significant from the conversation at the DMC office is the invocation of a 'wrong time', remoteness or the reference to 'interior', and the absence of clarity as the interviewees said, 'We don't know'. This, in part, is the reason why we found the dog meat debate an important lens to highlight urban life in Dimapur as a limitless and timeless space that fits into a Naga tribal culture and ways of life narrative. It spatializes knowledge and practice simultaneously. Even though urban Naga residents in Dimapur are unable to possess any knowledge about dogs (as food), it locates *real* Naga accounts in the remote and interior villages. Imposing such a worldview seemed to contradict accounts of the hunters living in Dimapur who possessed the skills to identify the smell of the forest and the animals, including the knowledge of sensing spirits.

The DMC office conversation seemed to suggest that any accountability to urban governance and life in the city is suddenly abandoned. Instead, the solution for dog meat stories involves 'going to the interiors' (referring to the villages) and asking elders for authentic accounts. Andrew Kipnis (2016: 15) notes how urban transformation and dynamics require 'close attention to the multiple, crisscrossing paths of various forms'. Kipnis refers to the memory of the residents and ideas of utopia, fantasies, and dreams. His ethnographic work about urbanization in Zouping, China, is closely associated with industrialization. For example, the establishment of the Development Zone, public plazas, and parks, including free heating and gas pipes transformed the lives of residents. Unlike Zouping, Dimapur transformed from a small town into one of the fastest-growing urban hubs in Northeast India as a consequence of the Indo-Naga ceasefire in 1997. Residents in Dimapur experience long hours of power cuts (as we noted in Chapter 3) and take up initiatives (which we refer to as community infrastructure in Chapter 1) to clean up the streets to save the neighbourhood from water logging and rotting garbage. The dog meat debate is important for understanding how discussion about city space and urban matters is relegated as issues raised at a 'wrong time' and replaced with insights about Naga culture. In this regard, the challenges of governing a conflict city and the struggles of its residents are obvious. But the most important point is the establishment of Dimapur as a Naga ceasefire territory. Dimapur, in this context, continues to be part of a contested territory among competing authorities—armed groups, business bodies, cultural associations, law and order agencies—where the ceasefire negotiation can break down any moment. In this urban landscape, there is constant anxiety as governing is contingent on the stability of the ceasefire itself and the durability of community infrastructure.

5

Dying in Dimapur

In this chapter, we dwell upon the topic of death and dying. By highlighting corporeal elements (dead bodies) and material artefacts (coffins), we examine living and dying in Dimapur as a process of place-making. Processes of place-making are social and are often characterized by contestations of belonging (Friedmann 2007). In Dimapur, this contestation is a deeply moral one because the concept of home is somewhere else and not located within the city. In this sense, it remains a migrant city where a sense of impermanence always dwells among the numerous tribal residents settled here. The final home, according to many residents, is never Dimapur. This thought is most obvious during conversations about dying and burials. The desire to be buried in one's village—perceived as a final resting place for the corporeal body—usually means returning to one's ancestral village. Dimapur becomes immensely attractive as a city that offers the stability and cosmopolitan life one desires, but the rituals of burials and the dead in Dimapur capture anxieties of the tribal modernity.

An increasing number of Nagas living in Dimapur are not associated with their rural villages in their everyday lives. They enjoy the benefits of modernization and consider their lives in Dimapur as an improved way of living, given the easy accessibility of the market, communication, and mobility. Yet, conversations about dying in the city present a compelling portrait of tribal alienation, exclusion, and the disenchantments of modern living. The anxieties and struggles to connect the city and the village are carried to the grave. Where do these conversations take place? In what kinds of gatherings can we identify these emotions about living and dying in Dimapur?

These questions led us to different locations and sites within the city, from a meeting of a tribal women's association and reflections on an NSCN-IM leader's funeral, to the memorial schools and parks dedicated to the deceased that have come up across the city. The cultural and social aspect of living and dying, as we will elaborate in the following sections, emerges from everyday lives, imaginations, objects, and sights.

Gathering

On a December morning in 2017, Kikon attended the Lotha Eloe Ekhung (Lotha Women's Association) meeting in Purana Bazar. As women gathered in twos and threes at the community centre, the volunteers arranged the tea and biscuits on a wooden table. The programme coordinator took to the podium and announced the schedule of the meeting, and an officious air dawned upon the hall. Gradually, participants settled down on the plastic chairs. Women from different tribal communities across Dimapur are part of various cultural associations. They share information about current happenings within the community and plan out social activities and cultural events.

There are many tribal associations in Dimapur and all of them have official designations such as presidents, secretaries, and treasurers. All the apex traditional councils are predominantly headed by male members, and youth groups and women's associations are regarded as extended units of these tribal councils. The youth groups and women's associations operate as networks to coordinate meetings and make connections with kin groups and also to create inter-tribal relations. For example, members from any tribal group—Angami, Sümi, Ao, Lotha, Rengma, Chakhesang, and so on—living in Dimapur seek to recreate a homogenous and unified sense of tribal structure. Women's association meetings, such as the one Kikon attended, seek to maintain a sense of social order in the community. Given the rapid urbanization and the increasing settlements of tribal communities, cultural associations like the women's group seek to create a community with a sense of value and meaning. For instance, members of the women's association carry out social services such as visiting one another's homes during times of illness, festivity, or grief.

That particular morning, the women's association meeting at Purana Bazar began with a mass prayer. Wearing a traditional stole and sarong, the secretary thanked the participants and read out a list of names: members who were unwell and admitted to hospitals, families who had experienced death in recent times, and so on. When Kikon enquired about the relevance of such associations in Dimapur, a member replied, 'To make sure we have not forgotten one another. So that our presence can bring beauty to [the] community and enhance our spirit, but more importantly [to ensure that] we are connected to one another.'[1]

The social order and the spatial history of Dimapur as a ceasefire city call for a deeper understanding of engaging with emerging forms of frontier urbanism in Northeast India. Herscher and Siddiqi (2014) underline the importance of recognizing the histories of spatial violence and how categories of peace or progress are propagated. As such, we extend this conversation and present stories and experiences of dying and memorials and rituals around death to illustrate the relationship between the living and the dead in the city. Engaging with themes of living and dying is crucial to illustrate the significant experiences of militarized urbanism. Accounts of living and dying are deeply associated with tribal community life in Dimapur, and as a result they influence the meanings of politics, kinship, and belonging.

The women's association meetings, as an informant shared with Kikon, keep the community spirit alive in the city. Through these activities, tribal values about service and obligations are propagated. These associations stress that attending funerals, visiting the sick, or arranging food and clothing for the aged are important missions. In many ways, these activities are perceived as exemplary tribal practices in Dimapur. However, such values and practices defined as 'tribal' in nature have come up with the expansion of urbanization. As social relationships among tribal groups have undergone a transformation due to the market, conflict, and militarization, new understandings about tribal culture, kinship ties, and values have also emerged. By

---

[1] All quotes from the members of the Lotha Eloe Ekhung (Lotha Women's Association) were taken during their meeting held at Purana Bazar in Dimapur on 1 July 2017.

focusing on the theme of living and dying in Dimapur, we go beyond the understanding of the city as a spatial geography, to one that is 'embedded in and constituted by a broader set of processes and social relations' (Brash 2006: 343).

None of the stories we heard during our fieldwork in Dimapur were simple accounts. They intersected with experiences of migration, unemployment, addiction, poverty, debt, or suffering. In this sense, conceptualizing the subject of dying in Dimapur allows us to engage with death rituals and burials as social practices that are both symbolic and political, and, therefore, are experiences that are part of the socio-cultural life of militarized societies. As a migrant city, scores of tribal communities who settle down in Dimapur organize themselves and maintain kinship networks, and dedicate their services and time to attend social events.

Among all activities, it is the news of dying and funerals that witness large turnouts. The support and hospitality (or the lack of it) in the house of the dead are testimonies of the political and social standing of the respective families, and they become examples of keeping ties and connections with one's kin groups. Young children who are born and raised in Dimapur are reminded of their 'weak roots' to their village, and when they refuse to go for tribal events, parents remind them, 'Who will come when you die?' These reminders are meant to instil the importance of remaining united with their respective kin groups.

Yet, these moral lessons are about finding a sense of belonging in a city that is ultimately seen as a migrant city and a place that is detached from tribal values. This is the marker of place-making in Dimapur. It resonates with Michael Smith (2001: 107) as he notes, '[p]lace making is shaped by conflict, difference, and social negotiations among differently situated and at times antagonistically related social actors, some of whose networks are locally bound, others whose social relations and understandings span entire regions and transcend national boundaries'. Therefore, rituals and conversations about dying are strongly tied to the social worlds of the living. The values and ties attached to dying in the city are also situated within the militaristic culture of the place.

In Dimapur, opposing armed groups seek to control and impose their authority and power on the city. From taxes to regulating the flow of movement, the activities of the Naga armed groups in the city are visible. What is distinctive about this city, as noted earlier, is also the presence of two ceasefire camps in the peri-urban areas of Dimapur. This means many Naga armed cadres and their families have adopted this city as their home. Under such circumstances, Naga nationalism and meanings of homeland and belonging have become part of the city's story. Non-state actors who control this city are equally invested in situating a Naga nationalist mark on the city.

A National Funeral

Gun salutes, hymns, prayers, and the vision of a Naga nation are part of a nationalist eulogy. On 3 March 2010, the funeral programme of Khodao Yanthan, the vice president of the NSCN-IM, was held in Hebron, the headquarters of the NSCN-IM. Kikon was in attendance and also witnessed the funeral preparations. Camp Hebron—the designated ceasefire camp of the NSCN-IM in the peri-urban area of Dimapur—witnessed hundreds of mourners who arrived to pay their respects to the departed Naga leader. Khodao Yanthan passed away on 1 March 2010 in Lakhuti, his ancestral village, but the NSCN-IM made arrangements to bring his body to Camp Hebron. The Lotha community members (Khodao's tribe) and the armed cadres carried out this daunting task of carrying the corpse of the Naga leader from Lakhuti to Hebron (and back to the village to bury his body); the journey took approximately 16 hours (one way) by road.

As the funeral convoy made its way to Dimapur, Kikon was staying in a household that was preparing meals and tea for the volunteers. She witnessed how community members from the Lotha tribe gathered to mourn the death. The village council leaders and elders from the Sovima area and its adjoining localities like Chumukedima and Dimapur also poured in. Yet, this was done in the absence of the body, and anticipation for the corpse was overwhelming. Throughout the night, Kikon heard phone conversations between volunteers at the Sovima house and the funeral convoy about the journey. The community members and volunteers observed an informal wake as visitors and mourners poured in through the night. In the early hours of 3 March, Khodao's funeral convoy arrived at Camp Hebron. Soon, the road to the ceasefire camp was lined with Indian security forces and NSCN-IM soldiers. At the entrance of the camp, NSCN-IM soldiers manned the check gate. Hundreds of cars lined up on the roads outside the boundary of the ceasefire camp and a multitude of people walked to the venue.

A large stage was built for the funeral to accommodate around 100 mourners who were designated as very important persons or VIPs. This was symbolic. Even in death, the VIP mourners were elevated. Their mourning demanded higher recognition and attention than that of the masses who had gathered there. In front of the stage, the organizational flag flew at half-mast. Three rows of plastic chairs on the stage were occupied by members from the NSCN-IM, members of the Naga Hoho (the apex tribal customary body), representatives from tribal associations, and families of the late Khodao Yanthan. A blue-and-white banner on the wooden stage announced, 'Funeral Service of Late Khodao Yanthan. His Excellency, the Vice-President of Nagalim. March 3, 2010 at Council Headquarters'. Images of the star, representing the Star of David that adorns the NSCN-IM national flag, featured on the banner. Below the banner, a raised platform was erected to hold the coffin of the deceased leader. White and pink flowers in cane vases tied to bamboo poles adorned the coffin. NSCN-IM soldiers in olive green uniforms, wearing blue berets carried out last-minute checks and surveyed the area.

As the crowd of mourners settled down under a red tent with blue, green, and white hexagonal designs, the afternoon sun illuminated the colours. The mourners got up from their chairs as a truck covered in white cloth and pasted with white wreaths made its entrance. A group of NSCN-IM soldiers held two thick ropes that were tied to the truck to imitate a Naga traditional rock-pulling ceremony, a symbol of honouring the corpse. Three men sat inside the truck with the portrait of Khodao Yanthan in a suit. Once the hearse came to a halt, six soldiers carried the coffin draped in the NSCN-IM national flag and placed it on a raised platform (see Images 5.1 and 5.2). A line of mourners took turns to place wreaths representing various cultural, political, and tribal organizations on the coffin.

As NSCN-IM leaders and the Naga Hoho representatives took their place on the podium to deliver their eulogies, there was a squall. The wind began to shake the tent and uprooted the bamboo poles. The tent began to unravel. Mourners and NSCN-IM soldiers hurried to

Image 5.1   Mourners await Khodao Yanthan's coffin at Camp Hebron

Source: Dolly Kikon

Image 5.2   Coffin draped in NSCN-IM flag, Camp Hebron

Source: Dolly Kikon

hold the bamboo poles. The programme continued. A gun salute to honour the departed leader was followed by speeches about Khodao's life. The speakers focused on the significance of fighting for Naga sovereignty and the right to self-determination. After the eulogy, the NSCN-IM choir sang an American Christian hymn titled 'I Will Meet You in the Morning' (Brumley 1956):

> I will meet you in the morning
> By the bright riverside
> When all sorrow has drifted away
> I'll be standing at the portals
> When the gates open wide
> At the close of life's long dreary day.

The choir's melodious voice echoed across Camp Hebron. The mourners, despite the squall unravelling the tent, were caught up in the melancholic rendition of the hymn. The mourners at the funeral were part of a complex political community in a peri-urban area of Dimapur. A community with disparate views and perceptions of the Naga armed struggle and experiences assembled in an urban location to mourn the passing away of a leader. It is during these death rituals like funerals, according to Katherine Verdery (1999: 122), that 'people situate themselves socially and in time, providing fundamental elements of their identity'. Many mourners were residents of Dimapur and returned to the city, while volunteers carried Khodao Yanthan's corpse back to Lakhuti village (via Kohima and Wokha, places where additional condolence services and prayers were performed). As the mourners left Camp Hebron for Dimapur, they were anxious of cadres and kept their voices low and their heads down. The fear and anxiety that mourners experienced brings our attention to issues of militarization and what constitutes safety or 'feeling safe' in the city. The transformation of the city involved more than just spatial and structural changes such as construction of malls, private mansions, or commercial hubs. The city remains a contested site among opposing political actors.

The period of the Indo-Naga ceasefire that started in 1997 witnessed a series of overlapping claims about who—politicians, armed groups, or traditional councils—represents the Naga people. The ceasefire period has given rise to complex political networks and developments in the city (Kikon 2019). For example, in Dimapur, the formation of new Naga armed factions has led to new spatial configurations. The NSCN-IM headquarter and the NSCN (Unification) ceasefire camps are built in peri-urban places like Bade, Sovima, Niuland, and Hovishe. These camps are connected to the neighbouring localities where families of armed cadres have set up homes and businesses.

Therefore, new understandings of 'safe' or 'peaceful' neighbourhoods in Dimapur have come up during the period of ceasefire. For families of armed groups, safety and being at peace might be felt in places closer to ceasefire camps, while it might be the opposite for civilians who wish to keep away from military and security operations. This was not the case during the pre-ceasefire period (prior to 1997). What constituted an 'unsafe' neighbourhood then was concentrated around the first cinema halls that came up in Dimapur, such as Latika Hall, Eros, and Friends, including the famous intersections around Dhobinala. The neighbourhoods and settlements that came up around these entertainment hubs were populated by food joints, bars, video game parlours, and gambling dens. These places were the centre of nightlife in the city and attracted people from across the state.

Young crowds who wanted a nightlife, travellers passing by, or movie goers who watched the 9 p.m. to 12 a.m. show frequented these places. These were civilian spaces and played a significant role in offering the city its first urban experiences of nightlife, bars, and cafés. These were not high-rise buildings or structures. A predominant feature of these places was the straight line of shops. The kitchens and bathrooms were extensions constructed with makeshift bamboo or wood. These shops (with extensions) accommodated families who operated the business. These areas were quickly condemned as immoral and disagreeable places. Vernacular phrases such as *Eros Line laga maiki* (woman from Eros Line) connoted a woman with dishonourable character. These places offered refuge to poor families who arrived in Dimapur escaping counter-insurgency operations and violence in the villages. Thus, these neighbourhoods became the first suburbs in the city where tribal working-class families in Dimapur built their lives.

After the ceasefire of 1997, the conception of what constitutes 'unsafe' and 'dangerous' changed. Instead, for the general civilians, neighbourhoods around the ceasefire camps (with high concentrations of armed cadres and their families) were perceived as unsafe and dangerous. The oscillation of value attached to these spatially bound units within the city influenced the consolidation of power, including manning law and order among different political actors. For example, the Nagaland police would seldom file First Information Reports (FIRs) or official complaints for disputes in neighbourhoods around the ceasefire camps. Given that many such cases would involve families/relatives/friends of armed cadres, the police preferred that the armed groups handle their own cases inside the ceasefire camps (see Kikon 2016). In this context, the funeral of Khodao Yanthan, and the enactment of nationalizing his corpse in the peri-urban area of Dimapur, is as an important political act.

The celebration of Khodao's life and Naga nationalism during the funeral at Camp Hebron gives us an idea about belonging and negotiating one's presence in a ceasefire city. Khodao's funeral highlights how Naga nationalism and militarism are reconfigured in an urban space and enacted as an event. Here, the process of dying in a ceasefire city captures the cosmology of everyday militarization and demonstrates how political actors claim their own territory and ways of belonging to the city during the time of ceasefire. This form of banal militarism, by which we mean the everydayness of militaristic displays of force and authority, shows the continuity of militarization during the ceasefire period.

Camp Hebron, located in a peri-urban area of Dimapur, is a transitory operational space that has come up during the ceasefire and functions as a de facto headquarter. There is a constant struggle between the national imagination of a Naga homeland versus the reality of belonging shaped by everyday practices in the ceasefire city. Today, meanings and experiences of safety and danger in Dimapur are coalesced around activities in ceasefire camps like Hebron and Vihokhu. These sites are townships consisting of residential quarters for its cadres, churches, canteens, kitchens, offices, and ration shops. It is here that taxes collected by the armed groups are sorted out, recruitments listed, and official meetings with the media organized. The political universe(s) of the Naga nation influences the everyday politics in Dimapur.

There is a routine performance of Naga nationalism in the city, like the visible banner of armed leaders and mourning rituals that are put up in billboards and posters. These are testimonies of the rise of a militarized memorialization in this city and new configurations of power even at the time of death. The profound inequality between the tribal elite and the poor, illustrated by the existence of wealthy gated neighbourhoods next to ghettos, is a regular feature of the city. But residents living inside the mansions and the ghettos both experience death. Along with stories of patched up sidewalks, private waste collections, and the dilapidated roads in the city, there is a configuration of power as spaces are appropriated, either temporarily (in the context of the funereal event at Hebron) or more permanently (in the context of the overcrowded graveyards in Dimapur).

Burying in Dimapur

As a migrant city, Dimapur is characterized by movement and migration. Many families in Nagaland make a concerted effort to have a home or a 'rest camp' here. Over the years, the real estate prices in Dimapur have skyrocketed. And although there are no statistics available to measure the property prices, the international brands and goods that flood the market and proliferation of medical hospitals and schools reflect the flow of capital and trade in this militarized city. This city also has a dark past. The escalation of fratricidal killings in the 1980s and the 1990s turned many sites into dumping grounds for dead bodies. The local football ground (near Nagaland gate) and the half-built abandoned stadium in Dimapur (near the Dimapur Government College) became sites to dispose of bodies (of their enemies) for the NSCN-IM and NSCN-K.

In addition, Dimapur also attracted people from all the districts of Nagaland for medical treatment and education. Growing up in Dimapur, Kikon reminisced how such hospital visits often turned into peculiar outings as the atmosphere was often festive in the patient's hospital room. Adults exchanged information about their villages and updated their kin members and relatives about their lives. While alive, the ailing tribal bodies are identified with their villages, clans, and tribal affiliation. At the time of death, these tribal corpses generate similar identities and meanings. As news about death travels across the city, the identity of the deceased and the corpse are expected to retain these tribal features. Therefore, news of a tribal death is followed by questions such as 'Which tribe? Which village? Which clan?' Tribal identity is bestowed on the dead to establish a social connection between the living and the dead. Katherine Verdery (1999: 28) argues that: 'A dead body is meaningful not in itself but through culturally established relations to death and through the way a specific dead person's importance is variously construed'.

There is a vibrant practice of memorializing the dead in Dimapur. While there are neighbourhood burial grounds in the peri-urban areas of Dimapur like the Naga United Village and Chumukedima, for many residents of Dimapur, the Naga Cemetery is the preferred place to bury their loved ones. Given the bad roads, few mourning families are prepared to travel with a coffin to the outskirts of the city to the new designated cemetery in Chumukedima. But there are no funds for the upkeep of the Naga Cemetery within the city. It is overcrowded and, hence, it is difficult to accommodate new graves there (see Image 5.3). Families and relatives of the deceased maintain the site. Some families erect iron grills and tombstones to make sure the graves of their loved ones do not disappear.

But stories of overcrowding in the Naga Cemetery are not new. As early as the 1980s, some families we interviewed in Dimapur noted, burying their loved one in the Naga Cemetery was traumatic. They

Image 5.3 Overcrowded Naga cemetery

Source: Duncan McDuie-Ra

found human remains while digging fresh graves. It was evident that families who were unable to afford wooden coffins wrapped the dead bodies in white sheets and buried them. If families failed to mark the graves with tombstones or a concrete structure, those sites were dug up by other families who were looking for fresh graves. Michael Taussig (2006: 4) notes: 'One of the most important events in life, namely, death, is so shrouded in secrecy and fear that most of us would never dare to check'. He continues, '[M]aybe none of the graves have the right body or any at all?' (Taussig 2006: 4). What if that is the case in the overcrowded Naga Cemetery in Dimapur too? Yet, it is the living families, relatives, and friends who harbour the need to conceive monuments and memorials. The graves, irrespective of the irony about whether they possess the right body, are marked for sentimental (and religious) reasons.

When we walked around the Naga Cemetery, the entrance to the graveyard was blocked with a fresh marble tomb. We noticed many small tombstones under rubble and mud. At times, there was cement and sand piled on top of existing graves. In the mid-1990s, the Dimapur Town Committee launched a drive requesting families not to erect large monuments. In the following years, regulations to stop gigantic monuments and guidelines to standardize graves came up. The officials allowed families to only erect headstones. But all these plans fell through. Wealthy families of politicians and tribal leaders continued to erect memorials and large structures for the deceased.

In 2018, the official authority overseeing the management of the Naga Cemetery, the Naga Council Dimapur (NCD), announced that there were no funds to maintain the graves. The NCD thanked the volunteers and the Pastor Fellowship of Dimapur for their service in taking care of the place, and appealed to the public, including families and organizations within the city, to volunteer in maintaining the cemetery (*Morung Express* 2018a). But such developments do not affect the wealthy. They have land and resources to maintain private graves. In some cases, families create memorial sites such as parks to symbolize the significance of the deceased. Dedicated to H. Khekiho Zhimomi, the memorial park in Sovima, along with his tomb, is one such example (Image 5.4). Zhimomi was a former MP of the Rajya Sabha, representing Nagaland at the national level after a long career

Image 5.4 Khekiho Memorial Park, Sovima

Source: Duncan McDuie-Ra

in state politics. The memorial park features landscaped gardens, a gazebo, and a tall stone monolith. The monolith features a crucifix on the front and an inscription at the back, comprising a long list of Zhimomi's achievements and a eulogy, perhaps explaining its considerable height. The inscription is a fascinating public account of political power in the state. It tracks his political life from village headman to student politics to election at the state level and then to the national assembly. Notable is Zhimomi's role in boycotting the state general election in 1998 and 2003, a move intended to give leverage in ceasefire talks with the Government of India. It portrays

Zhimomi as a 'true philanthropist' and a man with a 'lifelong objective to provide free land', leading to the establishment of Khekiho Village in 1989, Nitophu Village in 2009, and Khekiho Colony in 2011—all in Dimapur. The inscription describes Zhimomi as a 'pioneer in the timber trade', a 'self-made business personage', and a 'true industrialist'. The final line of the inscription calls Zhimomi 'a politician of incorruptible integrity' and 'a statesman till the end'. What makes the inscription so insightful is the story it tells about the city and the nature of political power. Zhimomi was part of customary authority, student politics, and mainstream politics with cognizance of—rather than antagonism towards—the Naga movement. He was also involved in the timber trade and in granting land to settlers and urban migrants. These roles are mutually constitutive—common rather than exceptional.

Irrespective of the tribal identity given to the dead in Dimapur, the city has gradually become home for many Naga and non-Naga residents as well. Unlike the previous generation who were buried in the village, more burials now take place in the city. That the cemetery has run out of space indicates that few tribal families carry the dead to their ancestral village. This also signifies how many more residents identify the city as their home. It is here that we witness the city as a home for the living and dead alike. This means there are new demands, which brings us to the story of coffins in the city.

Philosophy of a Coffin Maker

The following three scenes were part of a long conversation between Temjen, a 47-year-old coffin maker who grew up in a village in Mokokchung district before settling in Dimapur, and Kikon. For the most part, the scenes consisted of the ongoing political accounts about the ceasefire and the political negotiations.[2]

Scene one: 'I start my day at 5 a.m. I start working and then thoughts come to my head. As I polish the wood, I think about different designs, I think about new techniques. Then my mind drifts. Conversations

---

[2] All quotes by Temjen in this chapter are from a personal interview held with him in Dimapur on 25 July 2018.

from the previous evening come to my mind. Listen, this conversation we are having today will come to me tomorrow. It will come. I think about all these things. Because the process is not merely making a coffin. It is about cleaning the farm, solving disputes among friends, or managing my boys [workers]. I think about the coming election and politics. I also think about death. Some of my workers have died [while] working with me. They were buried in the coffins they had built. There is no certainty about life. I might die tonight or tomorrow. That is why we are all animals at the end of the day. Whenever boys are making the coffins, they go inside the coffins and test it. They see how it is coming along and whether the fitting is correct. The coffin has utility in our lives. We use it for our needs. Just like making a door frame, a window frame, a table, I make coffins. It is work.'

Scene two: 'Listen, when someone dies in Dimapur, they will not wrap up the body and take it to the village. In many cases, when people die here, they are often short of cash. So, they tell me, "The other two shops are asking this much [quoting a price]. But we are short of cash." I respond, "Ayah, come here. Listen. This is a one-time thing. We are born once and we die once. These two moments are important. Look around the showroom and select the coffin that makes you happy. You pay me the money after you have completed the work [referring to the funeral] or whenever you can pay."'

Scene three: 'When Indian soldiers die, their bodies are brought to Rangapahar, the Indian Army camp in Dimapur. These corpses will have to be sent back to their families in Bihar, Rajasthan, Jammu, etc. One day, the officers asked me for help. They enquired, "How will we carry these corpses? You must help us with this matter. We have to respect the family and show them the bodies of the soldiers." I replied, "Sure." I thought about it and worked out an idea. I made the coffin for the deceased soldiers, and then created a lining inside the coffin with a plastic sheet that is used in construction. Then I suggested that we either use ice or tea leaves to preserve the bodies.'

These three scenes highlight the relationship between the living and dead during the time of ceasefire. The first scene is a reflection about life, death, and work; the second one is an explanation about poor families who take coffins on credit; and the third scene is about working with the Indian Army. Stories following the death of a member in the family or locality are rarely discussed.

Temjen's reflections give us an insight into the everyday practices of dealing with the dead. 'Representational pathos', a term that Michael Taussig (2006: 161) offers, explains the dilemmas of 'representation transgression', by which he means 'crafted contradictions ... and unusual forms of narrative'. In dealing with the topic of living and dying, Temjen's experiences present us with the contradictions and meaning of what constitutes community as he gives us a sense of death and corpses, and the symbolic meanings and values around them. Temjen's work of packing dead bodies of soldiers belonging to the Indian Army and designing coffins for hostile factions of the Naga armed groups presents the city as a place that renders services that might be otherwise perceived as a transgressive action. For instance, during the pre-ceasefire period, a Naga entrepreneur from Dimapur helping the Indian Army to pack corpses of dead soldiers would be defined as a traitor to the Naga nation. Such developments are consequences of the ceasefire period where militarism and death have become mundane affairs. It is in transient moments like this, when corpses require a wooden body before they [the wood and the flesh] are bestowed with meanings and both the coffin and corpse are claimed by kin-folk and identified as part of them, that the coffin maker becomes the architect of memorializing the journey of death. Naga society continues to be portrayed as a community steeped in tradition and culture, but Temjen's stories cannot be contained within a fixed and immutable tribal narrative. His accounts that we highlight are an important political and social conceptualization of urban life.

Joy Pachuau (2014) describes death and the practices around it in Mizo society as an important process of marking boundaries and identity formation. Death rituals, she elaborates, are practices whereby societal links with place (such as locality) and identity (Mizoness) come alive. Pachuau explains how death practices are both place-making and identity-forming markers. Therefore, every death is a moment when group identities are reiterated and the boundary of the community manifested. In the case of Temjen's practices in Dimapur, we present how neither life nor death is experienced in a singular manner. Instead, highlighting the everydayness of making coffins and the lives who build these frames, we depart from analysing death as a community bonding and identity-marking occasion. Temjen's voice offers us a critical and fundamental way to imagine forms of life and death in a militarized city. What do coffins and the lives of those who design these boxes tell us?

Much of the work on militarization and violence during the ceasefire has centred on the factional killings and the mechanics of the peace process. As early as the 1980s, the construction of coffins was perceived as a community activity in Dimapur. At the time of death, clans and relatives came together and volunteered their time and labour to construct the coffins. Decorations such as silk linings, ribbons, and artificial flowers were added around the coffins by the women folk. Yet, with the increasingly high rate of migration from the hills of Nagaland to Dimapur, practices around tribal solidarity underwent a transformation. Unlike the Mizo society that Pachuau (2014) describes in Aizawl, in Dimapur the local and moral values of belongingness are grounded in not forgetting one's 'roots' and the 'village'. But given the rapid urbanization and the number of deaths in the city every day, community activities like making coffins have vanished.

As decisions to bury the dead in the city become routine, there is a distinction between mourning deaths from wealthy families and those from the margins of tribal society. Widows and members of poor families often find themselves alone and bereft of a collective to mourn for their deceased family member.

As with celebrating culture and tradition in Naga society, the death practices in Dimapur are increasingly focused on decorations, performing a Christian funeral, and feeding the mourners. Similar to organizing weddings where poor families took loans for the event, it is common to witness bereaved families with debts after burying their loved one. The disappearance of collective practices like making coffins for grieving families as signs of sociality and community activity means many things. Among them, loss and mourning are moments of encountering isolation and detachment from the tight-knit tribal community and sensing the alienation of an urban life. Even traditional wake practices where friends and relatives sing and remember the dead are disappearing. Perhaps city people are busy and cannot commit their time to it. But this might be a simple explanation. These developments do not take place overnight. While it is true that tribal sociality and tradition are reiterated as clans and tribal members assemble whenever someone from their clan/tribe passes away, the loss and the pain are equally felt beyond kin relations as well. Non-Naga neighbours, friends, and colleagues from diverse ethnic and religious backgrounds in the city also mourn the loss.

References to a Naga past where urban life or accounts about a tribal city feature continue to be thin. The context of the city and an urban experience is often elsewhere: outside the state, somewhere outside in an Indian metropolitan city, or overseas. Such perceptions tell us how urbanism in Dimapur is linked to a sensory and imaginative extension of 'remoteness', in line with policy documents where development progress is stressed as the way forward out of remoteness (see Kikon 2019). This practice of obliterating any associations with urbanization comes from maintaining, among other things, a sense of nationalist imagination where Naganess is inherently timeless and pristine and located out of the city space.

But assertions of authority and power across the city are marked by different Naga actors. Besides the state law enforcing agencies like the police and civil authorities, the Naga insurgents also exercise their power and collect tax within the city. At the level of the suburb or colony (a term of reference for different localities in Dimapur), there are overlapping tribal and urban authorities as well. From municipal corporation and traditional councils to youth associations and church bodies, these various bodies present Dimapur as a distinct urban space. For example, during funerals, the activities are divided among different groups. If traditional bodies and the church arrange for the funeral service, the traffic police regulate vehicles as the hearse makes its way to the cemetery, and the youth groups from the locality arrange the parking site for the mourners who drive to the funeral service.

Daily Life of a Coffin Maker

Beside a busy road along Nagarjan, a suburb in Dimapur, a small bamboo hut with three rooms functions as Temjen's living space and a coffin showroom as well. During his meeting with Kikon, Temjen spoke of his life and the events that led him to start designing coffins. He said, 'My story has appeared in the papers' to assert that his profession has attracted the attention of local media in the city. In the process of preparing for the interview, he sat down for a photo session.

'I am ready,' he announced. Laughing and appearing embarrassed, his wife threw a shirt at him and asked him to put it on. He threw it away, saying he was comfortable as he was. The wife commented that her husband was a peculiar man. 'He sleeps in the coffin workshop and does not come home for days,' she commented. Bare chested and smoking a hand-rolled cigarette, Temjen laughed and admitted that his wife was speaking the truth. When Kikon first met Temjen, he was working in his workshop. Pieces of wood lay on the floor. 'I am busy today,' he said and requested Kikon to return the following day. During the interview, as Kikon listened to Temjen's experiences about constructing coffins, it came as a surprise when he said, 'People tell me you are happy only when someone dies. I tell them that I will be very happy if human beings never died. I will find some other job. I do not feed myself only when someone dies.' Temjen was distraught when he narrated similar stories about people's reactions towards his profession. Then he explained the Naga people's attitude towards his business.

The Naga business logic is this: People think if we put in 100 rupees, the return should be 200 rupees. That is why we are never successful as owners. People will think that a coffin shop has 50 per cent profit. See, I give my 10 per cent to the church even though I drink and smoke. But it is not 50 per cent, highest is 30–35 per cent after I pay off the workers and keep money aside for the accessories. The most expensive coffin we have made so far cost 1 lakh [one hundred thousand] rupees.

See, things are only becoming expensive. When I go to the market for an item I have paid 100 rupees for earlier, the next time it costs 200 rupees. When I ask why this is happening, the shopkeeper tells me to look at the price tag on the item. I do not have education. So, it is not that the world is bad, it is the people in this world who are bad.

Coffin orders come; lots of orders do come. People download coffin designs from the internet and bring them to me. These are designs from London and all over the world. But I have to customize them accordingly. If a slight measurement goes wrong, the entire coffin is wasted.

Highlighting his commitment to the trade, he said, 'I really put in a lot. Once someone came to me and said, 'My father is on the Burmese side; I do not know if he will live or die. We have to take coffin today.'

Temjen designed a folding coffin that could be carried all the way
to the client's village. Given that there seldom are motorable roads
in many Naga villages, the folding coffin was an innovative item. As
Temjen described his profession, it became clear that he went beyond
building wooden frames and structures. Coffins also shaped the
future of the young men who worked in his shop. He affectionately
called his employees 'my boys,' and said:

> My boys have seven shops across the city now. I tell them, 'Boys, learn
> any work; bathroom cleaning, carpentry, sweeping the floor. You have no
> education; the time is over. But if you have skills you can maintain your
> tummy, have a livelihood.' On the last weekend of the month, we always
> eat together.

> The [prices of] coffins in my shop start from 1,500 to 35,000 rupees. All my
> employees are school dropouts. Why do I employ them? Because they will
> not get any loan to start a business. They do not have money and have no
> source [of income], so they work for me and I teach them the trade.

> Their salary starts at 3,000 rupees even though they have no idea about
> carpentry and the trade. But I teach them the skills and also instruct them
> to save 1,000 rupees every month. Once their savings reach 50,000 rupees,
> I give them the option to branch out and open their [own] coffin shops.

> All my former boys come to visit me and bring me a bottle of whiskey
> and meat. That makes me so happy! I do not need money. Some of them
> have also joined the Indian Army and the Indian Reserve Battalion (IRB).
> Those who come from the IRB and army during their holidays bring their
> savings. I tell them to go back to the village and look after the needs of
> their parents. They all go the village and spend time there. But before
> leaving for postings in Kolkata, Jammu and Kashmir, and other places,
> they come here. This coffin workshop is their transit camp.

During the interview, workers and visitors came in and sat with us.
Many more walked in and interrupted us to make enquires about new
coffins. When Kikon probed, 'When did you take up this profession?',
a question she had wanted to ask since she arrived to meet Temjen, it
was a personal loss in the family that led him to this profession. He
said:

> In 2000, my wife's brother died of tuberculosis. I bought a coffin for 1,200
> rupees. It was a plain one made of plywood. I had to search for sponge,

clothes, and ribbons to make it presentable. I told the Lotha and the Sema coffin makers, 'Don't do it like that. I suffered a lot.' They asked me, 'Why?' I said, 'I had to search for sponge, clothes, ribbons, etc. Why don't you make readymade coffins?' They did not make it.

After two years, I told them that I will open a coffin shop, and they said, 'Sure.' I told them, 'Look at the designs I create. You also have to learn to give customers readymade coffins.' Imagine having to search for sponge, clothes, ribbons in the middle of the night, to make the plain plywood coffins presentable! So, I began to make readymade coffins with flowers, and also offered coffins made with different kinds of wood so that people could choose [from the options].

During the ceasefire period, key activities like commerce, elections, and contracts in urban areas like Dimapur began to be determined by various factions of the Naga armed groups and the tribal elites. Yet, the malls and showrooms that are visible today did not come up overnight. Even though the power networks in the city were formed, neighbourhoods and shopping areas in the city centre were in a state of disrepair (Image 5.5). According to Temjen, his first coffin shop Home Trust Shop near Half Nagarjan Road was a rough place.

Image 5.5   Coffin making in the area around the Super Market

Source: Duncan McDuie-Ra

Today, a daily market sits in the area and there are scores of eating joints and shops. But this was not the case in the early years of the ceasefire. He recalled:

> When I opened the shop in the Super Market, the city was a dangerous place. The Super Market area was filled with drug addicts and alcoholics. It was a dangerous place, with sex work and peddlers. We started cleaning up the place. The deputy commissioner and the superintendent of police could not do anything. I took the initiative and made a regulation. I ordered that by 8 p.m. the shutters of all the shops will be down and there will be no business after that.

> It was not easy since there were single parents with children who could not afford even a pot of rice. The lines of buildings in the Super Market were allotted for shops but the rooms were taken up on rent and people started staying in single rooms meant for shops. They were neither shops nor apartments. All kinds of business went in there.

While the city has witnessed an economic transformation driven by the conflict economy, there is a demand for a long-lasting political solution to the ongoing Indo-Naga ceasefire negotiation. In addition, security experts have emphasized that the ceasefire period is a time for the Indian state to consolidate its power (Brar 2016). But on the ground, deep down in the localities and neighbourhoods across the city, the troubles and breakdown of law and order highlight the ordinariness of violence and militarization. Temjen's experience of mediating sites like the Super Market area as a dangerous space filled with drugs, alcohol, and immorality becomes one of the stories of a militarized city. The persistence of militarization is also marked on the urban landscape. The vision for the Super Market was something else. Completed during the time of conflict—around the 1980s—the Super Market was a line of concrete shops constructed for business. However, traders refused to move into that area since its location was not considered as an ideal site for trading. When the town municipal council offered subsidies to the Bengali and Tibetan traders to relocate their shops from bazaars like the Hong Kong Market and Shangri-La area, there was a brief glimmer of hope. But traders rejected the offer and the Super Market became an abandoned site until a new daily bazaar was set up there in the ceasefire period. Today, there are shops and offices in the area and civilians frequent these shops.

The political negotiations between the Naga political groups and the Government of India are central during the time of the ceasefire. This means intimate and out-of-context accounts are relegated to the margins. In that view, conversations with ordinary residents like Temjen allow us to reposition one's understandings about urban life under militarism. Dimapur is the hub of all kinds of infrastructure schemes and projects, ranging from accountants and business companies who draft proposals for the construction of roads, bridges, and commercial centres to establishing various networks and connections with politicians, suppliers, and hardware material agents. Yet, the business of readymade coffins in the city highlights how projects on the ground take off. The desire to honour the dead is not limited to the residents of the city. Insurgents and Indian security forces alike believe in this project.

'Now the Indian Army [has] also started visiting my shop,' Temjen said. Some years ago, the Indian Army stationed at the Rangapahar military station in Dimapur came looking for him. As mentioned earlier, there was a crisis when highly decomposed corpses of soldiers arrived at the army station. Temjen began to design coffins for carrying the decomposed corpses by lining the coffins with plastic sheets and packing the bodies with ice. He said:

> For example, if the body from Dimapur reaches Delhi today, then they will change the ice there and prepare the body to be taken to Rajasthan. The army sat down with me and we discussed these matters. I worked closely with them. Soldiers die under unpleasant circumstances sometimes, and sometimes they fall ill and die.

> No one would make these coffins, so it was problem for them. The army officers said that earlier they would cremate the decomposed bodies here [in Dimapur] and inform the parents. But the families of the deceased soldiers fought with the officers. They wanted the bodies back. That is the reason they came to me. I said, 'Alright, let's work together.'

The story underlines the everydayness of militarism and a militarized economy. The question is not about who constitutes the enemy during the ceasefire period. In Dimapur, business deals between insurgents, traders, ex-insurgents, and the Indian Army showcase the flow of labour, money, and ideas in this period. Naga armed groups and the Indian Army visit the workshop and order coffins for their dead soldiers. Stressing the frequency and the ease with which both state and non-state actors come to the shop, Temjen's wife described how the Indian Army officers from the Rangapahar station came to visit them recently. It was a Sunday, but they came with an urgent order. The Indian Army officials were unable to find a seven-feet-long readymade coffin in the city and arrived at the workshop looking for the same.

'Are there any distinctions between the coffins made for a Naga insurgent and the Indian Army?' Kikon enquired. Temjen appeared amused and said that the Indian Army had specific coffin designs, unlike the Naga insurgents. For instance, the Indian Army required a seven-foot coffin with six handles because a battalion body is carried by six people. It had to follow a military protocol. The coffin is straight—two feet all along in breadth and then seven feet in length. The design is also given keeping in mind that the Indian flag must cover the coffin. For the Naga insurgents, they come and buy the regular coffins. Their requirements were, according to Temjen, 'Just like us.' When Kikon asked 'Why?' Temjen responded, 'Listen, they [Naga insurgents] have not got their independence as yet. So where is the chance for all these coffin protocols?' According to Verdery (1999), burials allow us to see how authorities and nations order (and reorder) the political memories and national identities. The differences in designs and protocols during death between the Naga armed groups and the Indian Army show us how rules and systems of governance are applied during the time of death. This is an important aspect. Here, experiences of dying and the activities that follow reveal what lies behind the neat tribal narratives of customs and traditions around death ceremonies.

We learnt that prior to his current business, Temjen was a member of a Naga armed group. He was captured and served prison time in Tihar jail before the ceasefire in 1997. When he got out of prison, he surrendered and came to Dimapur. Some of his friends were still in the Naga armed movement and lived in ceasefire camps. When he met them in the city or on occasions when they visited his workshop, a desire to 'carry the gun again' crossed his mind. But he began to think about his children. And when he heard firings in the city, he would feel, 'Is it my child? Is anyone hurt?' All such kinds of thoughts came to his head. He was able to identify the gunshots and the type of weapon used, and his mind drifted back to the days when he used to carry guns and fire similar weapons.

After he was released from jail, he surrendered his membership with the Naga armed group; he came to Dimapur and took up carpentry. It was a hobby for him. He spent time fixing things in the neighbourhood for free. These are the unscripted moments of people's lives that are often erased by grand narratives of conflict and violence. Temjen's experiences show how people try to give meaning and service—no matter how peculiar and modest—as members of a society during the time of ceasefire.

Temjen said:

> My friends are still in the armed movement. They come to my workshop and watch me. They put down their guns and bombs and watch me. They come to visit me because it makes them happy. Sometimes they come and ask me for money, 2,000 or 3,000 rupees.

> See, I do not trust the banks and I do not have a bank account. I do not want bank loans either. I feel secure as long as I have 10,000 rupees in my pocket.

> I do not want to live in a building and be very rich.

> I want to live a happy life. I want to eat well and hope I have no illness.

> Even if people come in the middle of the night, and I am very tired and sleeping, I am happy to wake up and help them out with a coffin.

While Temjen expressed his worldview and his commitment towards society through his trade, as someone dedicated and hardworking, he invoked the language of 'trust' to emphasize the need to care for one another and be self-reliant. He was a school dropout and recognized early on the importance of acquiring skills to economically sustain oneself. By contrasting the written culture in Naga society with its oral past where 'our forefathers did not write and everything was through word of mouth,' Temjen emphasized how the social relationship among Naga people in the city have deteriorated. He was cautious about the written text. Indeed, his suspicion about the Naga people's dependency on written documents and texts was related to his reluctance to open a bank account. He said: 'The bank might open tomorrow, but it will not be open at night.' His notion of mistrust extended from the written text to the people and he explained why:

> Temjen: Now we are writing, but who can trust the written text? Today one writes something, tomorrow there is an error that is found. Whom can we trust? We need to work, trust our practice, and feed ourselves. That is the way to go.

> Kikon: You mean we should not trust anyone?

> Temjen: We should not trust even our brothers and sisters! Do not beg from others to feed yourselves. Work. That is what I teach my children. I work from morning till night. I had two brothers who worked with me. One of them was very naughty. But eventually he set up his own shop in the 4th Mile area [a suburb in Dimapur]. If they continue working with me, they will not change. So, I let them branch off. Now he is married with kids and has opened a second coffin shop. I have a shop in 4th mile, one in 3rd mile, one near Zion Hospital, one near Eden Hospital in Kashiram, and two in Nagarjan.

> Kikon: What about government jobs?

> Temjen: We should do government jobs; I am not opposed to that, but [there] we are working under someone. We should be the owner of our work. In India, there is a president, a prime minister; Modi is the owner of India for 5–10 years. But my belief is that we should always be the owner of our own life; we are Naga people, it is our land, our village, and that is the reason why we should be the owner. If Modi decides not to send money to Nagaland, people will not get their salaries. But if one works for oneself then we will not starve.

> Kikon: What is your idea about work?

> Temjen: When we are done making coffins here in the workshop, I do not sit idle. I take the boys to clean the farms of people or to chop wood in the forest. Being the owner of the coffin shops, I do all kinds of work as well. It is not enough to know only one kind of work. There is no point in demanding sovereignty from India if we are not willing to work hard.

Corsín (2011: 177) notes that 'crisis' in trust draws our attention towards a larger political and moral impasse in society. Temjen's reflections show how violence and insecurity are inscribed deeply in militarized societies. Perhaps he drew from the experiences of unemployment and the violence he witnessed as a member of a Naga armed group and the existing political uncertainty in the Indo-Naga ceasefire talks. But his account of trust, politics, and caring for grieving families highlights that death and dying is a social experience. The alienation of grieving families or officials (state and non-state actors alike) struggling to find a presentable coffin is an important story of living in Dimapur.

Dying and death shape social relations, politics, and ways of belonging during the time of the Indo-Naga ceasefire. The everydayness of dying in Dimapur is a way of bringing attention to urban life and social practices in a militarized city. Learning to bury the dead with nationalist protocols or living with memorials and buying customized coffins allows us to pay attention to the significance of modern tribal societies in urban spaces. By focusing on experiences of living and dying in Dimapur, this chapter illustrates experiences of community activity, isolation, and alienation in a militarized city. As a result, accounts of nationalizing corpses, restoring honour to the dead at the time of their burial, and the choices families make to bury the dead in Dimapur capture the complex fabric of urban life in Dimapur during the ceasefire period.

Epilogue

In July 2017, a bridge connecting Naga United Village to the rest of Dimapur collapsed into the Chathe River. Four people were killed and five were injured as the supporting pylons in the middle of the bridge were washed away in the flow of the rain-bloated river. The road across the bridge was sliced in half, and vehicles on the collapsed half of the bridge dropped into the river. Other vehicles remained on the metal road, wedged against the rest of the standing structure. Built in 1988 as a single-lane bridge for lightweight traffic, use of the bridge increased as the settlement in Naga United Village grew on the eastern side of the river and the edges of tribal territory extended into ambiguous zones around the Assam border and into the foothills towards Nuiland.

Amateur videos, shot on cell phones, of the bridge collapse were quickly uploaded to YouTube and shared on other social media platforms. In some videos, bystanders can be heard weeping over the general din of shouting and the sound of rushing water. In others, the owners of the video clips have added music and subtitles with facts about the incident and about the bridge itself. The videos and images of the bridge collapse invited streams of comments in various languages expressing anger, frustration, and sadness, but rarely surprise. When viewing these videos online, algorithmic prompts offer suggestions for similar content. Clearly, there is a whole genre of videos that focuses on the terrible condition of almost everything in Nagaland. One can pass hours looking at footage of Nagaland State Transport buses bogged in deep mud, cracks in government buildings spewing forth torrents of rainwater, and many, many dilapidated bridges still being used by auto rickshaws, cars, and small trucks.

The collapse of the Naga United Village bridge was a catalyst for public outrage, coming as it did in the conjuncture we have explored in the preceding chapters: poised between order and crisis. It shames a familiar target, the government, while leaving issues like customary authority well alone. At the present conjuncture, it seems almost everyone can get behind chastising the government for their corruption and ineptitude. Indeed, as evident in comments and in quotes to the media, most residents of the area knew that the bridge was in a terrible condition and would likely collapse at any moment. So too did the Public Works Department, which reported the bridge as unsafe for commuting in 2015 (*Morung Express* 2017b). The Public Works Department claimed that the bridge became unsafe due to sand mining activities in the river (for cement and other construction needs), directing blame to the construction industry, its notorious greed, and the faceless low-end labourers mining along the riverbanks, rather than the authorities charged with building and maintaining infrastructure. And perhaps the bridge epitomizes the argument we make throughout this book: Dimapur 'looks' like a city but does not function as one. It is an experimental territorial form, an enclave of gathered settlements with limited sense of shared place and limited capacity to be governed cohesively.

After the collapse, local press also revealed that funding for a new bridge had been sanctioned in 2016, after the Government of Nagaland appealed to the Ministry of Roads and Transportation based in Delhi (*Morung Express* 2017b): a standard practice in the dependent frontier. With limited prospects to raise revenue independently for public works, the state and municipal authorities request and wait. Waiting for funds from Delhi may not always be financially necessary but it is deeply embedded politically. However, when the funds actually come through there is only a slim chance that they will be utilized for their intended purpose. Once the bridge collapsed, the Central Nagaland Tribes Council alleged that the Public Works Department had drawn on the funds for the bridge 62 times between mid-2016 and mid-2017, yet no work was undertaken (*Morung Express* 2017b). Then the bridge collapsed, people died, and the eastern edge of the city was cut off from the rest of Dimapur for almost a year. The outrage was understandable. Though it is what happened next that was most revelatory.

In early 2018, six months after the collapse, we visited the site together on an early winter morning (Image E.1). It was a beautiful clear day, and with the water level of the river being very low, vehicles were able to drive down to the riverbank and use a makeshift bridge

Image E.1   Ruins of the collapsed bridge looking up at Naga United Colony from the dry riverbed

Source: Duncan McDuie-Ra

built on top of sandbags and concrete pipes to get across to the other side and then churn through dust and dirt to ascend the opposite bank. Everything was covered in dirt and dust. In the dry riverbed below, a crew of workers, all non-tribal labourers, assembled grids of bamboo and lowered them into deep holes sunk into the ground for the eventual pouring of concrete for the replacement bridge.

The site could be viewed from all angles from a suspended footbridge running parallel to the former bridge, wide enough only for foot traffic (Image E.2). Most of the original bridge had been removed, though ruins remained. On the Naga United Village side, a section of the old bridge lay marooned on top of a tall concrete pylon, cut off from the empty space where the bridge once stood, though still connected to the village on the far bank. Where the bridge would have once met the bank, a beautiful village gate stands with a sign reading 'WELCOME: NAGA UNITED VILLAGE, Est. Feb. 8th 1968' affixed to the steel and

Image E.2   Marooned over the river with a temporary footbridge in the background, Naga United Colony

Source: Duncan McDuie-Ra

timber roof, an entry point now inaccessible without traversing the eroding bank pulled away by the collapsed bridge. On the reverse side of the gate, the side facing the village through which vehicles would have once travelled across the river to the rest of Dimapur, a white-and-blue sign reads 'Safe Journey!', a now-impossible task with a sheer drop only metres away. The sides of the gate have finely crafted Naga motifs set in thick concrete pillars. A marble sign embedded in the gate honours the laying of the foundation stone for the construction of this version of the gate in 2011 by, not without macabre irony, the deputy transport commissioner of the Government of Nagaland. Safety railings were still intact on the side of this marooned patch of bridge facing the river, as if the small section was purposely left as a memorial to civilian tragedy and government ineptitude, though it is more likely no one has worked out how to take this part of the bridge down.

While the archiving of the tragedy in the marooned bridge section may be unintended, the use of the site to send a political message is impossible to miss. Along with new signs by the village council reminding visitors and residents of the alcohol ban and fines administered by the council for littering, the site is covered with messages printed on white A4-size papers glued to trees, poles, and bamboo hoardings. Some examples include:

'Have a Vision? Make the right decision. Bad officials are elected by good citizens who do not vote for right candidate [sic]'.

'Due to pathetic road condition for 15 years, citizens have already memorise the potholes in every corner of Nagaland [sic]'.

'No proper drainage system in Nagaland because there is no system. Nagaland itself have become a drainage [sic]'.

'Pollution by corruption leads to destruction. Be honest and fight corruption'.

These were all attributed to the Dimapur branch of the Aam Aadmi Party, a national party that grew out of the anti-corruption movements of the early 2010s and, at the time these signs were posted, was in power in the Delhi National Capital Territory. Our visit occurred just a month prior to the Nagaland state elections, and thus the collapsed bridge was an opportune site for one of the smaller parties to paste its campaign notices for anyone passing by, though given the lack of a bridge, there was not much traffic aside from weary residents of Naga United Village crossing the suspended footbridge and labourers working on the new construction. As a side note, the Nagaland branch of the Aam Aadmi Party merged with the Naga People's Front in late 2018 after failing to win a seat in the 2018 election.

It stands to reason that the party that identifies almost solely as an anti-corruption group would choose this site to symbolize their campaign. And further, it is striking that they performed so poorly in the election just one month later. The collapsed bridge may have been symptomatic of blatant corruption and government failure, yet perhaps these are things residents of Dimapur have come to expect from the state, or at least come to expect in the (limited) patches of the city where the state exercises spatial control. Anti-corruption sentiment is widespread in the city, appearing in graffitis and on car bumper stickers, is widely reported in the media, and debated in various political arenas (Image E.3). Yet elections are won and lost on the promises made to channel more funds to the frontier, to *deepen*

Image E.3 Anti-corruption signs, 4th Mile bank of the river

Source: Duncan McDuie-Ra

dependency, to ensure protection of customary laws and avoid any threat to hard-won entitlements.

As a catalyst for public outrage, the collapsed bridge continued to be present, even in ruins. Yet it is the response to the solution that is perhaps more instructive of the fabric of everyday life in Dimapur. Ten months after its collapse, a temporary bridge was installed, and like its predecessor, it is a prefabricated 'baily' bridge with a single traffic lane. This will be in place until a more permanent structure is built, if at all. At the opening of the temporary bridge in May 2018, a ceremony was held which was attended by the village council of the Naga United Village and members of the Public Works Department, and prayers were led by Reverend Dr P. Dozo (*Morung Express* 2018b). At the end of May, an open letter appeared in the *Eastern Mirror* newspaper, titled 'Appreciation to the PWD (Roads & Bridges) Nagaland' (*Eastern Mirror* 2018a), signed by notable public figures impacted by the bridge collapse, including school principals and village council members from areas beyond Naga United Village, located at the edges of the city, in enclaves, and on tribal territories. The letter is probably sincere, but it could just as easily be read as satire. The authors 'express profound gratitude' to the Public Works Department for completing the temporary bridge 'against all apprehensions we had that this project would never be actualized' (*Eastern Mirror* 2018a). After the bridge collapsed, these villages were 'totally cut off from the mainland', which produced a great deal of suffering and hardship (*Eastern Mirror* 2018a). They refer to the temporary bridge as a 'great achievement' that shows a 'concern for public welfare' (*Eastern Mirror* 2018a). Along with naming the key civil servants involved, the letter thanks the members of the affected villages and those who prayed for the bridge's completion. The letter casts the temporary bridge as remarkable, even a little magical. And the very public gratitude for the minimal municipal service rendered may prove valuable when the next dire infrastructural situation arises. As loudly as residents of Dimapur may grumble about corruption, patronage appears a more reliable strategy than resistance.

The gratitude expressed in the letter also reflects the gravity of the bridge collapse, symptomatic of the patchwork city where the infrastructure connecting the villages, colonies, and settlements that constitute its parts is unreliable and even ethereal. Naga United Village and the settlements to the east had one feasible route to the rest of the city. When it collapsed, they were almost completely isolated and cut-off from the rest of the city. Unlike the community infrastructure fashioned in neighbourhoods and settlements to compensate for the failures of the government, as discussed in Chapter 2, building a bridge across the Chathe River was too big a task, especially once the water level began to rise and the improvised bridge operating along the riverbed through the winter months could not be used.

Almost a year later, the provision of a prefabricated temporary bridge was celebrated, not just because it made the lives of residents much easier and even more possible, but because the Public Works Department actually fixed something. This warrants a public outpouring of gratitude. The fact that the very same department was accused of ignoring the original problem and of appropriating funds allocated to fix it is less remarkable. Dependency, corruption, and moral bankruptcy are the norm; actually getting public works completed where they are needed is the exception, the surprise. These acts, these moments of municipal responsiveness and action, provoke gratitude; they warrant prayer. And this reflects the way in which people experience the city, and how they respond—or not—to its dysfunction.

Belonging in the Ceasefire City

Throughout this book, we have explored spaces and stories of Dimapur to grasp at the ways in which it has shaped the lives of its inhabitants and the way they have in turn shaped the city. From advertisements plastered on the walls of Super Market ('Introduction') to the coffins and graveyards of the city's deathscapes (Chapter 5), from the stories of hunters traversing modern urban space and traditional hunting grounds on the city's edges (Chapter 4) to the anxieties and violence of the failed municipal elections (Chapter 2), and from the spatial experiments that constitute the city's territoriality (Chapter 1) to the sounds, lyrics, and music of the audible landscape (Chapter 3), we have sought the ways in which the city appears, feels, and (dys)functions. There is much about the city we have failed to understand, but we are comforted that almost everyone we know in Dimapur feels the same way. Indeed, beyond complaints about the poor condition of infrastructure and rumours about powerful elites or secret casinos or devil-worshipping cults, there are a few common narratives of the city. And perhaps this is the point.

For a city that is the largest in a tribal majority state in India's much-researched Northeast frontier, Dimapur has almost no public presence. As we have argued throughout the book, Dimapur is 'off the map'; there is no single public achievement, no shared public memory, and no contrivance about what Dimapur should be. The 'authentic' Nagaland of festivals, culture, and exotic costumes does not even start until you leave the city through Chumukedima and cross the Chathe River. With no dominant narrative of the city to latch on to, Dimapur is experienced in fragments. There is no shared urban sensibility to call upon when discussing the past, the future, or the character of the place or its people. There is no city museum, no old photos mounted in a public square, and no public repository of the areas settled or by whom. There are, however, fragments: oral histories of settlement, of events, of crises; visual archives in foundation stones, settlement names, dates on religious buildings; and lived experiences of violence, occupation, migration and return, and rapid urban change lodged in memories, bodies, monuments, and memorials.

To explore these fragments, we adopted a two-part focus. In the first half of the book we focused on Dimapur's spatial order and disorder and its moments of crisis that characterize the present conjuncture, and in the second half we have gone deeper into the lives of residents, migrants, sojourners, and interlopers, and the worlds within and outside the city they traverse, create, and occupy. We have argued that in the present conjuncture, Dimapur's urban environment, the spatial whole of Dimapur—as much as such a concept can be imagined—is shaped by militarism, capitalism, and urbanism. These historic forces produce the conditions of the present as manifest in the built environment, the spatial order, and the ways in which the city is governed and transformed. Dimapur's urban environment is shaped by capitalism (the commercial boom following the ceasefire and its role in rearranging the city spatially), militarism (the military infrastructure, surveillance, extraordinary laws, and continued presence of the Indian military and paramilitary, Nagaland state police, and other battalions, as well as the insurgent and separatist groups), and urbanism (the fantasies and failures of urban imaginaries and their attendant governance mechanisms). However, we assert that these conditions are not simply an obstacle course for Dimapur's urban dwellers that must be navigated and survived. Communities and individuals shape these dynamics and they shape the city created in their wake. Our position resonates with the provocations of Amin and Thrift to consider the mutually constitutive subjectivities produced by bodies and the material urban environment. They write:

> It is often assumed that in cities with rudimentary technologies, poor infrastructures and failing bureaucracies, where humans are left to do the heavy lifting, inhabitants proceed without prosthetics, challenged rather than formed by their habitat. Rarely in writing on the world's urban majority living in challenging circumstances does the habitat feature on the inside of subjectivity. Slums, suburbs, congested public spaces, tower blocks and busy city centres tends [sic] to get narrated as uncongenial spaces that urban dwellers learn to negotiate or survive, distorting subjectivity from the outside, for example, by encouraging opportunistic, feral or furtive behaviour. In contrast, a new genre of urban ethnography is emerging, showing that humans are equally of their habitat in these environments, with agency very much a hybrid of mind, body, machine and matter. (Amin and Thrift 2017: 19)

We have tried to show, through analysis of spaces and stories, the ways in which Dimapur is an integral component of subjectivity, identity, and lived experience. From the lyrics of Tali Angh to the hunters fleeing the Assam security forces for the safety of the city, Dimapur shapes its denizens in ways that are articulated consciously and in ways that are harder to find and harder to know; ways that are felt but perhaps not spoken about often. We do not seek to downplay the everyday struggles of people in Dimapur, instead we seek immersion in their experiences; the pain and the joy, the defeat and the mischief, the anxiety and the pride.

Communities and individuals make place in Dimapur through ritual, practices, codes of behaviour, physical and material boundaries, symbols and texts, buildings and gates, physical intimidation and monitoring, and violence and its possibility. Place-making in Dimapur produces belonging *and* exclusion, and from time to time, transgressions—actions judged to be 'out of place' (Cresswell 2015:

165). Some communities seek to establish firm territorial boundaries and claims in the city, while others prefer less visibility, at least until they have either human or financial capital to make stronger claims on space. For those outside the dominant tribal, ethnic, or religious groups, creating belonging in Dimapur is a sensitive and delicate task, especially for new arrivals, for non-tribals, and even for tribals from non-Naga communities. To establish some kind of belonging in the city without kin, clan, or familial networks is difficult, and for these communities their place in the city is 'unstable and unbounded but not ungrounded' (Roberts 2016: 9). Belonging is also temporal. As we have discussed in the moments of crisis that affected the entire city in Chapters 1 and 2 and in the moments that have affected individuals and communities in Chapters 3–5, there are periods of calm when life can take root and routines and rhythms can be established, the city experienced with minimal anxiety, and there are periods when this is impossible.

Dimapur Matters

We argue that studying Dimapur matters for many reasons. First, it matters not only for increasing the depth and variety of knowledge produced about Northeast India, but also for urban studies, especially ethnographies of urban space emerging from periods of prolonged conflict. Second, Dimapur matters because it is the largest city in a tribal majority state. This is deeply significant in Northeast India where cities in tribal areas are growing rapidly and taking on renewed significance in economic, political, and cultural lives. Is Dimapur the teleos of urbanization in the region or an outlier, an exception? We believe that Dimapur is indicative of the kinds of urban futures that will shape the region in the coming decades, but of course we do not know for sure. This brings us to our third point, which is that further research in other cities in tribal majority districts and states will help answer these questions. There is immense value in comparative urban ethnography in the Northeast, yet there is also value in thinking of frontier urbanism or tribal urbanism as a research agenda that can travel beyond India and connect to researchers working in other similar environments in Asia and beyond, answering the call to better situate urban ethnography in the Global South, engage comparatively, and move away from the mega city (Bunnell and Maringanti 2010; Simone and Pieterse 2017; Zérah and Denis 2017).

Fourth, Dimapur matters because it is more than just a city; it is an experimental territorial form. Dimapur is an in-between zone: an enclave that was established by the British administration as a transit space and a site that Dimasas claim as part of their kingdom. Today, it is the economic lifeline of Nagaland. It is also a swathe of terrain straddling Nagaland and Assam. It is simultaneously hills and plains, remote and connected, and parochial and cosmopolitan. As we have explored throughout the book, as an enclave surrounded by Assam on three sides, the boundaries and the edges of the city constitute different legal orders that are overlapping at times. Extending the city means extending tribal territory, Nagaland territory, and the area under special constitutional provisions. The zone also acts as a refuge, as a place of safety, as with the hunters in Chapter 4. Yet, outside the zone, there is the possibility of pleasures being frowned upon in the city itself, particularly legal access to alcohol. The city is also an enclave, separated from the rest of Nagaland. It is left off the map, outside the images of Nagas as exotic and traditional cultural specimens, and of the economy generated by these imaginations, epitomized by the annual Hornbill Festival. Dimapur may be Naga territory, but Nagaland—as an idea, as a particular landscape—begins where Dimapur ends.

Fifth, Dimapur matters because it unveils the coexistence, and in many ways the cooperation, between commercial, military, and insurgent groups during the commercial boom in the ceasefire period. Despite the city's commercial boom, it is still under extraordinary laws protecting the military and paramilitary and there is a large military presence adjacent to residential areas (and sometimes even within them) and on the outskirts. There are also large ceasefire camps, Camp Hebron and Camp Vihokhu, on the outskirts of the city (Image E.4). While the events and experiences of the conflict in Nagaland and the ways in which it has played out in Dimapur are no doubt unique, there are many cities all over the world where similar dynamics of occupation, encampment, and civilian life coexist, including within the Northeast, within South Asia, and in other parts of the world entirely. Dimapur adds to the corpus of work on these cities with its similarities and divergences.

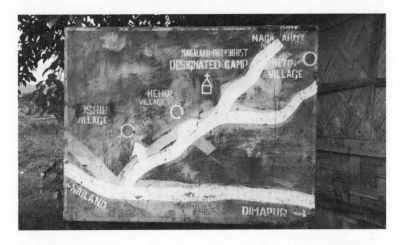

Image E.4   Self-made map on the way to Unification Ceasefire Camp

Source: Dolly Kikon

Sixth, Dimapur matters because it has been a city of refuge. The city has grown as migrants within Nagaland and from surrounding polities have settled here to escape armed conflict, military occupation, extortion, and all of the flow-on effects of a long-running insurgency: from poor employment and education prospects to the desire to escape horrific memories and follow relatives who have already decamped. Its history of settlement and place-making offers an alternative set of narratives of the Naga movement. Although we have not placed the Naga movement at the centre of our focus in this book, it lurks behind almost everything we have explored.

Finally, Dimapur matters as a manifestation of modernity. It is the largest city in a tribal state and thus gives us the opportunity to start an account of Nagaland and Nagas with modernity as the taken-for-granted element. Dimapur as a focal point for understanding the present conjuncture gives us the opportunity to, returning to Mbembé and Nuttall (2004: 352), 'throw people off their routine readings'. Like in cities across the region, the urban is a vantage point that avoids common traps in analysing the Northeast and its communities while also taking seriously the acceleration of urbanization, the growth of cities in the region, the connections maintained (and severed) with ancestral lands in rural areas, and the complex inter-legalities of producing urban space and metropolitan governance in these cities.

And while we are confident that we have made a strong case for why Dimapur matters while also unravelling aspects of its fabric, we close with an open question, perhaps a dilemma of sorts. Does Dimapur play a role in understanding urban India? As scholars of Northeast India, we are commonly entangled in the torturous task of giving layers and layers of context that can distinguish the region and smaller polities within it from the generalized set of assumptions made about India. Prior to launching into the particular story being told, scholars have to explain the difference of a community from the rest of India, its place on India's 'mental maps' (Guyot-Réchard 2015), differences from tribes in other parts of India, differences of tribe from caste, internal differences, cross-border similarities, decades of conflict, conversion and re-conversion, and various incarnations of identity formation and identity crisis—depending on which is thought to have come first. The extension of this task into urban ethnography is to explain what makes cities in the frontier different and then relate what we have explored, our arguments and claims, back to cities in mainland India.

In our case, beyond some of the accounts of failed infrastructure and corruption, we find making comparisons with cities in other parts of India difficult. There is little about Dimapur that would help to understand the spatial order and the ways in which residents experience large cities like Chennai or Kolkata, or similar-sized cities like Dehradun or Mangalore. To be clear, there is immense value in research on these cities, but the findings that are transferable to Dimapur are not necessarily more valuable than findings about cities outside India. There are obvious parallels within the Northeast region (Imphal, Agartala, Guwahati) and to frontier cities such as Siliguri (commercial, migrant settled, refuge from conflict) and Srinagar and Jammu (militarized, crisis, anxiety). However, we feel Dimapur is deeply relevant for urban studies and urban ethnography for cities like Sittwe or Myitkyina (Myanmar), Aceh or Pontianak (Indonesia), and even Hargesia or Mogadishu (Somaliland/Somalia).

Despite major advances in area studies of the past two decades that have challenged national and region geographical boundaries, we are still compelled to churn Dimapur and other parts of the Northeast back through national frames of reference, noting that scholars of sites in mainland India are not required to explain how their work may be relevant to the Northeast. Indeed, it would be far easier for us to give in to temptation and offer a vague list of resonances between Dimapur and better-known cities in India. However, we believe that cities offer us a better chance at liberation from the straitjacketed national and area studies by casting Dimapur as a frontier city, a borderland city, and a ceasefire city; a zone shaped by decades of militarism, capitalism, and urbanism; and a zone that resonates with similar urban environments across the globe.

Anand, Nikhil. 2016. *Hydraulic City: Water and the Infrastructures of Citizenship in Mumbai*. Durham: Duke University Press.

Angh, Tali. 2016. 'I Am a Revivalist'. Nagaland: Tali Angh.

———. 2018. 'City of Lights'. Nagaland: Tali Angh.

Atal Mission for Rejuvenation and Urban Transformation (AMRUT). 2015. *State Annual Action Plan (SAAP) 2017–18 To 2019–20 Nagaland*. New Delhi: Ministry for Housing and Urban Affairs.

———. 2016. *Annual Report 2015–16*. New Delhi: Ministry of Housing and Urban Affairs.

Baishya, Amit R. 2018. *Contemporary Literature from Northeast India: Deathworlds, Terror and Survival*. New York: Routledge.

Barpujari, S.K. 1997. *History of the Dimasas: From the Earliest Times to 1896 AD*. Haflong, Assam: Autonomous Council, NC Hills District.

Barton, N.H. and G.M. Hewitt. 1989. 'Adaptation, Speciation and Hybrid Zones.' *Nature* 341(6242): 497.

Baruah, Sanjib. 2003. 'Nationalizing Space: Cosmetic Federalism and the Politics of Development in Northeast India.' *Development and Change* 34(5): 915–39.

———. 2015. 'Reimagining Dimapur.' *Indian Express*, 18 March. Available at http://indianexpress.com/article/opinion/columns/reimagining-dimapur/; last accessed on 9 February 2017.

Basavapatna, Sahana. 2012. 'Chins in Mizoram: The Case of Borders Making Brothers Illegal.' *Journal of Borderlands Studies* 27(1): 61–72.

Basistha, P.S. 2016. *Assessment of Impact of Urbanisation on Deepor Beel Wetland*. Guwahati: Assam Science Technology and Environment Council.

BBC. 2018. 'The Indian Tribe that Gave Up Hunting to Save Forests'. *BBC Online*, 18 September. Available at https://www.bbc.com/news/world-asia-india-45328322; last accessed on 23 March 2019.

Bell, David and Mark Jayne. 2009. 'Small Cities? Towards a Research Agenda.' *International Journal of Urban and Regional Research* 33(3): 683–99.

Bera, Sayantan. 2015. 'Intanki National Park-Haven for Encroachers.' *Down To Earth*, 17 August. Available at https://www.downtoearth.org.in/coverage/intanki-national-park-haven-for-encroachers-2776; last accessed on 23 May 2017.

Bhan, Gautam. 2009. '"This Is No Longer the City I Once Knew": Evictions, the Urban Poor and the Right to the City in Millennial Delhi.' *Environment and Urbanization* 21(1): 127–42.

Bhattacharya, Rajesh and Kalyan Sanyal. 2011. 'Bypassing the Squalor: New Towns, Immaterial Labour and Exclusion in Post-colonial Urbanisation.' *Economic and Political Weekly* 46(31): 41–8.

Biehl, João. 2005. *Vita: Life in a Zone of Social Abandonment*. Berkeley: University of California Press.

Bibliography

Achumi, Ilito H. 2019. 'Perceived Illegality of the Body: Reclaiming the Space in Nagaland.' *Sociological Bulletin* 68(2): 204–20.

Agamben, Giorgio. 1998. *Homo Sacer: Sovereign Power and Bare Life*. Palo Alto: Stanford University Press.

———. 2005. *State of Exception*, translated by Kevin Attell. Chicago: Chicago University Press.

Agarwala, Tora. 2018. 'Meet Alobo Naga, Award-Winning Musician from Dimapur Who Sells his Albums on Pen Drives'. *The Indian Express*. 24 August. Available at https://indianexpress.com/article/north-east-india/nagaland/meet-alobo-naga-the-award-winning-musician-from-dimapur-who-is-selling-his-albums-on-pen-drives-5131616/; last accessed on 29 June 2020.

Agnew, John. 2011. 'Space and Place.' In *The SAGE Handbook of Geographical Knowledge*, edited by John Agnew and David N. Livingstone, pp. 316–31. London: Sage.

Agrawal, Ankush and Vikas Kumar. 2012. *An Investigation into Changes in Nagaland's Population between 1971 and 2011*. IEG Working Paper 316. New Delhi: Institute for Economic Growth.

Ambrocia, Medolenuo. 2019. 'Nagaland: Music Task Force Renamed as Taskforce for Music & Arts.' *East Mojo*. 26 July. Available at https://www.eastmojo.com/nagaland/2019/07/26/nagaland-music-task-force-renamed-as-task-force-for-music-arts; last accessed on 25 September 2019.

Amin, Ash. 2014. 'Lively Infrastructure.' *Theory, Culture & Society* 31(7–8): 137–61.

Amin, Ash and Nigel Thrift. 2017. *Seeing Like a City*. Cambridge: Polity.

Amnesty International. 2013. *The Armed Forces Special Powers Act: Time for a Renewed Debate in India on Human Rights and National Security*. Bangalore: Amnesty International ASA 20/042/2013.

Bollens, Scott A. 2012. *City and Soul in Divided Societies*. Abingdon: Routledge.

Bourgois, Philippe and Jeff Schonberg. 2009. *Righteous Dopefiend*. Berkeley: University of California Press.

Brar, N.S. 2016. 'The Naga Imbroglio and Conflict Resolution. Indian Defence Review,' 10 July. Available at http://www.indiandefencereview.com/news/the-naga-imbroglio-and-conflict-resolution/; last accessed on 1 February 2019.

Brash, Julian. 2006. 'Anthropologies of Urbanization: New Spatial Politics and Imaginaries.' *Urban Anthropology and Studies of Cultural Systems and World Economic Development* 35(4): 341–53.

Brosius, Christiane. 2012. *India's Middle Class: New Forms of Urban Leisure, Consumption and Prosperity*. New Delhi: Routledge India.

Brown, Trent, Tim Scrase, and Ruchira Ganguly-Scrase. 2017. 'Globalised Dreams, Local Constraints: Migration and Youth Aspirations in an Indian Regional Town.' *Children's Geographies* 15(5): 531–44.

Brumley, Albert. 1956. 'I Will Meet You in the Morning.' USA: Albert E. Brumley & Sons.

Bunnell, Tim and Anant Maringanti. 2010. 'Practising Urban and Regional Research Beyond Metrocentricity.' *International Journal of Urban and Regional Research* 34(2): 415–20.

Calhoun, Craig. 2003. '"Belonging" in the Cosmopolitan Imaginary.' *Ethnicities* 3(4): 531–53.

Capila, Pranav. 2018. 'The Naga Hunter Who Gave Up Hunting and Made Sure His Village Did Too'. *The Hindu*, 22 December. Available at https://www.thehindu.com/sci-tech/energy-and-environment/the-naga-hunter-who-gave-up-hunting-and-made-sure-his-village-did-too/article25799098.ece; last accessed 2 May 2020.

Census of India. 2011. 'Census Info India.' Available at http://censusindia.gov.in/2011census/censusinfodashboard/index.html; last accessed on 3 December 2015.

Chakravarti, Paromita. 2010. 'Reading Women's Protest in Manipur: A Different Voice?' *Journal of Peacebuilding & Development* 5(3): 47–60.

Changkija, Monalisa. 2013. 'Not Be Dead.' *Emerging Literatures from Northeast India: The Dynamics of Culture, Society and Identity*, edited by Margaret Zama Ch., pp. 134–46. New Delhi: Sage.

———. 2017. 'Equality's Time Has Come.' *Indian Express*, 7 February. Available at https://indianexpress.com/article/opinion/columns/naga-land-violence-kohima-protest-against-women-reservation-4511227/; last accessed on 14 November 2017.

Chasie, Charles and Sanjoy Hazarika. 2009. *The State Strikes Back: India and the Naga Insurgency*. Washington, DC: East-West Center.

Chatterjee, Partha. 1993. *The Nation and Its Fragments: Colonial and Postcolonial Histories*. Princeton: Princeton University Press.

Cheah, Pheng. 2006. 'Cosmopolitanism.' *Theory, Culture & Society* 23(2–3): 486–96.

Chu, Julie Y. 2014. 'When Infrastructures Attack: The Workings of Disrepair in China.' *American Ethnologist* 41(2): 351–67.

Collier, Stephen J., James Christopher Mizes, and Antina von Schnitzler. 2016. 'Preface: Public Infrastructures/Infrastructural Publics.' *Limn* 7: 2–7.

Corsín Jiménez, A., 2011. 'Trust in Anthropology.' *Anthropological Theory* 11(2): 177–96.

Cresswell, Tim. 1996. *In Place/Out of Place: Geography, Ideology and Transgression*. Minneapolis: Minnesota University Press.

———. 2015. *Place: An Introduction*, 2nd ed. Sussex: Wiley and Sons/Blackwell.

Darieva, Tsypylma. 2011. 'Rethinking Homecoming: Diasporic Cosmopolitanism in Post-Soviet Armenia.' *Ethnic and Racial Studies* 34(3): 490–508.

Datta, Ayona. 2015. 'New Urban Utopias of Postcolonial India: "Entrepreneurial Urbanization" in Dholera Smart City, Gujarat.' *Dialogues in Human Geography* 5(1): 3–22.

de Certeau, Michel. 1984. *The Practice of Everyday Life*. Berkeley: University of California Press.

Debbarma, Rhaikwchak, K. 2017. 'Agartala as a Settler-Colonial Town.' *IIAS Newsletter* (77): 35–6.

Denis, Eric, Partha Mukhopadhyay, and Marie-Hélène Zérah. 2012. 'Subaltern Urbanisation in India.' *Economic and Political Weekly* 47(30): 52–62.

Dhillon, Amrit. 2017. 'Nagaland, Where Men Are on Strike Until Women Go Back to the Kitchen.' *Sydney Morning Herald*, 16 February. Available at https://www.smh.com.au/world/nagaland-where-men-are-on-strike-until-women-go-back-to-the-kitchen-20170214-gucdtw.html; last accessed on 17 February 2017.

Directorate of Urban Affairs Nagaland. 2017. 'About Us.' Available at http://municipalaffairsnagaland.com/Home/About; last accessed on 7 June 2017.

Doron, Assa. 2010. 'Caste Away? Subaltern Engagement with the Modern Indian State.' *Modern Asian Studies* 44(4): 753–83.

———. 2016. 'Unclean, Unseen: Social Media, Civic Action and Urban Hygiene in India.' *South Asia: Journal of South Asian Studies* 39(4): 715–39.

Dunn, Elizabeth Cullen and Jason Cons. 2014. 'Aleatory Sovereignty and the Rule of Sensitive Spaces.' *Antipode* 46(1): 92–109.

Dupont, Veronique. 2007. 'Conflicting Stakes and Governance in the Peripheries of Large Indian Metropolises—An Introduction.' *Cities* 24(2): 89–94.

Dwyer, Owen J. and Derek H. Alderman. 2008. 'Memorial Landscapes: Analytic Questions and Metaphors.' *GeoJournal* 73(3): 165–78.

Eastern Mirror. 2013. 'Dimapur: The Garbage Capital of Nagaland'. 2 August. Available at https://easternmirrornagaland.com/dimapur-the-garbage-capital-of-nagaland/; last accessed on 27 July 2020.

———. 2016a. 'Civic Body Polls as Per Nagaland Municipal Act 2001: Zeliang.' 26 October. Available at http://www.easternmirrornagaland.com/civic-body-polls-as-per-nagaland-municipal-act-2001-zeliang/; last accessed on 12 March 2017.

———. 2016b. 'Urban Development Plans Two Flyovers in Dimapur.' 30 July.

———. 2018a. 'Appreciation to the PWD (Roads & Bridges) Nagaland.' 31 May.

———. 2018b. 'Nagaland 4 Kerala Concert: Naga Musicians Raise Fund.' 24 August.

Edensor, Tim. 2010. 'Walking in Rhythms: Place, Regulation, Style and the Flow of Experience.' *Visual Studies* 25(1): 69–79.

Eilenberg, Michael. 2014. 'Frontier Constellations: Agrarian Expansion and Sovereignty on the Indonesian-Malaysian Border.' *Journal of Peasant Studies* 41(2): 157–82.

Forty, Adrian. 2012. *Concrete and Culture: A Material History*. London: Reaktion Books.

Freitag, Sandria B. 2014. 'A Visual History of Three Lucknows.' *South Asia: Journal of South Asian Studies* 37(3): 431–53.

Friedmann, John. 2007. 'Reflections on Place and Place-Making in the Cities of China.' *International Journal of Urban and Regional Research* 31(2): 257–79.

Gaikwad, Namrata. 2009. 'Revolting Bodies, Hysterical State: Women Protesting the Armed Forces Special Powers Act (1958).' *Contemporary South Asia* 17(3): 299–311.

Gooptu, Nandini. 2015. 'The Indian City after Economic Liberalisation.' In *Routledge Handbook of Contemporary India*, edited by Knut A. Jacobsen, pp. 216–31. London: Routledge.

Govindranjan, Radhika. 2018. *Animal Intimacies: Interspecies Relatedness in India's Central Himalayas*. Chicago: University of Chicago Press.

Government of Nagaland. 2001. *Nagaland & NBSP: Municipal Act, 2001*. Kohima.

———. 2006. *Nagaland Municipal (First Amendment) Act, 2006*. Kohima.

Guin, Debarshi. 2017. 'Urban Transition in West Bengal, India.' *Journal of Asian and African Studies* 52(8): 1258–76.

———. 2019. 'Contemporary Perspectives of Small Towns in India: A Review.' *Habitat International* 86: 19–27.

Guite, Jangkhomang. 2015. 'Against State, Against History: Rewriting the Pasts of the Tribes of Northeast India.' *Occasional Paper: History and Society* (New Series), No. 76. New Delhi: Nehru Memorial Museum and Library.

Guyot-Réchard, Bérénice. 2015. 'Reordering a Border Space: Relief, Rehabilitation, and Nation-Building in North-eastern India after the 1950 Assam Earthquake.' *Modern Asian Studies* 49(4): 931–62.

Hall, Stuart. 1986. 'Gramsci's Relevance for the Study of Race and Ethnicity.' *Journal of Communication Inquiry* 10(2): 5–27.

———. 1989. 'Then and Now: A Re-evaluation of the New Left.' In *Out of Apathy: Voices of the New Left Thirty Years On*, edited by Robin Archer, pp. 143–170. London: Verso.

Harms, Erik. 2011. *Saigon's Edge: On the Margins of Ho Chi Minh City.* Minneapolis: University of Minnesota Press.

Harms, Erik, Shafqat Hussain, Sasha Newell, Charles Piot, Louisa Schein, Sara Shneiderman, Terence Turner, Juan Zhang, Erik Harms, and Shafqat Hussain. 2014. 'Remote and Edgy: New Takes on Old Anthropological Themes.' *HAU: Journal of Ethnographic Theory* 4(1): 361–81.

Harvey, Penny and Hannah Knox. 2015. *Roads: An Anthropology of Infrastructure and Expertise.* Ithaca: Cornell University Press.

Herscher, Andrew and Anooradha Iyer Siddiqi. 2014. 'Spatial Violence.' *Architectural Theory Review* 19(3): 269–77.

Hindu, The. 2017. '*Bowing Down to Patriarchy.*' 10 February.

Hirschkind, Charles. 2006. *The Ethical Soundscape: Cassette Sermons and Islamic Counterpublics.* New York: Columbia University Press.

Hoelscher, Kristian. 2016. 'The Evolution of the Smart Cities Agenda in India.' *International Area Studies Review* 19(1): 28–44.

Hoelscher, Steven and Derek H. Alderman. 2004. 'Memory and Place: Geographies of a Critical Relationship.' *Social & Cultural Geography* 5(3): 347–55.

Homegrown. 2014. 'Decoding Nagaland's Music Task Force: An Interview with Gukhato Chisi.' Available at https://homegrown.co.in/article/5693/decoding-nagalands-music-task-force-an-interview-with-gukhato-chisi; last accessed on 21 March 2019.

Hubbard, Phil. 1998. 'Sexuality, Immorality and the City: Red-Light Districts and the Marginalisation of Female Street Prostitutes.' *Gender, Place and Culture: A Journal of Feminist Geography* 5(1): 55–76.

Human Rights Law Network (HRLN). 2017. 'Guwahati HC Quashes Cabinet Decision Postponing Municipal and Local Council Elections in Nagaland;

Naga Women to Avail One-Third Reservation.' Available at https://hrln.
org/guwahati-hc-quashes-cabinet-decision-postponing-municipal-and-
local-council-elections-in-nagaland-naga-women-to-avail-one-third-reser-
vation/; last accessed on 12 January 2017.

Human Rights Watch (HRW). 2008. *These Fellows Must Be Eliminated: Relentless
Violence and Impunity in Manipur*. New York: Human Rights Watch.

Humane Society International (HSI). 2016. 'India's Brutal Dog Meat Trade
Exposed as Humane Society International Launches Campaign to End
"Nagaland Nightmare"'. Available at http://www.hsi.org/news/press_
releases/2016/07/nagaland-india-dog-meat-trade.html; last accessed on
15 July 2018.

Hutton, John Henry. 1922. 'Carved Monoliths at Dimapur and an Angami
Naga Ceremony.' *The Journal of the Royal Anthropological Institute of Great
Britain and Ireland* 52: 55–70.

Indian Express. 2016. 'Nagaland Is in Process of Banning Dog Meat'. 10 July.

———. 2018a. 'Nagaland Hunts for a Way Out of Its Bloody Tradition, Shows
Some Success.' 29 April.

———. 2018b. 'NSCN-IM Cadre Killed in Factional Clash in Manipur'.
22 November. Available at https://indianexpress.com/article/north-
east-india/manipur/nscn-im-cadre-killed-in-factional-clash-in-mani-
pur-5460009/; last accessed on 30 June 2020.

Ingold, Tim and Jo Lee Vergunst. 2008. 'Introduction.' In *Ways of Walking:
Ethnography and Practice on Foot*, edited by Tim Ingold and Jo Lee Vergunst,
pp. 1–19. Abingdon: Routledge.

Iralu, Kaka D. 2003. *Nagaland and India: The Blood and Tears*. Nagaland: Kaka
D. Iralu.

Jaffrelot, Christophe. 2015. 'What "Gujarat Model"?—Growth without
Development—and with Socio-political Polarisation.' *South Asia: Journal
of South Asian Studies* 38(4): 820–38.

Jain, Manisha. 2018. 'Contemporary Urbanization as Unregulated Growth in
India: The Story of Census Towns.' *Cities* 73: 117–27.

Jamir, Moa. 2015. 'Hornbill Festival Kicks Off in Nagaland – Though Locals
Suggest There Isn't Very Much to Celebrate.' *Scroll*, 3 December.

Jeermison, R.K. 2011. 'Politics of Population Growth in Nagaland.' *Sangai
Express*, 9 November. Available at http://e-pao.net/epSubPageExtractor.
asp?src=manipur.Census_of_Manipur.Politics_of_Population_Growth_
in_Nagaland; last accessed on 13 March 2017.

Jeffrey, Robin. 2015. 'Clean India! Symbols, Policies and Tensions.' *South
Asia: Journal of South Asian Studies* 38(4): 807–19.

Jessop, Bob. 2005. 'Gramsci as a Spatial Theorist.' *Critical Review of
International Social and Political Philosophy* 8(4): 421–37.

Joshi, Vibha. 2007. 'The Birth of Christian Enthusiasm among the Angami of Nagaland.' *South Asia: Journal of South Asian Studies* 30(3): 541–57.

Kaisii, Athikho. 2017. 'Globalization, Hybridization and Cultural Invasion: Korean Wave in India's North East.' *Asian Communication Research* 14(1): 10–35.

Kar, Bodhisattva. 2009. 'When Was the Postcolonial? A History of Policing Impossible Lines.' In *Beyond Counterinsurgency: Breaking the Impasse in Northeast India*, edited by Sanjib Baruah, pp. 49–77. New Delhi: Oxford University Press.

Karlsson, Bengt. 2017. 'Shillong: Tribal Urbanity in the Northeast Indian Borderland.' *IIAS Newsletter* 77: 32–3.

Kikon, Dolly. 2005. 'Engaging Naga Nationalism: Can Democracy Function in Militarised Societies?' *Economic and Political Weekly*: 40(26): 2833–7.

———. 2009a. 'From Loincloth, Suits, to Battle Greens: Politics of Clothing the 'Naked' Nagas.' In *Beyond Counter-Insurgency: Breaking the Impasse in Northeast India*, edited by Sanjib Baruah, pp. 81–100. New Delhi: Oxford University Press.

———. 2009b. 'The Predicament of Justice: Fifty Years of Armed Forces Special Powers Act in India.' *Contemporary South Asia* 17(3): 271–82.

———. 2015a. 'The City of Sorrow: Revisiting the 2015 Dimapur Lynching.' *Scroll*, 24 July.

———. 2015b. 'Fermenting Modernity: Putting Akhuni on the Nation's Table in India.' *South Asia: Journal of South Asian Studies* 38(2): 320–35.

———. 2015c. 'What Is Unique about Naga History?' *Economic and Political Weekly* (50): 35.

———. 2016. *Life and Dignity: Women's Testimonies of Sexual Violence in Dimapur*. Guwahati: NESRC.

———. 2017a. 'From the Heart to the Plate.' *IIAS Newsletter* 77: 38–9.

———. 2017b. 'Nagaland and the Fight for a Women's Quota.' *Open Democracy*, 17 March. Available at: https://www.opendemocracy.net/5050/dolly-kikon/nagaland-fight-for-women-quota; last accessed on 19 March 2017.

———. 2019. *Living with Oil and Coal: Resource Politics and Militarization in Northeast India*. Seattle: University of Washington Press.

Kikon, Dolly and Bengt G. Karlsson. 2019. *Leaving the Land: Indigenous Migration and Affective Labour in India*. New Delhi: Cambridge University Press.

King, Ross. 2011. *Reading Bangkok*. Singapore: NUS Press.

Kipfer, Stefan and Gillian Hart. 2012. 'Translating Gramsci in the Current Conjuncture.' In *Gramsci: Space, Nature, Politics*, edited by Michael Ekers, Gillian Hart, Stefan Kipfer, and Alex Loftus, pp. 321–43. Malden, MA: Wiley.

Kipfer, Stefan, Parastou Saberi, and Thorben Wieditz. 2013. 'Henri Lefebvre Debates and Controversies.' *Progress in Human Geography* 37(1): 115–34.

Kipnis, Andrew B. 2016. *From Village to City: Social Transformation in a Chinese County Seat*. Berkeley: University of California Press.

Kohn, Eduardo. 2013. *How Forests Think: Towards an Anthropology Beyond the Human*. Berkeley: University of California Press.

Koivisto, Juha and Mikko Lahtinen. 2012. 'Conjuncture, Political-Historical.' *Historical Materialism* 20(1): 267–77.

Kolås, Åshild. 2011. 'Naga Militancy and Violent Politics in the Shadow of Ceasefire.' *Journal of Peace Research* 48(6): 781–92.

Kshetrimayum, Jogendro. 2009. 'Shooting the Sun: A Study of Death and Protest in Manipur.' *Economic and Political Weekly* 44(40): 48–54.

Küchle, Andreas. 2019. *Class Formation, Social Inequality and the Nagas in North-east India*. New York: Routledge.

Kuldova, Tereza. 2017. 'Guarded Luxotopias and Expulsions in New Delhi: Aesthetics and Ideology of Outer and Inner Spaces of an Urban Utopia.' In *Urban Utopias: Excess and Expulsion in Neoliberal South Asia*, edited by Tereza Kuldova and Mathew Varghese, pp. 37–52. London/New York: Springer.

Kunreuther, Laura. 2018. 'Sounds of Democracy: Performance, Protest, and Political Subjectivity'. *Cultural Anthropology* 33(1): 1–31.

Kuotsu, Neikolie. 2013. 'Architectures of Pirate Film Cultures: Encounters with Korean Wave in "Northeast" India.' *Inter-Asia Cultural Studies* 14(4): 579–99.

Kurian, Anna. 2015. 'Dimapur Lynching and the Impossibility of Remembering.' *Economic & Political Weekly* 50(51): 25–6.

Lakoff, George and Mark Johnson. 1980. *Metaphors We Live By*. Chicago: University of Chicago Press.

Larkin, Brian. 2013. 'The Politics and Poetics of Infrastructure.' *Annual Review of Anthropology* 42: 327–43.

Laskar, Nurul Islam. 2015. 'The Dimapur Lynching: A Fire that Will Continue to Simmer.' *Economic & Political Weekly* 50(10). Available at https://www.epw.in/journal/2015/10/reports-states-web-exclusives/dimapur-lynching.html; last accessed on 10 February 2016.

Lees, Loretta. 2004. *The Emancipatory City?: Paradoxes and Possibilities*. London: Sage.

Lefebvre, Henri. 1991. *The Production of Space*, translated by Donald Nicholson-Smith. Cambridge, MA: Blackwell.

———. 2003. *The Urban Revolution*, translated by Robert Bononno. Minneapolis: University of Minnesota Press.

Li, Tania Murray. 2014. *Land's End: Capitalist Relations on an Indigenous Frontier*. Durham: Duke University Press.

Longkumer, Arkotong. 2015. '"As Our Ancestors Once Lived": Representation, Performance, and Constructing a National Culture amongst the Nagas of India.' *HIMALAYA: Journal of the Association for Nepal and Himalayan Studies* 35(1): 51–64.

——. 2016. 'Rice-Beer, Purification and Debates over Religion and Culture in Northeast India.' *South Asia: Journal of South Asian Studies* 39(2): 444–61.

——. 2018a. '"Nagas Can't Sit Lotus Style": Baba Ramdev, Patanjali, and Neo-Hindutva.' *Contemporary South Asia* 26(4): 400–20.

——. 2018b. 'Bible, Guns and Land: Sovereignty and Nationalism amongst the Nagas of India.' *Nations and Nationalism* 24(4): 1097–116.

——. 2019. '"Along Kingdom's Highway": The Proliferation of Christianity, Education, and Print amongst the Nagas in Northeast India.' *Contemporary South Asia* 27(2): 160–78.

Lotha, Abraham. 2016. *The Hornbill Spirit: Nagas Living Their Nationalism.* Dimapur: Heritage Publishing House.

Low, Kelvin E. Y. 2013. 'Sensing Cities: The Politics of Migrant Sensescapes.' *Social Identities* 19(2): 221–37.

Lowenthal, David. 1975. 'Past Time, Present Place: Landscape and Memory.' *Geographical Review* 65(1): 1–36.

Manchanda, Rita. 2001. *Women, War and Peace in South Asia: Beyond Victimhood to Agency.* London: Sage.

Mao, Caisii. 2012. '"The Dogs of Nagaland" with Caisii Mao.' *Strays.* Available at https://www.strays.in/index.php/2012/03/the-dogs-of-nagaland-with-caisii-mao/; last accessed on 12 January 2019

Maretina, Sofia A. 1978. 'The Kachari State: The Character of Early State-Like Formations in the Hill Districts of Northeast India.' In *The Early State,* edited by Henri J.M. Classent and Peter Skalnik, pp. 339–358. Den Haag: Mouton.

Massey, Doreen. 1993. 'Questions of Locality.' *Geography* 78(2): 142–149.

Mathews, Gordon. 2011. *Ghetto at the Center of the World: Chungking Mansions, Hong Kong.* Chicago: University of Chicago Press.

Mathur, Shubh. 2012. 'Life and Death in the Borderlands: Indian Sovereignty and Military Impunity.' *Race & Class* 54(1): 33–49.

Mbembé, Achille and Sarah Nuttall. 2004. 'Writing the World from an African Metropolis.' *Public Culture* 16(3): 347–72.

McDuie-Ra, Duncan. 2009. 'Fifty-Year Disturbance: The Armed Forces Special Powers Act and Exceptionalism in a South Asian Periphery.' *Contemporary South Asia* 17(3): 255–70.

——. 2012a. 'Leaving the Militarized Frontier: Migration and Tribal Masculinity in Delhi.' *Men and Masculinities* 15(2): 112–31.

————. 2012b. *Northeast Migrants in Delhi: Race, Refuge and Retail.* Amsterdam: Amsterdam University Press.

————. 2012c. 'Violence against Women in the Militarized Indian Frontier: Beyond "Indian Culture" in the Experiences of Ethnic Minority Women.' *Violence Against Women* 18(3): 322–45.

————. 2013. '"Beyond the 'Exclusionary City'": North-East Migrants in Neo-liberal Delhi.' *Urban Studies* 50(8): 1625–40.

————. 2015a. *Debating Race in Contemporary India.* London/New York: Palgrave MacMillan.

————. 2015b. '"Is India Racist?": Murder, Migration, and Mark Kom.' *South Asia: Journal of South Asian Studies* 38(1): 304–19.

————. 2016. *Borderland City in New India: Frontier to Gateway.* Amsterdam: Amsterdam University Press.

————. 2017. 'Learning to Love the City in Northeast India.' *IIAS Newsletter* 77: 29–31.

McDuie-Ra, Duncan and Lauren Lai. 2019. 'Smart Cities, Backward Frontiers: Digital Urbanism in India's North-East.' *Contemporary South Asia* 27(3): 358–72.

Mehta, Deepak and Roma Chatterji. 2001. 'Boundaries, Names, Alternities: A Case Study of a Communal "Riot" in Dharavi, Bombay.' In *Remaking a World: Violence, Social Suffering, and Recovery*, edited by Veena Das, Arthur Kleinman, Margaret Lock, Mamphela Ramphele, and Pamela Reynolds, pp. 201–25. Berkeley: University of California Press.

Mepfhü-o, Ketholenuo. 2016. 'Conversion: Perception of the Christian "Self" and the "Other".' *Asian Ethnicity* 17(3): 370–83.

Merrifield, Andrew. 1993. 'Place and Space: A Lefebvrian Reconciliation.' *Transactions of the Institute of British Geographers* 18(4): 516–31.

Ministry of Urban Development (MUD). 2016. *Annual Report 2015–16.* New Delhi: Ministry of Urban Development.

————. 2017. *Annual Report 2016–17.* New Delhi: Ministry of Urban Development.

Misra, Udayon. 2003. 'Naga Peace Talks: High Hopes and Hard Realities.' *Economic and Political Weekly* 38(7): 593–7.

Mitchell, Katharyne. 2003. 'Monuments, Memorials, and the Politics of Memory.' *Urban Geography* 24(5): 442–59.

Mitra, Dola. 2015. '"The Attempt Was to Create A Law and Order Crisis" Nagaland CM on the Dimapur Mob Violence.' *Outlook*, 30 March.

Moitra, Aheli. 2017. 'Learning a Native Culture.' *Morung Express*, 22 February. Available at http://morungexpress.com/learning-native-culture/; last accessed on 10 March.

Morung Express, The. 2011. 'Taking a Bite on Dimapur's Emerging Restaurant Culture'. 4 January.

———. 2015. 'Separate Directorate of Municipal Affairs in Urban Development Dept.' 13 April.

———. 2016a. 'BCCI Prez Weaves Big Dreams for Cricket in NE.' 31 May.

———. 2016b. 'Election with 33% Reservation: CM Assures Naga Women.' 3 October.

———. 2017a. 'NPF Legal Cell Explains Amended Nagaland Municipal Act.' 22 January.

———.2017b. 'Bridge Collapse: The Day After.' 14 July.

———. 2017c. 'Wildlife Conservation Efforts in Nagaland Continues'. 23 September.

———. 2018a. 'NCD Proposes Facelift of Old Naga Cemetery'. 22 April.

———. 2018b. 'Temporary Bailey Bridge over Chathe After a 10-Month Wait'. 7 May.

———. 2018c. 'Power Shutdown in Dimapur from July 26 to Aug 2'. 25 July.

Naga, Alobo. 2010. 'Kumsujulo'. Dimapur, Nagaland: Musik-A.

———. 2017. 'Mistry Gaana'. Dimapur, Nagaland: Musik-A.

Nagaland Post. 2011. '2001 Census Report Fake: CM.' 10 April.

———. 2013. 'Two New Flyovers for Dimapur.' 5 May.

———. 2018. 'Dimapur City Grapples with Mounting Garbage Problems'. 10 November.

Narayanan, Yamini. 2017. 'Street Dogs at the Intersection of Colonialism and Informality: 'Subaltern Animism' as a Posthuman Critique of Indian Cities.' *Environment and Planning D: Society and Space* 35(3): 475–94.

Nielsen, Kenneth Bo and Solano Jose Savio Da Silva. 2017. 'Golden or Green? Growth Infrastructures and Resistance in Goa.' In *Urban Utopias: Excess and Expulsion in Neoliberal South Asia*, edited by Tereza Kuldova and Mathew Varghese, pp. 53–73. London/New York: Springer.

Oakes, Timothy. 1997. 'Place and the Paradox of Modernity.' *Annals of the Association of American Geographers* 87(3): 509–31.

O'Neill, Bruce. 2017. *The Space of Boredom: Homelessness in the Slowing Global Order.* Durham: Duke University Press.

Outlook India. 2012. 'Send Stray Dogs to North-East States: Cong MLA'. 29 June.

Pachuau, Joy L.K. 2014. *Being Mizo: Identity and Belonging in Northeast India.* Delhi: Oxford University Press.

Pachuau, Joy L.K. and Willem van Schendel. 2015. *The Camera as Witness: A Social History of Mizoram, Northeast India.* New Delhi: Cambridge University Press.

Pandian, Anand and Stuart J. McLean. 2017. 'Introduction: Archipelagos, a Voyage in Writing.' In *Crumpled Paper Boat: Experiments in Ethnographic Writing*, edited by Anand Pandian and Stuart J. McLean, pp. 11–28. Durham: Duke University Press.

Patnaik, Prabhat. 2016. 'From the Planning Commission to the NITI Aayog.' *Economic and Political Weekly* 50(4): 10–12.

Pearson, Chris. 2012. 'Researching Militarized Landscapes: A Literature Review on War and the Militarization of the Environment.' *Landscape Research* 37(1): 115–33.

Pieris, Anoma. 2014. 'Encampments: Spatial Taxonomies of Sri Lanka's Civil War.' *Architectural Theory Review* 19(3): 393–413.

Pisharoty, Sangeeta Barooah. 2016. 'BJP-Ally Naga People's Front Attempts to Ban Dog Meat in Nagaland.' *The Wire*, 13 July.

———. 2017. 'Nagaland to Hold Urban Local Body Polls with 33% Reservation for Women.' *The Wire*, 28 January.

Pollock, Sheldon, Homi K. Bhabha, Carol A. Breckenridge, and Dipesh Chakrabarty. 2000. 'Cosmopolitanisms.' *Public Culture* 12(3): 577–89.

Pongen, Sashinungla. 2016. '"I Perceive That in Every Way You Are Very Religious" (Acts 17: 22): Naga Spirituality and Baptist Mission.' *Journal of World Christianity* 6(2): 291–310.

Prakash, Gyan. 2002. 'The Urban Turn.' *Sarai Reader* 2(7): 2–7.

Ramirez, Philippe. 2007. 'Politico-Ritual Variations on the Assamese Fringes: Do Social Systems Exist?' In *Social Dynamics in the Highlands of Southeast Asia*, edited by François Robin and Mandy Sadan, pp. 89–108. Leiden: Brill.

Rasmussen, Mattias Borg and Christian Lund. 2018. 'Reconfiguring Frontier Spaces: The Territorialization of Resource Control.' *World Development* 101: 388–99.

Rawat, Rachna Bisht. 2017. 'The Call of the Naga Tribes.' *The Hindu*, 7 January. Available at https://www.thehindu.com/todays-paper/tp-features/tp-metroplus/The-call-of-the-Naga-tribes/article17003019.ece; last accessed on 12 February 2019.

Robbins, Bruce. 1998. 'Actually Existing Cosmopolitanism.' In *Cosmopolitics: Thinking and Feeling beyond the Nation*, edited by Pheng Cheah and Bruce Robbins. Vol. 14, pp. 1–19. Minneapolis: University of Minnesota Press.

Roberts, Jayde Lin. 2016. *Mapping Chinese Rangoon: Place and Nation among the Sino-Burmese*. Seattle: University of Washington Press.

Roy, Ananya. 2009. 'Why India Cannot Plan Its Cities: Informality, Insurgence and the Idiom of Urbanization.' *Planning Theory* 8(1): 76–87.

Sami, Neha. 2013. 'From Farming to Development: Urban Coalitions in Pune, India.' *International Journal of Urban and Regional Research* 37(1): 151–64.

Samyal, Sanjjeev. 2016. 'Major Hurdles in Bid to Bring North-East into National Cricket Mainstream.' *Hindustan Times*, 17 May.

Santoshini, Sarita. 2016. 'In India's Nagaland, a Tale of Taxes and Corruption.' *Al-Jazeera*, 14 April. Available at https://www.aljazeera.com/indepth/features/2016/04/india-nagaland-drowning-taxes-corruption-160411062725238.html; last accessed on 1 March 2017.

Schiller, Nina Glick, Tsypylma Darieva, and Sandra Gruner-Domic. 2011. 'Defining Cosmopolitan Sociability in a Transnational Age: An Introduction.' *Ethnic and Racial Studies* 34(3): 399–418.

Schwenkel, Christina. 2013. 'Post/Socialist Affect: Ruination and Reconstruction of the Nation in Urban Vietnam.' *Cultural Anthropology* 28(2): 252–77.

Shillong Times. 2016. 'Nagaland Ao Senden Asks CM to Amend Municipal Act.' 3 November.

Shimray, A.S. Atai. 2005. *Let Freedom Ring?: Story of Naga Nationalism*. New Delhi: Bibliophile South Asia.

Shimray, Ungshungmi A. 2004. 'Socio-political Unrest in the Region Called North-East India.' *Economic and Political Weekly* 39(42): 4637–43.

Simone, AbdouMaliq and Edgar Pieterse. 2017. *New Urban Worlds: Inhabiting Dissonant Times*. Cambridge: Polity.

Sircar, Srilata. 2017. '"Census Towns" in India and What It Means to Be "Urban": Competing Epistemologies and Potential New Approaches.' *Singapore Journal of Tropical Geography* 38(2): 229–44.

Smith, Michael P. 2001. *Transnational Urbanism: Locating Globalisation*. Malden: Blackwell Publishers.

Suhasini, Lalitha. 2013. 'Nagaland's Music Task Force Launches Monthly Gig Series'. *Rolling Stone India*, 19 August. Available at http://rollingstoneindia.com/nagalands-music-task-force-launches-monthly-gig-series/; last accessed on 10 June 2016.

Sundar, Nandini. 2011. 'Interning Insurgent Populations: The Buried Histories of Indian Democracy.' *Economic & Political Weekly* 46(6): 47–57.

Taussig, Michael. 2006. *Walter Benjamin's Grave*, 2nd ed. Chicago: University of Chicago Press.

Telegraph Kolkata. 2016. 'Maneka Targets Dog Meat Sale.' 28 October. Available at https://www.telegraphindia.com/india/maneka-targets-dog-meat-sale/cid/1513920?ref=search-page; last accessed on 14 September 2018.

Thomas, John. 2015. *Evangelising the Nation: Religion and the Formation of Naga Political Identity*. New York: Routledge.

Tir Yimyim. 2017. 'Asür Bendangnungsang Aser Asür Khriesavizo Nem Tetushi Agütsü,' 27 February. Available at http://tiryimyim.in/asurbendangnungsang-aser-asur-khriesavizo-nem-tetushi-agutsu/; last accessed on 12 March 2017.

Toy, Senti. 2010. *The Politics of Affect and Acoustemology in Nagaland*. PhD Dissertation. New York: New York University.

Vajpeyi, Ananya. 2009. 'Resenting the Indian State: For a New Political Practice in the Northeast.' In *Beyond Counterinsurgency: Breaking the Impasse in Northeast India*, edited by Sanjib Baruah, pp. 25–48. New Delhi: Oxford University Press.

van Duijne, Robbin Jan. 2019. 'Why India's Urbanization is Hidden: Observations from "Rural" Bihar.' *World Development* 123: 1–13.

van Schendel, Willem. 2011. 'The Dangers of Belonging: Tribes, Indigenous Peoples and Homelands in South Asia.' In *The Politics of Belonging in India*, edited by Daniel Rycroft and Sangeeta Dasgupta, pp. 19–43. Abingdon/ New York: Routledge.

Verdery, Katherine. 1999. *The Political Lives of Dead Bodies: Reburial and Postsocialist Change*. New York: Columbia University Press.

Verstappen, Sanderien and Mario Rutten. 2015. 'A Global Town in Central Gujarat, India: Rural–Urban Connections and International Migration.' *South Asia: Journal of South Asian Studies* 38(2): 230–45.

Von Stockhausen, Alban. 2014. *Imag (in) Ing the Nagas: The Pictorial Ethnography of Hans-Eberhard Kauffmann and Christoph von Fürer-Haimendorf*. Zurich: Arnoldsche Verlagsanstalt GmbH.

Wouters, Jelle J.P. 2015. 'Polythetic Democracy: Tribal Elections, Bogus Votes, and Political Imagination in the Naga Uplands of Northeast India.' *HAU: Journal of Ethnographic Theory* 5(2): 121–51.

———. 2018. *In the Shadows of Naga Insurgency: Tribes, State, and Violence in Northeast India*. New Delhi: Oxford University Press.

Wouters, Jelle J.P. and Michael Heneise. 2017. 'Introduction to Nagas in the 21st Century.' *The South Asianist* 5(1): 3–19.

Yi'En, Cheng. 2014. 'Telling Stories of the City: Walking Ethnography, Affective Materialities, and Mobile Encounters.' *Space and Culture* 17(3): 211–23.

Yimchunger, Tsukhumla L. 2016. 'Dimapur – Hell or Heaven?' *Morung Express*, 21 June.

Zérah, Marie-Hélène and Eric Denis (eds). 2017. 'Introduction: Reclaiming Small Towns'. In *Subaltern Urbanization in India: An Introduction to the Dynamics of Ordinary Towns*, pp. 1–35. New Delhi: Springer.

Index

About the Authors

Dolly Kikon teaches anthropology and development studies at the University of Melbourne, Australia. Her previous publications include *Living with Oil and Coal: Resource Politics and Militarization in Northeast India* (2019), *Leaving the Land: Indigenous Migration and Affective Labour in India* (2019), *Life and Dignity: Women's Testimonies of Sexual Violence in Dimapur* (2015), and *Experiences of Naga Women in Armed Conflict: Narratives from a Militarized Society* (2004).

Duncan McDuie-Ra is professor of urban sociology at the School of Social Sciences and Humanities, the University of Newcastle, Callaghan, Australia. His current research focuses on 'emerging urban forms': towns, cities, and industrial zones undergoing rapid growth or slated for new interventions, especially digital and networked infrastructure. His previous publications include *Borderland City in New India: Frontier to Gateway* (2016), *Debating Race in Contemporary India* (2015), and *Northeast Migrants in Delhi: Race, Refuge and Retail* (2012). His work has appeared in journals such as *Contemporary South Asia, Development and Change, Energy Policy, Geoforum, The Geographical Journal, Men and Masculinities, Political Geography,* and *Urban Studies*. He has also edited several articles in *Contemporary South Asia, South Asia: Journal of South Asian Studies,* and the *IIAS Newsletter*. He holds various editorial roles with journals (such as *South Asia: Journal of South Asian Studies, Contemporary South Asia*) and book series (Asian Borderlands, Amsterdam University Press, and ASAA South Asia Series). His forthcoming book is titled *Skateboarding and Urban Landscapes in Asia: Endless Spots* (2021).